Women, Immigration and
Identities in France

Women, Immigration and Identities in France

Edited by
Jane Freedman and Carrie Tarr

Oxford • New York

First published in 2000 by
Berg
Editorial offices:
150 Cowley Road, Oxford OX4 1JJ, UK
838 Broadway, Third Floor, New York, NY 10003-4812, USA

Berg is the imprint of Oxford International Publishers Ltd.

Library of Congress Cataloging-in-Publication Data

A catalogue record for this book is available from the Library of Congress.

British Library Cataloguing-in-Publication Data

A catalogue record for this book is available from the British Library.

ISBN 1 85973 431 6 (Cloth)
ISBN 1 85973 436 7 (Paper)

Typeset by JS Typesetting, Wellingborough, Northants.
Printed and bound in Great Britain by Biddles Ltd
www.biddles.co.uk

Contents

Contents

Preface

This book arises from a day conference on 'Women and Ethnicities: Identities and Representations' that we organized at the Institute of Romance Studies (IRS), London (UK) in November 1998. A number of the essays gathered in this volume were originally given as papers at the conference; others were specially commissioned in order to extend the range of issues addressed and provide a coherent basis for further research and teaching in the area. The conference itself was prompted by a meeting of Women in French, which felt that a gendered approach to the understanding of ethnic minority experiences in France needed to be developed and articulated. Research into immigration, ethnicity and identity has tended to take the experiences of immigrant and 'second generation' men as paradigmatic of the experiences of immigrants more generally. This book's multidisciplinary analysis of post-colonial immigration and identities centres specifically on the experiences and cultural productions of women immigrants and their second (and now third) generation daughters.

Immigration and ethnicity studies are rightly preoccupied with issues of language and naming, symptomatic of the relations of power between majority and minority cultures. In our introduction, we discuss the problematic (and often inaccurate) use of the term 'immigrant' in France. We want here to register our difficulties in deciding how to refer to women 'of immigrant origin' and their children, members of the 'second generation'. This is particularly the case with regard to those of North African or Maghrebi (Algerian, Tunisian, Moroccan) origin (we have opted for Maghrebi rather than Maghrebian), the generic 'Maghrebi' being itself problematic in that it does not refer to a specific place of origin. Furthermore, the word 'Beur', commonly used to describe the sons and daughters of first generation 'Maghrebi' immigrants (a word which derives from Parisian backslang for 'Arabe' and was first coined by the 'Beurs' themselves) is one that they now often disclaim (Durmelat, 1998). The feminine derivative, the diminutive 'Beurette', is particularly patronizing and offensive. Since there are no easy alternatives, however, we have decided to use the terms 'Beur' and 'Beurette' in inverted commas to signal the way they have been appropriated by dominant discourses.

Preface

We would like to thank the IRS for hosting our day conference, as well as the British Academy and the Association of Modern and Contemporary France for helping to fund the conference. We would also like to thank Southampton University and Thames Valley University for help in funding our research trips to Paris. Finally we thank Stuart, Olivia and Frank for their support during this project.

J.F. and C.T.

List of Figures

Cover picture: The *sans-papières* women's march from Saint Ambroise to Matignon on 11 May 1996,where their delegation was turned away (photograph by Alejandra Riera).

Notes on Contributors

Sonia Dayan-Herzbrun is a professor in the Centre for the Study of Political Practices and Representations at the Université de Paris VII (France). She has published widely on women in the Middle East, and her current research is on Palestinian women's political engagement. She is the editor of *Ruptures*, a journal of political sociology.

Sylvie Durmelat is Assistant Professor of French and Francophone Studies at Georgetown University (Washington DC, US). Her research interests include urban and migrant cultural productions in metropolitan France and post-colonial cultures in the Caribbean and in North Africa. She has published articles in *French Cultural Studies* and in *L'écriture décentrée*, among others, and is currently working on a book-length study on processes of cultural reproduction and filiation in urban and migrant diasporic fiction and film.

Jane Freedman is a lecturer in French and European Studies at Southampton University (UK). Her research interests centre on questions of gender and politics in Europe. Her most recent book is *Femmes politiques: mythes et symboles* (L'Harmattan, 1997), and she is currently preparing a book on feminism, and working on a project on women in the European Parliament sponsored by the European Commission.

Camille Lacoste-Dujardin is an ethnologist and director of research at the CNRS (France). She has published widely on questions of family and gender in the Maghreb, and amongst communities of Maghrebi origin in France. Her books include *Yasmina et les autres de Nanterre et d'ailleurs: filles de parents maghrébins en France* (La Découverte, 1992).

Mark McKinney is Assistant Professor of French at Miami University (Ohio, US). He is co-editor with Alec G. Hargreaves of *Post-Colonial Cultures in France* (Routledge, 1997) and is currently writing a book on imperialism and (post-)colonialism in French and Belgian comics.

Notes on Contributors

Catherine Quiminal is a professor in the Centre for Research on Migrations and Society at the Université de Paris VII (France). Her research focuses on African women in France. Her books include *Gens d'ici, gens d'ailleurs* (Christian Bourgois, 1991), and she is co-editor of *Les lois de l'inhospitalité* (La Découverte, 1997), a study on French immigration laws and their consequences.

Emily Roberts is completing a doctorate on 'Cultural Identity and the Colonial Encounter in the Twentieth Century French Indochinese Novel'. She is a research associate at the University of the West of England (UK), working on a comparative study of regional identity and regional television in the West of England and the Aquitaine, and is co-editing a book on 'Group Identities on French and British Television'.

Mireille Rosello teaches French and Francophone literatures and cultures at Northwestern University (Chicago, US). Her most recent book is *Declining the Stereotype: Ethnicity and Representation in French Culture* (University Press of New England, 1998) and she is currently completing a project on hospitality and immigration in contemporary Europe and Africa.

Anissa Talahite is a lecturer in French at Manchester Metropolitan University (UK). Her research interests include the development of the French and francophone novel and post-colonial writing, particularly Maghrebi, 'Beur' and women's writing. She also researches questions of race and gender in the literature of southern African women writers, and has published articles on gender, race and representation.

Carrie Tarr is a research fellow at Kingston University (UK). She has published widely on gender and ethnicity in French cinema, including a recent book on the cinema of *Diane Kurys* (MUP, 1999). She is currently preparing a book on twenty years of women's filmmaking in France.

Introduction

Jane Freedman and *Carrie Tarr*

Studies about immigration and post-colonial society in France tend to ignore or marginalize the gendered nature of their subject.[1] The various contributions to this book attempt to redress the balance by demonstrating the ways in which the experiences and identities of women of immigrant origin in France differ both from those of their male contemporaries and those of white French women. Situated as they are at the intersection of a complex web of ethnic/'race', class and gender relations, these women are the victims of both gendered and racial oppressions; but at the same time they are forging new and positive cross-cultural identities within French society. This book addresses the ways in which gender and 'race' interact, both in French representations of women of immigrant origin, and in these women's political and cultural self-representations. Its focus both on general questions such as those relating to immigrant women and citizenship, and on more specific issues such as 'l'affaire des foulards' (the Islamic headscarves affair), together with its examination of the cultural productions of women of immigrant origin, highlight the specificity of these women's experiences and identities. This specificity is rarely recognized, despite the large presence of women amongst populations of immigrant origin living in France.

Perhaps one of the reasons for the lack of recognition of women's particular experiences of immigration is the fact that for some time there were few women amongst communities of immigrant origin in France. Post-war immigration into France was mainly composed of men from France's ex-colonies coming to find work. Since the suspension of immigration for work by the French government in 1974, however, the main source of immigration has been for family regroupment, which successive governments have not been able to outlaw, although they have tried to restrict its application (as will be discussed in chapter one). This immigration for family regroupment has led to a feminization of the population of immigrant origin as wives and children came to join the male workers already in France. In addition women have immigrated autonomously into France, and so it should not be assumed that all

-1-

women's migratory projects are dependent on men (Golub, Morokvasic and Quiminal, 1997). A 1990 census revealed that 48.4 per cent[2] of immigrants and those of immigrant origin in France are now women. This figure includes both women who have immigrated into France and those born to families of immigrant origin within France. A certain confusion may arise here as the French use the term 'immigré' (immigrant) to refer not only to those who have actually migrated from another country into France, but also to those of ethnic origin within France, and particularly those whose ethnic origins lie in France's ex-colonies in Africa and Asia. Thus a woman who was born in France, has been brought up in French society and has French nationality, but whose grandparents originally migrated to France from Vietnam, for example, will still find herself labelled as an 'immigrant'. The same is true of ethnic minority communities in France originating from Martinique and Guadeloupe, even though these are still French territories. The choice of words to describe those of immigrant origin is a clear sign of the way in which dominant French discourses construct their post-colonial minorities as 'Other', a consequence of which is their exclusion from full citizenship rights. This problem is exacerbated for women from these communities by the double bind of sexism and racism. Within the context of this book we have chosen to use the term 'women of immigrant origin' rather than a direct translation from the French 'femmes immigrées' (immigrant women), to indicate that many of those we are talking about are not actually immigrants, that is they have not crossed any borders to arrive in France, and they do, in fact, have French nationality.[3]

Whilst they make up very nearly half of the populations of immigrant origin in France, within dominant representations women of immigrant origin are more often than not either ignored or represented in stereotyped categories. Older women are portrayed as wives and mothers, responsible for the 'integration' of the family into French society, whilst when young people of immigrant origin are discussed it is usually the problems of young men which come to the forefront. Young women are often forgotten, 'as if their experiences posed no problem' ('comme si leur vécu ne soulevait aucun problème') (Bentichou, 1997, p. 9). Only an explosion of media and public interest in an issue like that of the Islamic headscarves in French schools brings the problems of young women of immigrant origin to the foreground, albeit in a very limited manner. These stereotyped representations, which portray women of immigrant origin as wives, mothers or daughters, supports for the process of 'integration' of immigrant communities into France, or 'victims' of patriarchal Muslim cultures, are clearly obstacles to the full understanding of the heterogeneity of

Introduction

identities and representations and the multiple dimensions of problems and difficulties that touch these women's lives. One of the most important facts to remember is that these women have their origins in many different cultures and countries in Europe, Asia and Africa, and there are obviously various different ethnic communities within French society. Clearly one should not assume that the process of immigration overrides these differences of origin and ethnic identity. Similarly, within different ethnic communities there are differences of class, age, sexuality, ability, and so forth. This book will seek to capture this heterogeneity and multiplicity whilst at the same time highlighting certain themes that are of concern to all women of immigrant origin, especially women from France's ex-colonies.

The first part of the book focuses on social and political representations and identities. The hardening of the political debate on immigration and nationality in recent years in France, together with the rise in popularity and electoral success of the extreme-right Front National, has meant that the position of immigrants and those of immigrant origin in French society has become increasingly difficult. As Chemillier-Gendreau argues: 'Through a continuing blind reinforcement of repressive policies concerning immigrants, successive Ministers of the Interior have contributed to the elimination of hospitality from the list of French virtues'[4] (Chemillier-Gendreau, 1998, p. 8). This 'failure of hospitality' has both political and cultural implications and will thus be an issue that recurs in both parts of this book. Politically and socially, it has affected women of immigrant origin in specific ways as their citizenship is brought into question. And whilst the French Republican model of citizenship has been criticized for the manner in which gender has been used as a category of exclusion, there has been little discussion of the ways in which the interactions of the categories of gender and 'race' produce multiple exclusions. This multiple exclusion of women of immigrant origin from French citizenship is discussed by Jane Freedman who examines the dominant political representations of women of immigrant origin in France and the ways in which the construction of policy and law based on these representations has defined their position in French society. She argues that recent changes in the laws on immigration have affected women in specific ways and have created situations of double oppression and double dependency on men.

Although women of immigrant origin find themselves at the intersection of dominations and exclusions based on gender and 'race', this does not mean that they are passive victims without voice and agency of their own. This is clearly shown in the example of the *sans-papières* (literally

— 3 —

Figure 1. The *sans-papières* participate in the demonstration of 1 May 1996 (photograph by Alejandra Riera).

'women without papers'), women who have been pushed by recent changes in immigration and nationality law into a situation of illegal residence in France. The very active and vocal role which these women have played in the *sans-papiers* movement is a demonstration of the way in which women can display formidable strength and solidarity in social movements and can act together in order to overcome both racist and sexist oppressions from the French authorities, and opposition from men within their own communities. In our interview with Madjiguène Cissé, who emerged as a leading spokesperson for the *sans-papiers* movement, she explains her experiences and her views on the role of women within this movement. Another, if less visible, example of the ways in which women of immigrant origin have organized to overcome exclusions and to forge new forms of citizenship, is that of the numerous women's associations which have sprung up in France. Catherine Quiminal examines the ways in which African women's associations create 'innovatory social networks', spaces within which women of immigrant origin can meet and redefine their identities and social positions.

It is also clear that the situations and identities of women of immigrant origin are in a process of continual transformation, and whilst it is important to be aware of the historically constructed identities and representations that result from these women's varied migratory experiences, it is also vital to realize that there is an ongoing process of negotiation taking place in their lives between the cultures and traditions of their communities of origin and their new social positions in France. The falling birth rate amongst women of immigrant origin is one of the indicators of the transformations taking place in their lives, as is their growing rate of economic activity (Lelièvre, 1997, p. 13). At the same time, however, the influence of their cultural heritage and traditions cannot be underestimated. This negotiation between 'tradition' and 'modernity' and the complexities it entails are apparent in the space of the family where the intertwining of two or more cultures leads to complex relations between men and women and between parents and children. Camille Lacoste-Dujardin analyses this complexity with regard to Maghrebi families in France. Within their families, as well as within society as a whole, women of immigrant origin are in a dynamic process, creating new social spaces and negotiating new identities. Dominant representations have often failed to take account of this dynamism and situated such women in fixed cultural universes, perceiving them as guardians of tradition incapable of developing new and original forms of knowledge and agency. As Beski argues, neither the 'culturalist' point of view, which celebrates this false representation of women as the unchanging guardians of culture, nor an 'assimilationist' view, which urges women of immigrant origin to abandon their cultural heritage and embrace 'modernity', provide adequate answers to the problems they face (Beski, 1997). In the case of the Islamic headscarf, for example, it would be wrong to accept the wearing of the headscarf unquestioningly as part of Muslim culture in France without acknowledging the patriarchal structures that force some women to cover their heads. But at the same time, an outright refusal of the headscarf on feminist grounds would ignore the varied reasons for which many women choose to wear a headscarf as an expression of their identity. As Sonia Dayan-Herzbrun argues, the French responses to the 'Islamic headscarves affair' are as much an indicator of a society that has not yet come to terms with its own multi-ethnic reality. In effect, media coverage of the affair, and of other issues such as the trials of women accused of excision, has demonstrated that dominant representations of women of immigrant origin and women of different 'race' have changed little since the colonial era: women are still represented as victims, trapped in traditional lifestyles and unable to express their agency (Bloul, 1996). This is of course far from the truth and, as Dayan-Herzbrun indicates, the wearing of the Islamic headscarves is not a throwback to tradition, but rather the sign of young women of immigrant origin trying to negotiate a new and 'modern' identity within contemporary French society.

The second part of the book is concerned with the way women of immigrant origin in France have been represented and, more importantly, have represented themselves across a range of media. The question of representation is particularly problematic in the context of a nation state whose universalist Republican principles make it reluctant to recognize difference (a problem which affects women of immigrant origin both as women and as ethnic or racial 'Others'). The dominant culture continues to obscure the problematic bicultural or hybrid identities of women of immigrant origin who are French residents and, in many cases, French nationals, but who also feel allegiance to their culture of origin (or the culture of origin of their parents in the case of the second generation). As Barlet notes, the French continue to require their post-colonial Others to assimilate into metropolitan French culture and are unable to imagine 'accepting a shift in our own identity, enriched by the experience of others and the confrontation with other cultures'[5] (Barlet, 1996, p. 134).

Mark McKinney investigates dominant representations in French comic books, a key component of French popular culture. French comics are aimed at a male readership but they enjoy a traditionally parodic, iconoclastic approach to social problems and taboo issues and imagery and provide a useful indicator of issues perceived as relevant to contemporary youth culture. McKinney analyses comics that depict France as a post-industrial, post-colonial society and provides a historical survey of their changing representations of ethnic minority women of different generations. Not surprisingly, perhaps, these characters, when present, generally occupy marginal social, economic and geographical positions and are also marginalized in terms of their narrative positioning. They are frequently represented as the victims of racist attacks and/or the targets of male abuse and there is a strong tendency towards the eroticization of the exotic, female ethnic Other, especially in the case of young Arab women detached from their Maghrebi milieu. In other words, comic books continue to be informed by neo-colonial perceptions of the former colonized Other. However, McKinney also identifies a number of Left-leaning and ethnic minority-produced comic books which offer more progressive, complex representations of women, particularly second generation women of Maghrebi origin.

Given the way in which the dominant culture excludes, marginalizes or stereotypes immigrant women and their daughters, it is important that women find a way of narrating and visualizing their own attitudes and experiences. In fact, since the early 1980s, and the change in the laws governing the formation of associations brought about by the new Socialist government, many such women have become active cultural producers. In particular, women of the 'Beur' generation, many of whom participated in political actions (like Rock against Racism, the March against Racism and for Equality, and Convergences), started to make an impact on French culture though their writing (Laronde, 1993; Hargreaves, 1997b). 'Beur' women writers, or 'les écrivaines beures' (Ireland, 1996), foreground the double oppression of second generation women, both as ethnic Others, and by their position within the Arabo-Berber-Islamic sex/gender system with its insistence on male authority, female virtue, arranged marriages and the segregation of the sexes. Though dominant French discourses may esteem that the path to liberation from an oppressive patriarchal regime lies in assimilation, the issue for many women of Maghrebi origin lies, consciously or otherwise, in negotiating freedom from the constraints of Arabo-Berber-Islamic conceptions of women's roles without losing sight of their Maghrebi identity (Geesey, 1995). The writing of the second generation foregrounds the pain and anguish of their split identities, and the difficulty of negotiating between different and sometimes conflicting cultures. Anissa Talahite examines a key aspect of this literary phenomenon, namely, the way in which individual 'Beur' women writers tackle the articulation of female subjectivity and identity and attempt to construct an autonomous self-representing narrative voice. Based on the postcolonial, feminist notion that the migrant woman's narrative can disrupt hegemonic colonial and patriarchal discourses (Woodhull, 1993a), she explores the different ways in which these texts attempt to re-locate the female subject within symbolic historical and linguistic discourses.

In addition to the 'Beurs', a number of francophone women writers find themselves centred in Paris and writing about immigrant experience in metropolitan France, including for example, Leïla Sebbar, a Franco-Algerian woman who is not herself a 'Beur', but who writes about the 'Beur' generation (Laronde, 1993; Tarr, 1994), and Calixthe Bayala, the award-winning writer from Cameroon (Hitchcott, 1997). Emily Roberts analyses novels by Kim Lefèvre and Linda Lê, women of Vietnamese origin now resident in France, who have made their mark on French literature with their narratives of exiled, migrant women. Roberts examines the metaphors they use to express the troubled identities of their central protagonists, in each case first generation immigrant women, and demonstrates how different historical moments and different degrees of acculturation produce significantly different effects, be it an acceptance of their problematic heritage and hybrid identity, or a continuing state of exile and loss.

As well as enabling oppressed women to express a personal voice, writing is also a means of articulating a critique, whether of the dominant culture or of oppressive aspects of the culture of origin. Regressive nationality and immigration laws have focused attention on France's 'failure of hospitality'. The theme of (in)hospitality and cultural difference is taken up by Mireille Rosello in her analysis of particular episodes from two key texts of the 1990s, François Maspéro's *Les Passagers du Roissy Express*, now a classic of post-colonial literature, and Yamina Benguigui's *Mémoires d'immigrés* (the text published in the wake of her better known documentary film of the same title, discussed below). Rosello discusses the representation of those crucial moments when the 'host' culture comes into contact with the culture of its 'guests' (in French the word for people in both situations is 'hôte'). As it happens, in each case an 'immigrant' woman tries to offer hospitality to an unwilling or uncomprehending 'French' person, and Rosello analyses what is at stake in the refusal of hospitality. However, she concludes on a note of optimism that other women acting as cross-cultural mediators (in the first case Maspéro's colleague, a white French woman photographer, in the second Benguigui herself, a young woman of Maghrebi origin) can bridge the gap between the provider and the refuser of hospitality. The theme of the young woman of Maghrebi origin as cultural 'entrepreneuse', to coin Sylvie Durmelat's term, is one that is taken up in the final chapters, which explore aspects of women's intervention as cultural mediators in film and television.

Although second generation 'Beur' women have been active as writers since the early 1980s, it has been more difficult for them to gain access to film and television. This is not surprising in a country where there is no policy of extending access either to women or to ethnic minorities. As Barlet points out: 'Supporting ethnic minority cultural production would be tantamount to admitting the existing of ethnic minority communities and the right to difference.'[6] (Barlet, 1996, p. 134). Black and 'Beur' women have featured in usually secondary and often stereotyped roles in French cinema, in certain *banlieue* films (films set in the working-class housing estates on the peripheries of major cities) and certain films by French women directors (Tarr, 1997b; Sherzer, 1999). Carrie Tarr analyses the first appearance of French feature films written and directed by young women of Maghrebi origin. Zaïda Ghorab-Volta's *Souviens-toi de moi* reworks the *banlieue* film from a woman's perspective, Rachida Krim's *Sous les pieds des femmes* the history of the Algerian War as it was fought out on French territory. Tarr argues that the shift between the two films is indicative of a shift in the concerns of 'Beur' generation women, the first articulating a young woman's struggle for identity, the second foregrounding the normally silenced immigrant mother in a process of commemoration, which both retrieves a lost history and establishes a female genealogy.

A similar line of argument is taken by Sylvie Durmelat in her analysis of Yamina Benguigui's television documentary, *Mémoires d'immigrés: l'héritage maghrébin* (1997), later released in the cinema. Durmelat analyses how Benguigui allows men and women immigrants of Maghrebi origin and their children to testify to their memories and experiences of immigration, aiming both to validate immigrant lives and history and to contribute to shifting majority perceptions of colonial history and the place of post-colonial Others within the (history of the) French Republic. Whereas television has hitherto been instrumental in circumventing the power and authority of first generation immigrants and marginalizing or demonizing their children, Benguigi's intervention provides a powerful space for mediation, bridging the gap between the second generation and their parents as well as between 'French' citizens and 'immigrant' Others.

The success of *Mémoires d'immigrés*, which closely followed the release of the three-minute campaign film, *Nous, sans-papiers de France* (1997) featuring Madjiguène Cissé,[7] may have contributed to (and been the result of) an awareness of the need for more, and more thoughtful, representations of France's post-colonial Others. Since 1998, a group of artists and intellectuals calling themselves 'Egalité' (Equality), led by Calixte Beyala among others, has been putting pressure on the CSA (Conseil supérieur de l'audiovisuel/Audio-Visual Commission), to introduce a quota system to ensure the adequate representation of the black and 'Beur' population of France on television (Delesalle, 1999, p. 98). Hopefully, cultural 'entrepreneuses' like Yamina Benguigi and Calixte Beyala will ensure that any attempts by the CSA to induce the public service channels to reflect the diversity of origins of the French are informed by gender as much as ethnicity. The work of women writers and filmmakers of immigrant origin, through the way it addresses the painful consequences of immigration and exile and the difficulties of integrating into metropolitan French culture, is clearly vital in validating the histories and identities of women readers and viewers of immigrant origin. It also invites majority French readers and viewers to call into question dominant notions of what it means to be French, so opening up the possibility of a France able to take account of the diversity of identities within its population and reinvent a politics of hospitality for a multi-cultural society.

Notes

1. For a recent example of a work on immigration in which gender issues are marginalized, see Dewitte, P. (1999), *Immigration et intégration: l'état des savoirs*, Paris: La Découverte.
2. INSEE 1990.
3. The use of the term 'French' presents similar problems in that it is commonly understood to refer to white French people (who may in fact also be of immigrant origin themselves). We acknowledge this difficulty by tending to refer to the 'dominant' or 'majority' French society, representations and culture.
4. 'Par le renforcement aveugle et continu de leur politique répressive à l'égard des immigrés, les ministres de l'Intérieur successifs ont contribué à éliminer l'hospitalité du champ des vertus françaises.'
5. 'Soutenir l'expression d'une communauté minoritaire revient à en admettre l'existence, et donc une droit à la différence.'
6. '[Cela supposerait] accepter une mutation de notre propre identité, enrichie de l'experience de l'Autre et de la confrontation des cultures.'
7. The film, shown in selected film theatres in Paris and the provinces in April 1997, was made by some fifteen filmmakers including Claire Devers (Powrie, 1999, p. 12). Of the sixty-six filmmakers who initiated a protest against the Debré law on 11 February 1997, twenty-three were women, including Pascale Ferran, Claire Denis and Catherine Breillat. After the mass demonstration of 22 February 1997, filmmaker Jeanne Labrune organized a meeting between intellectuals and the *sans-papiers*, one of the results of which was a policy of 'godparenting' the *sans-papiers*.

Part I
Social and Political Identities

–1–

Women and Immigration: Nationality and Citizenship

Jane Freedman

Questions of nationality and citizenship have provoked fierce and widespread debate in France in recent years. Immigration, and the 'integration' of those of immigrant origin into French society,[1] are issues which have been at the forefront of political discussion and, under pressure from the extreme right-wing Front National and its growing electoral support,[2] political parties of both the moderate Right and Left have taken a hard line on immigration policy, leading to changes in the laws on immigration and the acquisition of French nationality, and the residence of 'foreigners' in France. As elsewhere, these issues of nationality and citizenship are ones that affect women immigrants and women of immigrant origin in particular ways. Patterns of immigration into France have shown a gender differentiation with women generally arriving later than men. The arrival of women is linked in the French perception to the sedenterization of the immigrant community, with the idea of immigrants' return to their country of origin being replaced by a project of settlement in France. As Nicollet argues with relation to immigrants of African origin, the sedenterization of the immigrant community and the greater presence of women and children amongst the immigrant population has given gender relations a particular importance, and to the previous debates over immigrants and the labour force have been added questions over families, marriage, polygamy, excision etc. (Nicollet, 1993). This is true not only for African immigrants but for all other immigrant communities. The immigration of women rather than men poses different questions for French society, and the experience of immigration is clearly a gendered one, lived differently by men and women. Similarly, integration and the acquisition of citizenship and nationality are clearly gendered and racialized processes, lived differently by men and women of immigrant origin. In fact, the intermeshing of both sexist and racist forms of domination and exclusion places women of immigrant origin in France in sometimes very difficult and oppressive situations.

The politicization of the immigration question since the early 1980s has led to increasing mediatization and a proliferation of representations, often stereotyped, of immigrants and those of immigrant origin. These representations highlight a perceived crisis in French national identity and a questioning of what citizenship really means in contemporary France. And, as Yuval-Davis and Anthias point out, there has always been a close linkage between gender and national identity with women participating in ethnic and national processes in a number of specific ways: as biological reproducers of the ethnic community; reproducers of the boundaries of ethnic or national groups; key actors in the transmission of the community's values; markers of ethnic or national distinctiveness and active participants in national struggles (Yuval-Davis and Anthias, 1989). Political representations of immigrants in France have tended to concentrate principally on the image of the male immigrant worker, and have often ignored women's varied migratory projects and trajectories, either rendering women of immigrant origin 'invisible' (which seems particularly to be the case for women of Asian origin) or confining them to the family and representing them principally as wives and mothers (Barison and Catarino, 1997; Bentichou, 1997; Golub, Morokvasic and Quiminal, 1997). Those political representations that exist of women of immigrant origin in France have thus highlighted all of the aspects of women's roles in ethnic processes outlined by Yuval-Davis and Anthias, with particular emphasis placed on women's role in the reproduction of communities of immigrant origin, and the transmission of values to their children. On the one hand, racist stereotyping, typical of extreme-Right discourse, but not by any means the sole preserve of the Front National, highlights women's role in the biological reproduction of ethnic communities in France, creating fears of an 'immigrant invasion' boosted by the supposedly high birth rate amongst communities of immigrant origin. Research carried out amongst Front National supporters reveals their horror at the idea of women of immigrant origin producing numerous children and claiming benefits from the French state to support them. One Front National voter, for example, expresses his feelings of disgust: 'When I see these North African women who have fifteen or twenty children! Who claim benefits of thirty or forty thousand francs . . . it's abhorrent'[3] (Mossuz-Lavau, 1994, p. 170). There is a persistent image of women of immigrant origin bearing numerous, illegitimate children and expecting the French state to support them. Those, on the other hand, who maintain a discourse of 'integration' also place their representations of women of immigrant origin within the family. Their role as biological reproducers of the ethnic community is still highlighted, but in this instance, their importance in the transmission of community values, and in particular those values which will aid their childrens' integration into French society, is stressed. Represented in their role as 'mothers' of families, it is seen to be their duty to ensure the stability of the ethnic minority population and to see to it that their children integrate or assimilate and become 'French'. Women of immigrant origin are thus represented as both the bearers of 'tradition' and agents of 'modernity', responsible both for perpetuating the boundaries of ethnic groups within France and for ensuring that these boundaries are made permeable to French culture. These dominant representations are often both stereotyped and contradictory, and little has been done to moderate them by analysts of immigration or, indeed, by French feminist researchers. One can thus point to a *rendez-vous manqué* (missed rendez-vous) between feminisms and anti-racisms in France (Lloyd, 1998), with both sides tending to prioritize one axis of domination (either sexist or racist) and failing to take full account of the multiple nature of women of immigrant origin's identities, experiences and situations. As Barison and Catarino argue:

> Ignoring, or wishing to ignore that women immigrants are situated in a strategic position at the intersection of the social relations of domination which exist between sexes, classes and ethnic groups, the body of research on migration and feminist research on general themes (work, family, etc.) have respectively, for many years, neglected women and immigrants.[4] (Barison and Catarino, 1997, p. 17)

So we can argue that these women face a particular weight of expectation and are under specific pressure from French society. At the same time there are powerful forces acting to exclude these women from this same society, depending on their particular situation. For many first generation women of immigrant origin in particular, adaptation to French society may be difficult. They have broken with systems of solidarity and affiliation in their countries of origin and have to reconstruct their social position in a foreign society. They may find themselves isolated, especially if they have a limited command of the French language. Housing for immigrants is often poor, and one can argue that this has a particular effect on women, who, in many communities of immigrant origin, are almost entirely responsible for the management of the domestic space. In addition, for women of immigrant origin, access to salaried work has been limited both because of domestic and social pressure from within their communities – women of Maghrebi and Turkish origin have the lowest rates of formal employment due in part to the norms in their countries of origin (Hargreaves, 1995) – and because of reluctance by French employers to hire women of immigrant origin, especially those from the ex-colonies (there is a general differentiation in French opinion between immigrants of European origin and those from Africa and Asia who are more readily referred to as *immigrés* and can be seen to suffer greater discrimination from employers and others). Thus in contrast with many immigrant men who arrived in France to fulfil demands for manual labour, women of immigrant origin have not been able to count on integration through waged employment, particularly in a time of economic recession. Those who do find waged employment are often employed in low-paid service sector jobs, many in temporary and part-time positions with no security. As Quiminal explains, women of immigrant origin may be less prone to overt racist attacks than men, but at the same time, they are expected to occupy a particular place and there is no room in the French imagination for these women to expand their role, take advantage of education and job training opportunities and enter the labour force. French attitudes to women of immigrant origin, particularly from the ex-colonies can be summarized thus:

> They are tolerated as housewives, taking care of the domestic chores, bringing up the children, and taking responsibility for the integration of their family. Immigrant women are assigned to a particular place, and in a time of economic crisis and unemployment, they must not overstep the limits of that place. When they ask for education or training, for example, they are not heard.[5] (Golub, Morokvasic and Quiminal 1997, p. 25)

The situation for women of immigrant origin, and particularly women who are themselves immigrants has worsened in the past decade with the introduction of new laws restricting rights to residence in France and to French nationality.

Women, Citizenship and the Law

The political representations of immigrants as a threat both to French national identity and to France's social and economic future, have led to a series of laws restricting the rights of immigrants in France. The so-called Pasqua laws of 1986 and 1993 and Debré law of 1997 (named after the two Ministers of the Interior who instigated the legislation), concerning the conditions of entry and residence for 'foreigners' in France, have limited the rights of residence of numerous categories of immigrants in France, and have made it easier to expel those who are found to be residing in France 'illegally'. Under the terms of these laws it is more difficult to obtain a residence card to live legally in France. The conditions for family regroupment have been tightened, for example, and those immigrants who have a French partner can only obtain a residence card after one year of marriage during which they have lived in France in a legal situation. In addition, the laws have restricted the rights of immigrants to marry in France, giving mayors added powers to refuse to allow what they believed to be marriages of convenience. Access to social security and health care has been restricted to those immigrants who have a legal residence status. On top of these laws to limit access to political and social citizenship in France there have been reforms in the nationality laws. The Méhaignerie law of 1993, for example, restricted access to French nationality, most importantly, of children born in France to foreign parents. Whereas these children would previously have acquired French nationality at birth, they now have to wait until the age of sixteen. Between the ages of sixteen and twenty-one they must show a willingness to become French by presenting a request for French nationality. When the Left came back to power after the legislative elections of 1997, it was hoped that these repressive laws would be reformed, but in fact there has been little change, with the Chevènement law of 1998 doing little to reform the restrictive measures previously introduced. As a result the situations of many women and men of immigrant origin living in France have become increasingly precarious, with the creation of an increasing number of so-called *clandestins*, those without the necessary legal papers for residence in France, and who therefore risk expulsion. Since 1996 these 'illegal' immigrants have been highly visible in the French media and in political debate through the organization of the *sans-papiers* movement (literally meaning the movement of those without papers). In fact, the effects of the legislation on immigration and residence in France have been far reaching, going beyond a simple decision about who may or may not enter France and including, as Lochak argues:

> The destabilisation of young people born or brought up in France but deprived of the assurance that they will be able to live there permanently; the plunge into irregularity of thousands of people to whom the law had up till then guaranteed the right to live in France; the brutal restriction of the right to live as a family; the denial of the right to social protection and of a minimum income to anyone who is or is no longer in possession of residence papers, even if they have previously worked and contributed their social security payments.[6] (Lochak, 1997, p. 44)

These new immigration and nationality laws are, in theory, universal, and thus equally restrictive to men and women of immigrant origin. In practice, however, gendered social and economic conditions mean that the laws concerning immigration and nationality affect men and women in different ways. Formal equality is undermined by a gendered division of labour that places the onus for the care of children and family responsibilities on women, whilst sexual discrimination in employment means that those women of immigrant origin who do work generally earn less than men, and many women suffer from unemployment, or exploitation through black-market labour. Many women of immigrant origin in fact find themselves in a position of economic dependence on men, a position that is worsened by the fact that they may also depend on men to have the right to residence in France. Women's independent citizenship is thus denied in a number of ways, and they may find themselves in a position where they are victims of both racist and sexist oppressions, and are in a situation of double dependency.

The Family

Dominant representations of women of immigrant origin confine them, as argued above, principally to the context of the family. This is not a coincidence as one of the major concerns of the debate over immigration in France has been that of family regroupment. After the government's official suspension of immigration for work in 1974, it was hoped by many that France could put a stop to immigration altogether, but one of the factors preventing this (apart from France's membership of the European Union)[7] was international pressure to allow family regroupment (Prencipe, 1994). In practice, however, although the French are obliged under international law to respect families' rights to live together in France, the way in which the laws have been written and the manner in which they are applied make this right of family regroupment more and more tenuous. As Rude-Antoine comments:

> A more attentive reading of the legal texts alerts one to the more and more hypothetical right of foreign families to residence, and reveals the greater and greater divide between those who come from the European Union and those who do not.[8] (Rude-Antoine, 1997, p. 12)

In fact, those wishing to bring their family members to France from countries outside of the European Union, have to satisfy certain conditions, particularly concerning housing and financial resources. Because of the stringency of these conditions, and because it is up to local authorities to decide whether they are fulfilled, there are many occasions when the right to family regroupment is denied. The historical patterns of immigration into France, where men were encouraged to come alone to work in French industry, mean that although this law is phrased in gender-neutral language, it is more often the case that the family member already resident in France is a man, and those trying to join him are his wife and/or children. The difficulties involved in getting these women and children into France legally means that they are often forced to enter the country without the correct papers, often with a tourist visa which expires after three months, leaving them in a state of perpetual fear of discovery and deportation. Many women, therefore, live in a state of clandestinity because of these laws, and this reinforces their dependence on the men who they have come to France to join. It means that it is almost impossible for them to find work and if they do it will be on the black market, risking further exploitation. These women are oppressed because, in effect, their existence is denied. What makes this situation even more difficult is that the law forbids all regularization *sur place* (on site) on conditions of family regroupment – the demand for residence papers for those coming to join their family in France must be made when they are still in their country of origin; once they are already in France their case cannot be considered. This added restriction leads to cases such as that described by Quiminal, of a young Moroccan woman who came to study in France. In 1992 during the course of her studies she married a Moroccan man who had residence papers and they had a child. When this woman finished her studies in 1996 her student visa expired and so she applied to renew her papers on the grounds of family regroupment. This application was rejected because she was in France and not Morocco at the time she made the request (Quiminal, 1997). This inflexible application of the laws is used to deny many women in similar situations, who have been resident in France for some time, the right to stay and live legally with their families.

Problems also exist for those women of immigrant origin who wish to marry a French man (and vice versa) and to obtain the rights to French residence and citizenship through such a marriage. Although the problem of 'mixed' marriages is one that both men and women of immigrant origin encounter, again the restrictions are more important for women, as women have a higher rate of exogamous marriage than men (Tribalat, 1995). In addition to social and communal pressures against 'mixed' marriages (see for example Lacoste-Dujardin's analysis of Maghrebi attitudes to exoga-mous marriage in Chapter 5), there are now greater legal restrictions, which act to discourage such marriages. Under the new immigration laws, mayors are given the power to refuse to marry a French partner to a partner of immigrant origin if they suspect that this marriage is one of convenience, taking place in order for the immigrant partner to gain residence papers to live in France. Moreover, once married, in order for the request for residence papers to be successful, the partner making the request must have entered France and must have been living in France legally and the couple must have been married and living together for at least one year. For many, however, proving that they have entered France legally may involve a return to their country of origin to request a visa, and if they do this the French authorities may hold against them the period of separation from their partner, using this to argue that their marriage is not a genuine one. As Ferré argues, the law does not take into account personal histories and tends to perceive all 'mixed' marriages as suspect, thus problematizing personal relations and denying some couples the right to marry and others the right to live together in France legally (Ferré, 1997).

On a more fundamental level, the laws on immigration are geared towards the acceptance of families which not only discriminates against single people and homosexuals – whose couples are not recognized by law as grounds for family regroupment and the granting of residence permits – but in fact again discriminates against women by pushing them into marriages that they might not otherwise have accepted. As Morokvasic argues:

> In order to stay in the host country, immigrants are obliged to marry in a much larger proportion than the native population. The marriage rate amongst immigrants thus appears much higher than it would be if they benefitted from the same possibilities as the native population.[9] (Morokvasic, 1997, p. 27)

Once they are married, there is pressure to stay in a relationship, even though it may be one of oppression or dependence. Divorce or separation could lead to the removal or non-renewal of their residence papers. This constraint is added to that of communal norms, which may view divorce badly or may give the husband greater freedom to divorce than the wife (Lesselier, 1999). Again there is a risk of a double sanction as a husband may use the threat of removing his wife's legal right to residence in France (as Cissé points out in Chapter 2), to reinforce communal pressures against separation or divorce. The Réseau pour l'Autonomie Juridique des Femmes Immigrées et Refugiées (Network for the autonomy of immigrant and refugee women) or RAJFIRE, a campaigning group set up in 1997 to help immigrant and refugee women in France, is concerned that these women's oppression is worsened by the French law's insistence on the family as a framework for the admittance of immigrants. Their chairwoman, Claudie Lesselier, argues that: 'The attribution of residence permits and eventual regularisation of foreigners in an illegal situation are based, above all, on the family framework. This is especially onerous for women for whom the family is often a site of dependency and constraint'[10] (Lesselier, 1999, p. 46).

Further, the families which the policies and laws on family regroupment seek to promote are those modelled on the 'normal' family – a family composed of father, mother and children. This is a highly normative conception of the family – one that is based on an idealized version of the French family and one that does not take into account variants on this traditional family such as one-parent or polygamous families. The same representations which see women as the key to the successful integration of immigrants into France usually see this happening in the context of such a 'traditional' family, and other types of family living arrangement are therefore rejected as tending to increase instability and decrease chances of integration. For example, in his book *La famille: secret de l'intégration,* Christian Jelen argues that if immigrants have a 'quality' family model, which is coincidentally close to that of the French family, integration and social success will follow (Jelen, 1993). This conception of the family is an archaic one, untouched by feminism, a model which assumes the father as the chief of the family, responsible for providing for his family financially whilst the mother is engaged with bringing up the children and ensuring their proper integration into French society. These representations upon which French law is based not only serve to reinforce the inequality between men and women within families but also justify the discriminatory nature of immigration policies that regard the entry of women as another burden on both immigrant men and on French society. It is not considered that women may go out and work and provide for themselves and their children and families. In fact, this model of the 'traditional' nuclear family is one which is in decline amongst all of the French population, irrespective of their origins, but the multiple variants on the family that now exist in society are not recognized in the laws concerning immigrants into France and this is yet another cause of difficulties for women of immigrant origin.

One problem that some of these women face is that of polygamy. Although this is a problem that is more widespread in the French imagination than it is in reality, there are still a significant number of polygamous families living in France, and this is clearly a model which does not fit the French conception of a 'traditional' family unit. So again women in polygamous families are in a situation where they are doubly oppressed, firstly by the social and economic conditions under which they live, and secondly by the French law. The law against polygamy is in theory universal and does not recognize a difference between men and women, in other words it is illegal for a man to have more than one wife and a women to have more than one husband. In fact, however, it is clear that in the case of populations of immigrant origin where polygamy occurs it is men who have several wives. This situation makes life very difficult for the wives; not only do they suffer emotional and material difficulties, sometimes with two or more wives and their children living in the same flat, but they are in a situation where it is often impossible for them to live legally in France as only one of the wives can legally obtain a residence card and the other/s will remain in a clandestine situation. The condemnation of polygamy within dominant French discourse is framed in terms of the defence of women's rights, and it is true that this is of course a key issue in the debate. It is important to note, however, that the French state tolerated polygamy when it needed immigrant workers to boost its manpower and that the official opposition to polygamy and concern for women's rights only became operative when immigrants began to be represented as a threat to French national identity and a burden on the French economy. What is more, those politicians and officials who profess to oppose polygamy out of a concern for women's rights are often unconcerned by the negative effects the simple repression of polygamy, with no support for the women concerned, may have on women of immigrant origin in France.

The Problems of Children's Nationality

Another way in which some women of immigrant origin have been affected by the new legislation is in the changed legal status of their children and the resulting restrictions on access to healthcare and social security both for them, and for their children. In response to a perception within dominant French representations that foreign women came to give birth in France in order to obtain French nationality for their children, and therefore, ultimately for themselves, there have been amendments to the nationality laws (as mentioned above) so that children born in France to foreign parents resident in France no longer automatically obtain French nationality, but have to wait until the age of sixteen or eighteen to do so. This poses problems for many women, because, without wishing to essentialize their positions as mothers, it is usually the case that women are more involved in bringing up children. The fact that children do not obtain French nationality at birth means that many women's legal situation is made precarious. Under the terms of the Debré law, parents not living in a state of polygamy who have children under sixteen residing in France can obtain a residence card for themselves as long as they effectively provide for their childrens needs. Those in an illegal situation concerning residence at the time they make their request for a residence card may, however, find that they are refused on the grounds that they are not providing for their children properly. In fact, a vicious circle is created: because of their illegal situation they cannot work legally in France and thus it may be deemed that they are not providing properly for their children, but they cannot get legal residence papers until they prove they are providing for their children. In addition, parents of children who do not have French nationality cannot claim any family allowances for them, and are denied access to health and social security cover. A woman *sans-papières* (without papers) from Toulouse recounts her experience:

> I've lived in France for six years. I came to join my husband who is a craftsman. I have four children of fifteen, twelve, eight and five. The little one was born here. My husband left me and now I live alone with the four children. I became part of the collective of sans-papiers in Toulouse and I was one of the first to be regularized under the terms of Chevènement's circular. But that has hardly changed anything because my children have still not been regularized. It's as if they didn't exist. I don't have the right to any family allowance, I don't have any rights. How am I meant to live?[11] (Toulouse, 18 February 1998)

This problem of their children's nationality is not unique to those women who form part of the *sans-papiers* movement. Benani points to the example of Maghrebi single-mothers who, because of their status as women and immigrants, have children with no nationality:

> Women are in a more fragile position because of their status as women and immigrants, or daughters of immigrants. The phenomenon of Maghrebi single mothers is significant in this regard. Those who have not acquired French citizenship and who are mothers of children born on French territory, are bringing up children who are not recognized by any country. They are not French (and will not become French before the age of sixteen or eighteen) because of the Pasqua laws, and neither are they Moroccan, Algerian or Tunisian, because the family law codes in the Maghreb do not recognize the status of single mothers, and do not accord a legal status to their children . . . From birth, these children live in a position of exclusion.[12] (Benani, 1995b, p. 217)

Thus women of immigrant origin often find their status as mothers devalued and encounter both legal and material difficulties in bringing up their children in France. Whilst dominant representations portray them first as wives and mothers, responsible for bringing up children who will integrate into French society, the social and legal conditions of this same society make this a sometimes very difficult task.

Women, Work and Immigration Law

As argued above, the principle representations of women of immigrant origin portray them as wives and mothers, and thus see them as inactive outside the home. In fact it has been difficult for women of immigrant origin to find work in France. Unlike men who came specifically to fill gaps in the French labour market, most women immigrated later when economic conditions were more difficult, and it was not assumed that they would find work. In fact there is an increasing presence in the labour force among women of immigrant origin, but they are also a group who suffer from high rates of unemployment (38.4 per cent of all women of immigrant origin who come from outside of the European Union were unemployed according to a survey carried out in 1990),[13] and many who do work do so on the black market, either because they cannot find any other type of work, or sometimes because of the legal problems with residence papers outlined above. Sexist and racist discrimination by employers is thus reinforced by legal structures that do not take into account these women's desire to work.

The new Chevènement law on immigration of May 1998 is an example of how socio-economic and legal conditions can contribute to discriminate doubly against women. This new law makes it easier for certain categories of foreigner to receive residence cards in France. This includes those whose professional qualifications may be seen to benefit France: scientists, those with artistic and cultural professions, and anyone else whose residence is considered to be advantageous for France. Again, although this law is not gender specific, in reality it is clear that these categories will probably benefit men much more than women given the unequal access of women to education in their countries of origin (Cissé, 1999). So those who do want to work in France often have to do so illegally and this means that they are dependent on employers who will give them work on the black market. They have no employment rights, and are often isolated and exposed to the risks of sexual harrassment and sexual violence (Lesselier, 1999). This black market employment also militates against the possibilities of women of immigrant origin having access to legal residence cards in the future. The new Chevènement law allows for the 'regularization' of those who have been living in France for at least ten years, even if they have been doing so illegally. This clause, however, which gave hope to many *sans-papiers* has in fact delivered far less than it promised. For many women who have been living in secrecy and working on the black market, it may be impossible to convince the local authorities of their length of residence in France. *Le Monde* recounts the case of a young Haitian woman, living in Paris since 1989 and working as a black market cleaner. Her requests for residence papers have been rejected by the authorities because she does not have adequate proof of her length of residence in France, nor of the fact that she earns a living, as none of her employers will testify that she has been working for them because it is illegal to employ someone without declaring it. A voluntary worker trying to help in this case has persuaded her employers to sign letters acknowledging that they have known the woman in question for several years but she comments: 'The prefectoral offices know very well that this type of declaration is really an implicit recognition of work that has not been declared. But I have the impression that they do not want to regularize them because they are single women'[14] (*Le Monde*, 14 November 1999).

Women's Associations: A Recourse Against Discrimination

Throughout this chapter, I have argued that women of immigrant origin face a double discrimination within French society, and are often in a situation of double dependency on men. It is important, however, not to paint a picture of these women as helpless victims who are unable to defend themselves against these oppressions. One important manifestation of women's agency and of their desire to fight the discriminations of which they are victims is the formation of women's associations to provide solidarity and self-help for women of immigrant origin. A well-known example of a women's association is that of the Nanas Beurs (now known as the Meufs Rebeus or Voix d'Elles Rebelles) an association for young Maghrebi women. One of the founding members describes how she and other young women from the North African immigrant community set up this association to defend their interests as: 'Women's concerns were often overlooked in the ideological battle for equal opportunities for immigrants. None of the slogans or campaigns showed how young women of North African origin were the victims of discrimination or oppression' (Benani, 1995a, p.79).

Their association provides help for women having trouble with their residence or nationality papers, refugees, unmarried mothers and battered wives amongst others. They also stage debates and public meetings on topics of concern to women of immigrant origin and act as a point of liaison between women of immigrant origin and the French authorities in the forms of social and welfare workers, courts and police. And the *Nanas Beurs* are not the only such organization of women of immigrant origin, there are numerous other associations of women of immigrant origin of different origins (Catherine Quiminal analyses the functions of African women's associations in Chapter 3), providing self-help in negotiating a path towards an easier life in France. Women have also been active in the *sans-papiers* movement, and in fact have ensured the movement's survival and success (as Cissé argues in Chapter 2).

In addition, although French feminists and women's organizations may have been slow to realize the problems facing women of immigrant origin, and to organize to help them (Barison and Catarino, 1997; Lloyd, 1998), a campaigning network, RAJFIRE, has now been set up whose goal is to defend the rights of women of immigrant origin, to fight for the right of asylum for women who are victims of sexist persecution and violence, and to achieve the introduction of an autonomous legal status for women of immigrant origin. Until women of immigrant origin achieve such an autonomous status, they argue, they will be prevented from accessing the rights they should have as individuals. It seems that until the problems of women of immigrant origin in regard to nationality and citizenship are considered specifically and apart from general issues relating to these subjects, women will continue to be the victims of particular exclusions. Despite the efforts of women of immigrant origin to organize and struggle against these exclusions, there is still a long way to go before they overcome their double source of oppression and achieve equal citizenship status in France.

Notes

1. For a discussion of the use of the term *immigré* in France, see the introduction to this volume.
2. Although they have not made a significant breakthrough in elections to the National Assembly, except in 1986 when these elections took

place under a system of proportional representation, the consistently high scores of the Front National in local elections has put pressure on the other parties of the Right to enter into coalitions with the Front National. Similarly the high scores of their leader, Jean-Marie Le Pen in presidential elections has influenced the strategies and policies of other political parties. For more information on the Front National and their policies see, for example, Mayer, N. and Perrineau, P. (1996), *Le Front National à découvert*, Paris: Presses de Sciences Po.

3. 'Quand on voit des exemples des femmes Maghrébines qui ont quinze, vingt gamins! Qui touchent des trente, quarante mille francs d'allocations . . . c'est aberrant.'

4. 'Ignorant ou voulant ignorer que les femmes immigrées se situent dans une position stratégique, car à l'intersection des rapports sociaux de domination qui se jouent entre les sexes, les classes et les groupes ethniques, le corpus de recherche sur la migration et les recherches féministes qui ont porté sur des thèmes généraux (travail, famille . . .) ont respectivement, pendant des années, négligé les femmes et les immigrés.'

5. 'On les tolère comme femmes au foyer, s'occupant des tâches domestiques, de l'éducation des enfants, responsables de l'intégration de leur famille. Les femmes immigrées sont véritablement assignées à une place, et en période de crise, de chômage, elles ne doivent absolument pas "déborder" cette place, et lorsqu'elles demandent des formations, par exemple, elles ne sont absolument pas entendues.'

6. 'Déstabilisation des jeunes nés ou ayant grandi en France, privés de l'assurance de pouvoir y vivre durablement; basculement dans l'irrégularité des milliers de personnes auxquelles les textes donnaient jusque-là garantie de pouvoir demeurer en France; restriction brutale du droit de vivre en famille; dénégation du droit à la protection sociale et à un minimum de revenus à toute personne qui n'est pas ou n'est plus en possession d'un titre de séjour, même si elle a antérieurement travaillé et cotisé à la Sécurité sociale.'

7. The provisions of the various European Treaties mean that France cannot prevent immigration from countries within the European Union. European immigrants, however, are not perceived as a threat to French national identity and economic stability in the same way as immigrants from Africa and Asia.

8. 'La lecture plus attentive des textes législatifs alerte sur le caractère de plus en plus hypothétique du droit de séjourner des familles étrangères et révèle la césure de plus en plus accentué entre les ressortissants communautaires et les non-communautaires.'

9. 'Pour pouvoir se maintenir dans le pays d'accueil, les immigrés sont obligés de se marier dans une proportion plus importante que les autochtones. Les taux de mariage des immigrés apparaissent donc beaucoup plus élevés qu'ils ne l'auraient été s'ils bénéficiaient des mêmes possibilités que les autochtones.'

10. 'L'attribution des titres de séjour et la régularisation éventuelle des étrangers en situation irrégulière sont avant tout basés sur le cadre familial. Ce qui pèse donc avant tout sur les femmes pour qui il est souvent un espace de dépendance et de contrainte.'

11. 'Ça fait six ans que je vis en France. Je suis venue pour rejoindre mon mari, qui était artisan. J'ai quatre enfants: quinze ans, douze ans, huit ans, cinq ans. Le dernier est né ici. Mon mari est parti, je vis seule avec les quatre enfants. Je faisais partie du Collectif des sans-papiers de Toulouse, et j'ai été une des premières à être régularisées, avec la circulaire Chevènement. Mais ça n'a pratiquement rien changé, parce que mes enfants, eux, ne sont toujours pas régularisés. C'est comme s'ils n'existaient pas. Ça fait que je n'ai pas droit aux allocations familiales, je n'ai droit à rien. Avec quoi je vis?'

12. 'Les femmes sont plus fragilisées par leur statut de femmes et d'immigrées ou de filles d'immigrées. Le phénomène des mères célibataires maghrébines est à cet égard significatif: Celles qui n'ont pas acquis la citoyenneté française et sont mères d'enfants nés sur le territoire français élèvent des enfants qui ne sont reconnus par aucun pays. Ils ne sont pas français (et ne le seront pas avant l'âge de seize ou de dix-huit ans), en vertu des lois Pasqua, et pas davantage marocains, algériens ou tunisiens, les codes de la famille, au Maghreb, ne reconnaissent pas le statut des mères célibataires, et pas davantage un statut juridique de l'enfant naturel … Ces enfants, dès leur naissance, vont vivre sous le statut de l'exclusion.'

13. INSEE 1990.

14. 'Ce type de déclaration, les service préfectoraux savent pertinemment qu'il s'agit d'une reconnaissance implicite d'emploi sans déclaration. Mais j'ai l'impression qu'ils ne veulent pas la régulariser parce que ce sont des femmes seules.'

–2–

The *Sans-papières*: An Interview with Madjiguène Cissé

Jane Freedman and *Carrie Tarr*

On 18 March 1996, 300 Africans who had no residence papers and were, therefore, living 'illegally' in France, occupied the church of Saint-Ambroise in Paris to protest about their situation and to demand that the French authorities regularize their situation. Their protest continued throughout the Spring and Summer of 1996, as they moved from one location to another, eventually occupying the church of Saint-Bernard in Paris, from which they were evicted brutally by riot police in August. These protests and accompanying hunger strikes brought the plight of these *sans-papiers* (literally 'without papers') to the attention of the French public provoking a wave of support which included many prominent personalities. The French Government has remained unmoved, however, and despite the election of a new Socialist government in 1997, there are still thousands of *sans-papiers* throughout France, and a protest network has been established to organize regular occupations and demonstrations.

Madjiguène Cissé, a woman of Senegalese origin, emerged as one of the leading spokespeople for the *sans-papiers* movement. Overcoming both opposition from men within her movement, and sexist and racist discrimination from the French authorities and police, she has succeeded in bringing the plight of the *sans-papiers* to public attention both in France and elsewhere in Europe, and in arguing forcefully and persuasively for the regularisation of all of these so-called 'illegal' immigrants. In 1998 she was awarded a prize by the German Human Rights League in recognition of her work. Madjiguène has recently published a book, *Parole de sans-papiers! (A Sans-papiers Speaks!)*, in which she recounts her experience as a woman and a *sans-papiers*. She recounted this experience and discussed the lessons to be learned from it in an interview with the editors in September 1999.

Figure 2. Madjiguène Cissé at a meeting outside Notre-Dame on 12 August 1996, organized after 300 policemen had removed ten hunger strikers by force at 5.00 a.m. and sent them to six different hospitals (photograph by Alejandra Riera).

What was Women's Role in the *Sans-papiers* Movement?

Women were present in the *sans-papiers* movement from the beginning. In the first collective, out of 300 people there were already eighty of us women. And it was lucky that we were so numerous, because otherwise the *sans-papiers'* struggle would certainly have turned out very differently. It was important because the women were an important physical presence, but more importantly they played the role of what I would call a motor. This isn't really clear from the reports you read, but women played a key role in that each time the movement began to slow down and stagnate, when the media weren't paying us any attention and people began to become discouraged, it was the women who took on the role of encouraging the whole group and it was also the women who, by organizing meetings amongst ourselves (just the women), managed to find initiatives which allowed our campaign to reinvigorate itself. For example, right at the beginning, when we were at the Saint-Ambroise church, we held a meeting amongst the women to which we invited French women too, and we organized a women's demonstration, marching from Saint-Ambroise to Matignon.[1] And when we arrived they (the government) refused to meet us, so we held a sit-in for the whole afternoon, chanting 'the *sans-papiers* won't go away'. And that brought back the media attention to the movement. We also had the support of women artists, a famous singer of Moroccan origin came to the demonstration, for example, and that brought us lots of publicity and gave the movement back lots of energy. And it kept happening in the same way. Each time the movement began to run out of steam, it was the women who got together and said we've got to find ways to get over this, and that was how we occupied the town hall of the eighteenth arrondissement of Paris, just women and children. We also occupied the town hall of the thirteenth arrondissement of Paris, where the mayor was also Minister of Justice at the time. We organized demonstrations every Wednesday in front of the Elysee, Chirac's residence,[2] to protest to the politicians about the situation of the *sans-papiers*. And that weekly demonstration took place for almost a year. So the women really played a very dynamic role in the Saint-Bernard group and in all the other collectives of *sans-papiers* as well, because now there are collectives all over France.

Another way in which women helped the struggle was to keep the group together. The government kept trying to divide us, to break up the group. And each time there was an attempt at division, it was the women who saved the situation. Women are very perspicacious, they understand very quickly what's going on. For example, when someone comes to talk to us, when the women say 'that person is dubious', then a bit later you always realize that that person really is dubious. It's true. So each time there was an attempt at division, it was the women who saved the situation. When we started out, for example, we were a group of 300 at the beginning, and a group of three hundred is very visible. We were at the church of Saint-Ambroise and the priest and certain associations made a proposition to re-house fifty people. In other words, they were going to sort through the different cases and pick out the 'good' ones. And the 'good' cases were those of families, especially families with children. The others would have to go back where they came from. And each time this type of thing happened it was the women who said 'no, if they separate us, those who are single won't get their residence papers'. And that's how we managed to overcome these attempts at division. Personally, I think that if there hadn't been that number of women there from the beginning, then the *sans-papiers*' struggle would never have lasted so long. I think that the government is a bit scared of the women too, because we're numerous and we're combative. When there's a fight the women join in as well, and give punches and kicks — the government thinks that we're real devils!

Figure 3. Madjiguène Cissé, Place de la République, at a solidarity meeting for Algerian women, held on International Women's Day 1999 (photograph by Alejandra Riera).

So that is how women have played a role in the *sans-papiers'* fight, and not only foreign women, but French women too. There has been a lot of solidarity, which in my view, could only be found amongst women. I think that relationships are easier between women. When I went to Saint-Ambroise for the first time on the day of the occupation (I wasn't at the two preparatory meetings before the occupation), I spontaneously headed for the women there. It was instinctive. And I spent the first few days talking to the other women in small groups. I understood straight away that we'd have an important role to play, the complicity between us was there from the start. That's why at the first public meeting that we organized, where there were already 2,000 people, I spoke in public for the first time and my message was addressed to women: foreign women and French women as well.

There are many different nationalities within the *sans-papiers* movement. Just in Saint-Ambroise there were ten different nationalities. But there are collectives elsewhere where there are more than thirty different nationalities. And in the national coordination we counted forty-eight. It's really the United Nations of *sans-papiers*: we come from all over the place. Despite that we've managed to avoid community-based movements.

That was really vital: it's no good if all the Sengalese group themselves together, and all the Moroccans together, etc. In the collective everyone was united. It wasn't that easy to achieve. Before people got to know each other well it was difficult. In some collectives they had to call on a delegate from another collective to act as a referee. I've often been to other collectives to help sort out problems like that. We did even go through a kind of racism amongst the different communities: Chinese who didn't get on with Maghrebis, or Maghrebis who didn't like the sub-Saharan Africans etc. But that kind of thing is inevitable in a group like ours, and each time a dispute arose we settled it by negotiation. Each time a problem arose we brought it up in the General Assembly and we all expressed how we felt and we overcame the problem. That's how everyone learned to live together. But it was definitely easier for women from different communities to get on with each other. Right from the start the relationships between different women were easier than those between men from different communities: there was a real complicity between us women.

Did you Encounter any Sexism within the Movement?

There has been a lot of sexism in the *sans-papiers* movement. When the first election of delegates took place, the women who were there said that there must be some women delegates. But the men said no, there was no need for women delegates, they only wanted men delegates. They thought that only men had the right to be leaders. So we had to fight for our rights, and eventually we got two women delegates – but only two out of ten. The men really didn't want women delegates, they were so scared of us that they didn't want us to take a leading role. It even came to blows – I ended up breaking a chair over someone's head!

And there were some men who didn't even want women to be there in the movement at all. At the beginning of the movement there were men who didn't want women to be present in the General Assembly. And the women just said: 'Why shouldn't we be there, we have things to say too.' So in the General Assembly everyone was there, and everyone had the chance to express themselves, men and women. There were a lot of women who had very interesting and intelligent ideas, and often their husbands panicked and wanted to send their wives home and stop them coming to the General Assembly again. They discovered that their wives were intelligent, that they could keep up an argument, and that made them scared. There was a kind of rebellion where we had to defend these women against their husbands who didn't want them to be there.

There are men who are progressive, one shouldn't tar them all with the same brush. Luckily there are those who accept progress. But on the other hand, there are those who have never accepted me as a spokeswoman for the movement. It's contradictory in a way because they realize that you can be useful – they all recognize that. They know that I know how to write a tract and they don't. I speak much more fluent and proper French than most of the *sans-papiers*. But despite that there is still reticence about me being a spokeswoman, just because I am a woman. And that type of sexism isn't confined to the *sans-papiers*. Even amongst representatives of the French organizations who support the *sans-papiers* it's the same. They prefer to have a dialogue with Ababacar[3] who is a man, even if they don't really agree with his position, rather than to talk to me, Madjiguène, a woman. It's the same story with the administration. I think that in fact women disturb people, because they are intransigent and honest and they know what they want.

Is there any Tradition of Combat like this amongst African Women?

There is a real combative tradition amongst women of African origin, and in fact it's a tradition which comes from their upbringing and education. As a small girl one is brought up to manage a whole house, all alone. When the mother is absent it is the daughter who manages the house, and I think that's the root of our capacity to organize and to take the initiative. Because it's not everyone who has the ability to take the initiative, there are many people who are scared of responsibility. But as an African girl you're already going to the market to do the shopping at the age of eight. You go to market all on your own to do the shopping for the whole family. Your mother gives you the money she has and you have to make do with it, you have to buy fresh vegetables, rice, fish etc. and it's you who calculates how much money you have and how much you can spend on each thing. I think that it's a really good training.

It's also true that African women are women who work – the statistics show it. They are women who work and women who have a tradition of struggle. You can see that from our history. The stories of women of Mali and Senegal during the period of colonization spring to mind for example. These women fought fiercely to get their husbands out of prison. It was during the railway strike. The Dakar–Niger railway came from Mali and ended up on the Senegalese Coast and it was used to transport primary materials – cotton, phosphates etc. The Africans who worked on the railway worked in conditions that were frankly conditions of slavery. So in 1936 and 1947 there were two huge strikes when the workers rebelled and said that they wouldn't be treated like slaves. The colonial administration responded with a massive repression and imprisoned all the strike leaders in Dakar. And it was the women who managed to liberate their husbands by organizing a women's march. They marched from Thiès, one of the biggest railway towns in Senegal, to Dakar, which is about seventy miles away, demanding the liberation of their husbands. So you see that the women's march of Saint-Ambroise has historical precedents.

There are lots of other examples of women's marches in Africa too. In Guinea there was a women's march in 1984 against the high cost of living. In Dakar in 1988 there were riots against the high cost of living brought about by the economic restructuring etc. and again it was the women who were at the forefront of the fight. For three months we organized surprise demonstrations and 'saucepan concerts'. There was a curfew at the time and marching was illegal. But not only did we march, we went out with saucepans to make noise. And we made lots of noise in all the different quarters of the city from nine o'clock onwards. So there are lots of examples. There's also a tradition of women leaders and heroines. In my book, I cite the story of a woman from Casamance in the South of Senegal who organized a revolt against the colonial administration who were requisitioning rice from the villagers. There is a real tradition of struggle.

Do Women of Immigrant Origin have Particular Problems in France?

As women we have specific demands that men wouldn't take into account, for example, concerning the recognition of sexist violence as a justification for asylum. Only women can put this type of demand to the forefront. There are women who have fled from their countries simply because they can no longer bear the social pressures that exist for women, because their families want to marry them to old men of sixty, etc. We believe that these are valid motives for seeking asylum. As women we should be recognized as human beings like everyone else, which isn't always the case. We noticed, for example, that Police prefectures don't always treat women equally when they process their demands for papers. At Saint-Bernard we had the experience that when the first women were given their residence papers, the prefecture always gave them a visitors card, which doesn't give the right to work. It is as if women were there to look after the house and the family. And we women said 'no', we want to look for work outside the home as well. So we had to fight and mobilize ourselves in order to get the prefecture to agree to change these visitors cards into normal residence cards that allowed women to work. As an immigrant woman in Europe one is always perceived and represented either as someone's wife, or their mother, or their daughter. Even though you are a mother, your son will be considered more highly than you by the public authorities. And then there are cases, for example, where a woman rebels against her husband and leaves him, and her husband will go to the Police prefecture and tell the police to take away her residence card. And if the husband can he'll take the card himself and tear it up or hide it. There are a lot of ways in which repression against immigrant women goes on, and we're fighting to change that. There are sexist attitudes not only amongst the police but everywhere in the administration. So that's why we need to fight: for immigrant women to have an autonomous status quite simply as human beings.

In fact you could say that women immigrants suffer doubly. Above all single women. Single women are already considered as lost by their society of origin. Only a 'lost' woman, a woman who doesn't accept her family's and her community's authority, could travel thousands of kilometres all on her own. So you're already rejected over there. And then equally you're rejected over here, not just by French society but by immigrant men. I've talked to lots of men in the Saint-Bernard group who are originally from Mali, and they tell me that they wouldn't marry a woman who was here in France alone because those women are too independent. They would prefer to go back to Mali and marry a woman from a village over there. That is how it works. So single women suffer all these discriminations, and then if they are married it's not much better because in general they come to join their husband in France and the husband has the power of life and death over his wife.

The problems for women with children are very serious. Even those whose children do have French nationality can suffer serious problems because the changes in the law mean that once the children reach the age of majority their mothers can find themselves in an irregular situation concerning residence papers. Previously parents of French children would have their situation regularized, but now there is a problem once the children reach the age of sixteen. And the other problem for women with children is that of social security. In general, as it is the husband who came to France first, it's the husband who the administration deals with first, and it's to him that the administration pays family allowances etc. Even though it's usually the woman who spends more time bringing up the children and looking after them. So you get situations where men take all the family allowances and then go and marry a second wife, and the first wife and children end up living in hostels with no money.

Polygamy is a real problem that women have to face. Although it's illegal, there are men who do bring a second and third wife to France. And because only one of the wives is recognized under French law, polygamy being illegal, the other wives are there unrecognized and live in terrible conditions. They don't have any residence papers, they have no rights to social security, often it's very, very difficult. Even if they decide to leave their husband because they can't stand the situation any longer, it's very hard for them to manage alone, to find housing, a job etc. And the French authorities must bear some of the responsibility for this because they tolerated polygamy when they needed workers to come and work in industry twenty or thirty years ago. Because they needed workers they turned a blind eye to polygamy, and so the workers brought their wives. And now, those wives who may have been living in France for twenty-five years in a regular situation, because of changes in the law under the Pasqua law[4] in 1993, suddenly find themselves without papers. So a woman who has been here for twenty years, and whose children are French, from one day to the next finds herself a *sans-papières*. What is really shocking is that these laws are retroactive: they even affect those who have been living in France for thirty years. That can't be right. When you have been living in a country for thirty years your whole life is there.

As far as the *sans-papiers* are concerned, the Right and the Left are all the same. The laws have become more repressive in France since 1974 when they decided to close the borders and to stop immigration for work purposes. They needed immigrant labour after the war but then there was the oil crisis in 1973 and because of the depression it caused they limited immigration. That's when the laws started to become more repressive. And what has happened is that when the Right has come in to power they've really hardened the laws, and then when the Left is elected they may take one or two clauses and modify them to make them a bit better, but they keep the repressive basis of the laws. And sometimes the Left even strengthens the repressive dispositions that the Right has introduced. For example, Chevènement[5] has lengthened the period of administrative detention, in other words the time allowed for the administration to hold someone in order to expel them. And all the clauses of the Debré and Pasqua laws which are really objectionable have been kept. There have been a few little adjustments here and there: retired people have now got residence cards which allow them to come and go between France and their country of origin, and things have got a little better for students. But there is always a utilitarian aspect to the laws – they make it easier for intellectuals, doctors, people whom France needs, to get a visa and come and live in France. But for the others the repressive laws have been upheld.

Translated by Jane Freedman

Notes

1. Matignon is the residence of the French Prime Minister, at the time Alain Juppé.
2. Jacques Chirac, the president of France at the time of writing.
3. Ababacar Diop was another spokesperson for the *sans-papiers*.
4. For more details on this law, and others, see Chapter 1.
5. Chevènement is the Minister of the Interior in the Socialist government, at the time of writing.

—3—

The Associative Movement of African Women and New Forms of Citizenship
Catherine Quiminal

The situation of migrants (whether male or female) is an ambivalent one. It involves both the impossibility of continuing to live in the country that one has left for various reasons (whether economic, political, or familial), and difficulties in the country in which one has arrived. These difficulties which have to be endured are particularly in evidence in a period of economic or political crisis in the migrants' new country of residence. There are many constraints which have to be overcome in moving from one country or territory to another, but both women and men migrants plan to make their exile a valuable experience. In attempting to understand migratory histories we must be aware of their dynamic character, complexity and ambivalence. There is also an important gender difference. The hopes and fears of men and women are not the same; each sex has a different way of articulating their past, present and future, of relating to the society that they have left and the one in which they have arrived. It is important to take this difference into account, and to understand the individuality of migratory experiences. This helps us to understand the relationship between the social relations of gender and migrants' relations with French society.

Choosing to study the associations of African women in France is a means of privileging an analysis of the way in which these women mobilize against the different forms of domination to which they are subject in their lives in France. The development of the associational movement of African women in France is the expression at the local level (more rarely national or international) of modes of collective action whose logical end is to become involved in new forms of citizenship. We are not considering citizenship in its formal, legal aspect here – the fact of belonging to a political community – but as a process involving activities undertaken in an attempt to maintain social life and exchanges. As Madoc and Murard argue, citizenship is not just about the relationship between the individual and institutions but also about relationships between individuals (Madoc and Murard, 1995). African women's associations are involved in such citizenship activities, as will be shown throughout this chapter.

The Arrival of African Women in France

The flowering of African women's associations during the 1980s (there are more than fifty in the Paris region alone) corresponds to a change in the composition of migration from sub-Saharan Africa. In the 1960s immigrants from this region were mainly male and came from rural areas, particularly from the region of the Senegal River (Mali, Mauritania, Senegal). These men's experiences of immigration and of life in France were determined by the way in which they viewed their stay as a temporary one. Their patterns of immigration were based both on community networks and on their prospects for employment. Since the late 1970s and early 1980s three important developments have taken place. These are the diversification of the migrants' countries of origin, to include Cameroon, Ivory Coast, Ghana, Benin, Togo, Congo – Zaire; the arrival of relatively well qualified individuals, both men and women; and the growth of family reunification. These developments have had important effects on migrants' strategies, particularly on the positioning of women concerning the relationships they expected to have, and that they have attempted to maintain, both with their new country of residence and with 'Africa'. Of these three new developments the most important factor in this analysis is the much greater proportion of women migrants. Whilst there were only 4,712 women immigrants originating from sub-Saharan Africa in 1968, there were 16,470 in 1975, 42,400 in 1982, and 73,000 in 1990. That is an increase of 70 per cent between 1982 and 1990. It is a young population: 52 per cent are under twenty-five years of age, and 33 per cent between the ages of twenty-five and thirty-four. This development is observable for all African women, but is particularly relevant for Senegalese and Malien women. In 1968 there were 452 Senegalese and 256 Malien women in France. In 1990 there were 17,010 and 41,023 respectively. This demographic development of the female population from sub-Saharan Africa is largely because migrants from the Sahel have brought their wives to France. There still remains an over-representation of men in this population. Malien women for instance only make up 37 per cent of the Malien immigrant population, and Cameroonian women are 46 per cent of the total, but the gap between the number of men and that of women is falling. More generally, the female immigrant community is not just composed of women living in couples but also of women migrating autonomously. In addition, the female African population is far from homogeneous. These women come from and represent heterogeneous social backgrounds. They can be distinguished both by their migratory careers (their regions of origin, motives: family, economic or political), and by their social profile (from rural or urban origins, family structure, education, religion etc.). There is an important difference between a woman with no viable urban experience, who has never been educated, who comes to live in France at her husband's decision, and an educated woman, who knows how urban life works, who has decided to pursue her studies in France, or who has left her country for her own reasons, whether economic or political. This diversity is linked to the social changes which are affecting African societies. While they are the source if not of divisions, at least of distinctions, which are often marked in the country of origin, in the migratory situation they give rise to a remarkable development: the establishment of associations of African women.

Women have chosen to call their groupings 'African women's associations', rather than any more specific name, because they are attached to this rather vague and open framework. The cosmopolitan aspect of these associations, as well as the fact that they group together women from different social backgrounds, should not be under-estimated in the analysis of the dynamics of their organization. Nevertheless, this play on the indices of common belonging is reinterpreted in migration, which teaches us about the manipulation of cultural traits, and constitutes a new relationship with the receiving society. It also suggests the force of the other's gaze, the French ignoring the differences amongst African women immigrants and classifying them all as one dominated group.

The Difficulties of Family Immigration and the Emergence of the Associative Movement

The majority of sub-Saharan immigrant families are divided between the Île-de-France region (Paris and its surroundings) and Upper Normandy (Rouen, Le Havre).

According to national education statistics the Île-de-France region contains 70 per cent of the female population. As they arrived in the 1980s, women have come to live in a France that is in a situation of economic crisis. They have broken with the systems of affiliations and solidarities in their own society and they have to reinvent the social meaning of their presence in France, that is the meaning that they find in their relations with others as foreigners. It is a more difficult task because the receiving society is ill-prepared. The lack of social housing, made worse by the discriminatory attitudes of private and public landlords, is demonstrated by the strong concentrations of African families in poor, run down housing in Paris and its suburbs. This insalubrious housing situation, lacking in modern comforts, has a particular effect on women who are almost entirely responsible for the management of domestic space. At the same time they have to deal with the problems that face them in terms of the social insertion of their families: relations with the local community, schools, negotiations with different administrative structures and institutions of health and social welfare. They are at the centre of all the questions raised by their existence in public space. As with men, women's migratory projects involve the need to have access to money. Their employment situation, however, is not very favourable because of discrimination by employers and because many lack the characteristics required by the labour market. Consequently there is a very high level of unemployment amongst African women immigrants. Unlike men who arrived in the 1960s, a period of full employment, in which unqualified manual labour was needed, women cannot count on insertion through waged employment. In 1990 the level of unemployment of African women was around 45 per cent: 50 per cent for Senegalese women, 46 per cent for Malien women, 46.7 per cent for women from the Ivory Coast and 36 per cent for Cameroonian women.[1] This is important in a society where waged work is the basis of social recognition, and the means by which people are protected against insecurity and injury. Lack of employment constitutes a basic obstacle to the reinvention of social ties, which is necessary to prevent people from becoming completely excluded (Castel, 1995). Neither institutions, communities nor families are capable of responding to the new demands which women face today. The development of a vigorous African women's movement towards the end of the 1980s was an attempt by women to negotiate a new status suitable to their new life within their family and their new society.

Origins, Structure and Operation of Associations

Even the smallest event can give rise to an association. They usually originate in the difficulties encountered by young women who have recently arrived in France and who need to group together. Women's solidarity and self-help constitute the usual reasons for the establishment of these associations. There are many activities that need to be undertaken and to be given new meaning within a new society: finding housing, obtaining family allowances, obtaining regular residence papers, ensuring one's children receive a good education, looking after oneself, finding one's place in the family. Many African women choose to form groups with other women to deal with these issues together. Women go to other women who have dealt with difficult conditions themselves, and the process moves on to the formation of an association that will be used by an increasing number of women. This is not a natural, spontaneous or mechanical process. It is part of the histories of these African women which converge here in France, but it is also partly a response to institutional demands. In many African societies there is a very strong social division between the sexes. The masculine and feminine universes are strongly differentiated particularly in rural areas. Work is gendered, meals are taken separately, men's and women's budgets are autonomous. Thus women develop a reserve that is reinforced by the existence of social groups based on age (these include all women or all men in the same age range, of about four or five years, who have been initiated at the same time). Within the same age group solidarity operates regardless of the position of one's family in the social hierarchy. Today women often group together within villages around a common economic project: market gardening, crafts, small scale trading. In towns a common form of association between women are the *tontines* which involve a monthly subscription in order to accumulate capital which every woman takes it in turn to use in order to set up an enterprise (a shop or restaurant).

African women have responded to the repeated call (too often merely demagogic) from state and international organizations for women to participate in the development of their country through the establishment of women's sections within political parties. In France on the one hand there is the influence of the women's liberation movement, on the other the active and specific participation of certain African women in parties, trades unions or men's associations, which is giving rise to a remarkable potential cadre of women's associations. These women transfer their activism, their competencies, their ambition to support other women who are less hardened by experience but who nevertheless wish to take control of local space and of the conditions in which they enter civic life and French society. The meeting between these women from different social backgrounds and of different nationalities is for them a means of being recognized by local institutions, of demanding new positions in communal and family spaces, and also sometimes an opportunity to find employment when there is a possibility of them being paid by these associations. The expansion of this female associative movement takes either the form of networks so that activities then take place in the framework of the community outside institutions (undeclared groupings), or within the framework of the law on associations of 1901. This second type of association thus operates within the logic of local institutions. A minimum partnership requires a formal constitution and a declaration under the law of 1901. This is a necessary condition before associations can receive money. This Jacobin state institutionalization of forms of collective organization or action is a particularity of the French system which marks associational space. However, these associations have relatively flexible structures. They have the structure of the law of 1901, with a president, treasurer, secretary, a committee, and for the larger ones, an administrative council. Other roles are not clearly defined and vary according to the availability of people, knowledge and demands. The mode of operation is very variable according to the personality of the leaders, the number of women who are mobilized within the association, and whether or not they have their own premises. Having an office is the proof of a strong interest in these associations, their ability to be recognized as of public interest, and their knowledge of the workings of French society. An office and telephone are their main tools.

The choice of responsible actors in the associations is made according to two criteria: competence and confidence. The question of confidence is fundamental in this type of structure. The legitimacy of those responsible comes partly from their involvement, their effectiveness on the ground, the diplomas they may have acquired in Africa or since their arrival in France, or the social status of the family to which they belonged. This last factor plays a secondary role in these pluri-national associations. Numerous offices are composed of women from different nationalities, mainly from sub-Saharan Africa but also from the Maghreb, France and Turkey. One of the characteristics of these associations is that they know how to mobilize the most varied competencies independent of nationality. The constitution of associations of 'African women' immediately transcends national frontiers in a way that no previous migratory current has done until now. It is an almost inescapable process for several reasons. Firstly, housing policies are such that populations from very different parts of Africa are to be found on the same site. Secondly, in their daily living conditions African women have one factor in common that underpins their stigmatization: they are black. This construction by white people, which certain black movements have appropriated for themselves, has both discriminatory and identificatory effects. Within their associations, black women can understand one another, can make themselves heard by French society, and they can avoid being suspected of being 'westernized' by African men. The pluri-national character of their associations also corresponds to the demands of different grant-giving agencies. These associations have understood that being inter-cultural is often a condition for obtaining funds. This openness to others is nevertheless a reality. It corresponds to the demands of situations on the ground. As an association develops, the geographical origins of the office-holders and also of the members and users becomes more varied. The most cosmopolitan associations are those which have economic projects, such as finding or creating employment.

These associations are linked together in many ways. Their networks are a living base for what one can describe as the transmission of associational knowledge. Contacts between associations can go from the simple exchange of information to the training of leaders or the exchange of experiences. The journal *Regards, femmes d'ici et d'ailleurs* (Women From Here and Elsewhere) is a means of communication, each issue providing a profile of a particular association. The journal *Hommes et migrations* (People and Migrations) also reports the creation of different associations, illustrating the importance that it attributes to this movement of women's associations. But what is particularly of interest here is that this also demonstrates the desire and capacity of these associations to make themselves known and to make their activities public, so that the largest possible number of women can benefit from them. Most associations operate on a voluntary basis. Their funding which has never been very high, comes from subscriptions of between fifty and one hundred francs a year (between £5 and £10), from fund-raising activities (cultural activities, sales of craft objects), or other profit-making activities such as the renting out of offices, printing of leaflets, or legal consultations. There are various funding agencies, the most generous being the FAS or Fond d'Action Sociale (Social Action Fund). There is a surprisingly small amount of support from the Secretary of State for Women's Rights or from other initiatives specifically aimed at women. They rarely seek funding from European structures. But whatever their size, the level of their interventions at local or national level, the variety of problems with which they deal, these associations generally display a good knowledge of the funding circuits that can assist their activities. Information about this circulates among associations.

From Public to Private: a Great Diversity of Activities

Beyond their flexible structures and their way of operating, the activities and vocations of associations are not defined once and for all. These activities fall between the defence of values advanced by women's movements at an international level and a more pragmatic approach towards the family and social difficulties that women confront in their daily lives; between a radical transformation of certain practices of domination and a search for elements of negotiation in order to manage unacceptable social situations. The associations of African women have two major purposes: firstly, the transformation of the French national social order which assigns immigrants, particularly women, to a certain place and, secondly, contestation of the internal equilibrium in the communities from which these women originate. In searching for new forms of daily citizenship, new relations within their communities and their homes, they occupy a social space between that of the intervention of institutions and that of the social and domestic space of African families. Most of them attempt a dialogue with the institutional resources established by the state, regions, municipalities, and with community and family groups. They often define themselves as spaces for 'mediation'. These associations can be considered as creating innovatory social networks. As intermediary groups, in the Durkheimian sense, they are means of integration in today's world, spaces where women can meet one another and redefine their identities and their relations to others. They present themselves as a framework within which women offer their competences to other women, both their knowledge of French society and their understanding of the situation in which a large number of African immigrant women find themselves. This gift is not without reciprocity, they expect social recognition and a changed social status. These mediations operate in three directions.

Firstly, associations address different social partners who want to develop a better understanding of these populations in order to improve their effectiveness. Secondly, they intervene in order to familiarize African women with different social codes and different expected behaviours in the receiving country. Thirdly, they play an important role in the daily relations between wives and their husbands, a woman and her children, her family or even her community. These are crucial roles in as far as they constitute a real exchange with the receiving country. To know where to go and what to do in order to obtain housing, for example, is something that must be learned almost immediately after arrival in France and it is a process that is not without pitfalls, everything which affects relationships within the family sets complex mechanisms in operation, representations, behaviour, values inherited from elsewhere. African women, who have responsibilities within associations, use their personal experience, knowledge and know-how to help resolve problems encountered by women whose collection of values and understanding needs to be reconstructed in order to be adapted to their new conditions. These conditions are for many, precarious. Associations permit, if not the resolution, at least the improvement of tensions due to the gap between externally expected behaviour and behaviour accepted within the family or the community.

Integration and Culture: the Relationship between 'Received Categories' and 'Perceived Categories'

Social partners concerned with daily issues of integration are confronted by an important contradiction. On one hand, they have the mission of securing respect for individuals, laws, values and behaviour which express the republican model, but on the other hand, they are addressing a population that does not benefit from the social conditions that permit it to adhere to this model and that wants to preserve its identity even in the transitional situation of its migratory status, by reproducing more or less the system that it has left behind. In giving this contradiction its most rigid formulation, one can better understand the central importance of the associative dynamic of African women which helps to meet the demands of institutions. This associational dynamic identifies elements of possible negotiation, the points of contact between these two logics of state institutions and migrant communities, which if allowed to develop separately, risk increasing the process of segregation, negation of the Other and confinement. Associations attempt to make known the culture, practices and customs of African women. They use several means to this end. They respond to demands for direct contact from teachers, doctors, social assistants, magistrates and nurses. Most of the time these are individuals who are conscious of the impact of their work, convinced that a better understanding of their public would help them, and who make contact with an association they have heard about.

In order to go beyond the limits of individual contacts, associations also organize information days. These days require a considerable infrastructure, know how and a recognition by professionals. However, it seems that, even in their early stages, they succeed in mobilizing people and resources, thanks especially to the relations they have with other associations who are more experienced. It is important to note that these African women's associations know how to mobilize French people of all social categories around and in support of their actions. They use a social capital which circulates between associations. They are solicited in this way by almost all the major institutions: health, legal, educational, each with its own specific needs.

Associations also work to advance understanding that the kind of problems that women encounter are not simply economic but are also situated at a symbolic level, that of the representations which they have of relations with others. For fear that they will not be understood, not just because of language problems, but because of not understanding the nature of the relations in which they are becoming involved, certain women hesitate to seek medical advice or to go to a meeting at school, for example. Associations show that certain practices or behaviour are not 'obvious' to everyone, and thus help to avoid numerous misunderstandings. They make exchange possible; they help to set up communications. This task contains the major risk of ethnicization as the people with whom they dialogue may use this 'presentation' of African women to enclose them in an insurmountable alienness. The aim of these associations, however, is to offer substitutes for the images that oscillate between depictions of sordidness and exoticism, which place women in an archaic position, and to suggest instead a more complex, living image of women from Africa who are confronting the modern world in France. Some of the more institutionalized associations have relations with the mass media and broadcast information through these channels: newspaper and journal articles, radio and television programmes. They contribute to the re-valuing of the image of African women, which has an effect on these women's relations with institutions and also within their local communities.

These actions allow different social workers who are working to try and ensure integration of African women to know more about the women they are addressing. To appreciate all their richness and complexity but also to understand their difficulties, and as a consequence, to prepare the ground for a successful integration of these women. This must happen in such as way that they do not feel as though their history and identity has been denied, and at the same time that they are given the means to find their own space in French society. This model amounts to a critique of the Republican model of assimilation of immigrant communities.

Teaching French Society: Autonomy through Socialization

Associations all offer women a better integration through a better understanding of French society. They offer a certain number of services through individual relations with women. The nature of mediation here is based on concrete problems encountered by women who have to learn a certain number of rules, laws and customs particular to the receiving country. They aim to create a certain autonomy for women through a better understanding of the social situations in which they may find themselves. The great majority of associations do not want women to pass from one form of dependence to another in their relations with the social services: from ignorance to reliance on welfare. They see themselves as temporary intermediaries. They give themselves the objective of making these public spaces accessible to women so that they can use them. From an initial concern with women's individual problems they widen their actions, as for example in the relationship between mothers and schools, where instead of just dealing with individual cases, they establish offices where they can respond to calls from teachers to help place their children's education on an even footing. Similarly, starting from individual women's concerns about employment they widen the scope of their activities to include door to door visits to families to let them know about available jobs. The demands they face are of several kinds. They concern housing, health, problems to do with the education of their children, rights, employment and training. In order to accompany this nascent autonomy and to respond to the needs of women, associations offer specific activities: literacy classes, sewing, short courses in housework, cooking. This form of training has several aims. It offers precious moments for women to meet which fulfil similar functions to the meetings around wells which take place in Africa, and provides social spaces reserved for women where they can discuss their family or economic problems, exchange information or elaborate common plans. They constitute spaces for socialization through which women can find confidence in themselves, confidence to understand the meaning of the behaviour which is expected of them. Beyond that, going to these courses is part of a strategy of economic insertion. African women, whether they are rural or urban have, in Africa, access to monetary revenues that they alone control. When they arrive in France they expect, following the example of their husbands, to make their migration worth while, including financially. The African women's associations help them to achieve this financial ambition. Through these associations they hope not just to gain a basic training, but beyond this, to get to know about official circuits of training. They can also improve their knowledge of the African community in France to uncover profitable 'niches'. Associations are one of the bases for what Americans call 'ethnic business' and which African women practice so well: embroidered clothes for weddings, sales of African products, cooked meals, etc. Associations can support these activities. They often help to set up *tontines*.

We should also highlight the fact that several women's associations, following the example of village associations of men, aim to take responsibility for the problems faced by village women back home. After being solicited by or imposing themselves in village associations created by men, women are increasingly setting up autonomous associations. These associations are strictly composed of people from the village. They bring together women from a particular village now living in France to help a project for the women having stayed in the village, for example, the building of a well which may make it possible to extend the cultivation period, or help to re-establish older crafts. They subscribe towards the project and try to transmit techniques they have learnt in France to women in Africa.

Some associations emphasize the economic aspect of their activity. They see themselves as helping women to realize a particular economic project. They help them with the necessary formalities, to contact organizations, help them with small-scale market research and direct them towards appropriate courses. They train women to become 'social cultural mediators', who look to the public authorities to give them professional recognition and a salary. More and more of these women are looking for employment and certain associations focus on training beyond the level at which they provide it themselves. For instance they participate in European programmes of professional training, and help their members to find out about training courses run by professional bodies.

The place of festivals and various leisure activities in this autonomous dynamic cannot be ignored. Festivals have a double aspect, permitting women to go out together, but also to invite neighbours whatever their nationality. These events usually take place in public places such as a tent by the town hall. This has an effect on the way in which African women perceive these institutions, making them seem more welcoming, and also on the local view of African women, making these women much more visible. Associations also organize visits: to monuments, to the cinema, to the sea-side, forest walks, all unusual activities for African women, which open new horizons, presenting a different view of French society as not just a series of laws and constraints to be respected. They are initiations into French society, ways of lightening the load of problems encountered by women and introducing conviviality and relaxation.

New Identities and Changing Status

It is partly because they fulfil the two functions I have just outlined, (making information about African women available to French institutions, and giving information about means of insertion and integration into French society to African women), that these associations can mediate private tensions. Women can express themselves, give one another advice and help one another within associations. One of their objectives is to support solidarity between women. Whatever the size of the association or its local, national or international impact they mainly hear problems about relations between spouses or children. To give just one example, of all the problems expressed by women who consult the Association of African Women of the Val d'Oise,[2] AFAVO, more than 60 per cent were about threats by husbands to send their wives back to their country of origin, conjugal violence, divorce or problems with children. The situation is similar in smaller associations like that in Massy.[3] Associations do not just deal with women, they attempt to intervene within families, notably with the men. They can do this more effectively when they are recognized as competent at other levels, but they may still be considered with suspicion by a certain number of men who do not want any interference in their private life. Because they involve African women, these associations are often feared by men. This may even lead to a fear that men could attempt to control associations in order to restrict women's initiatives.

Associations do not aim in principle to intervene in internal family conflicts. However, especially in the situation of migrants, the limit between public and private is at its most flexible. Many young women go to associations for help in dealing with conflicts arising from family norms. The French family is very different from many African families and certain problems arise from the expectations that state institutions have of these families, but there are also problems that may be described as internal family problems. They all turn around the question of authority. Associations play a major role in the practical redefinition of this notion. By giving women the desire and the means to support their children's education, by encouraging them to acquire a certain financial autonomy, by transmitting the codes of French society thus helping them to manage the problems of housing or health, they are changing the place which they have been given in the family. When these changes give rise to conflict they represent a certain negotiating strength that women can use directly with men or in helping French law to intervene. The individual appropriation by women of their rights and duties often takes place through collective information exchanges. Meetings on the Pasqua laws,[4] on women's associations, on questions of employment, of health or of education, allow women to see that while what is demanded of them requires a personal effort, all African women are confronted with the same problems. We should also note the presence of men during demonstrations organized by women for women, showing that these associations have acquired a certain legitimacy amongst men, even though they may also be viewed with suspicion.

All these activities acquire added significance during public meetings. These meetings are real events in which women's demands are crystallized, affirmed and publicly articulated. Meetings are special events insofar as they put social groups who do not normally communicate into contact with one another. Certain organized days provide occasions for meetings and debates between women and lawyers, teachers, doctors or other health personnel. The protagonists, then, have the occasion to express themselves, sometimes violently, about the problems and inequalities they have encountered. Here it is interesting to note how important it is for social partners in French society to be mobilized, even though they may only be there on a voluntary basis. There is good will for mutual understanding on both sides. African women are particularly interested in the question of rights, which is not surprising when one knows that immigrants generally are subject to decrees and laws that are constantly being revised, that women are not always living legally in France, but that French laws could be more favourable to them than those back home. These meetings attempt to find and develop mediations that can simultaneously accompany acculturation and integration. Take the example of a public meeting about 'women's health, sexually transmitted diseases and AIDS', organized by AFAVO. African women of rural origins may find it difficult to talk about these problems with their husbands because of their status within the family and their conception of what the relationship between husband and wife within the family ought to be. The discourse of doctors is even less comprehensible to them because it often runs against their religious convictions. However, medical care will be less effective if they do not listen to doctors. Social intervention by an association in this case consists of assembling women who have problems with their health that may be aggravated by their situation as immigrants and giving them the opportunity to express their concerns. These meetings are valuable because such women may be ready to listen to doctors if they are listened to themselves. At such a meeting there would also be:

1. Doctors who are prepared to listen to women recount their experiences and to express their grievances about how they are treated in hospitals or how they experience medical treatments, notably those which affect the integrity of their bodies (such as caesarean section, sterilization, contraceptive methods).
2. Women's husbands or male representatives of the African community.
3. An Imam may also be present if a religious matter is to be discussed. Obviously these participants are not chosen by chance. They help to establish a compromise between the discourse of 'modernity' and that

of 'tradition', a compromise which is often acceptable to women for whom both modernity and tradition may be experienced as forms of oppression.

At such a meeting the women would expect to obtain information and knowledge from doctors. The doctors will explain how AIDS or sexually transmitted diseases are spread, and discuss preventative methods. However, even a non-racist doctor, known to African women professionally, who gives proper attention to their problems, holds free surgeries, and gives information about medical risks and means of avoiding them, may not be able to persuade women to take up the necessary precautions or treatments. Thus, the intervention of an African Imam who can affirm that it is not contrary to Islam to use contraceptives in certain cases, that a woman with AIDS can have an abortion, that husbands have a duty to tell their wives when they are carrying the virus, that spouses should discuss such questions among themselves, helps to justify change. They can use a new reading of the Koran more in keeping with the new situation of women, their religious convictions and their use of new practices. The choice of such a person is decisive, involving many attempts and considerable diplomacy.

However, if the meeting was just about the confrontation of two discourses, that of the doctors and that of the Imam, the event would be incomplete and could be interpreted as manipulative from the point of view of both the dominant and dominated groups. The second part of the meeting is about women's expression. This takes several forms and addresses several different interlocutors: the doctors, the Imam, the men in the room (depending on the aim of the meeting public authorities may also be involved). The most frequent form that this part of the meeting takes is that of the narration of the numerous problems confronted by women. It is important for them to realize that these are widely experienced and affect many women in their situation, so that they do not feel abnormal or responsible for these problems themselves. The sharing of such problems through public speech helps people to feel less personally culpable, and often makes it possible for them to realize that what is happening is because of the social condition in which they find themselves. Strengthened by the discourse of the doctor or the Imam, the size of their own presence (these meetings often assemble a hundred African women), women speak to the men present, often from the back of the room:

'I don't know the Koran but a good muslim does not put two wives and eleven children in the same room.'
'It doesn't say in the Koran that you can take a second wife because I, as the first, want to take a breath after having four children – there is no recommended number of children.'
'Is it normal for a wife to be beaten for refusing to have sex because she is tired?'[5]

We should note the importance given here to gender relations and the doubly normative register of these interventions. Women judge the practices of their husbands firstly in the name of Islam and secondly in the name of their liberty as women. For them it is about living as harmoniously as possible given the changes arising from their migration while indicating that they are maintaining a frontier beyond which they do not plan to venture.

Men are not the only ones to be addressed. They ask the Imam as an recognized religious authority, to give information on what is and is not permitted by the Koran. They ask the doctors for particular information, but also try to make them understand what it means to an African woman to have a caesarean or a forced sterilization on the pretext that she already has enough children. There are very few women who remain silent. They have come to listen but also to speak. Exchanges take place in several languages thanks to voluntary interpreters, who translate French and African languages.

On such days, the women wear their most beautiful African clothes. In this way they affirm their 'African' identity and the importance of the meeting. Their attitudes to their identity are cosmopolitan, interpreting ethnic constraints in a flexible way, maintaining its distance from the dominant group as well as looking for possible points of contact. It is a model for men who frequently accuse their wives of betraying their origins because they want to 'act Western', because it evokes the outlines of a new way of being faithful to oneself and to the group. The meeting gives rise to an exchange by which on the one hand African women and on the other the 'official' spokespeople voluntarily engage in a process of transformation of their representations and practices. This is certainly an unequal exchange, but it is never without its reciprocal effects. It allows the demands and aspirations of the women who are present to be made public in a systematic manner. Women are together searching for new norms appropriate to the two worlds that now make up their own universe: that of French society and that of their community of origins. They react against their private situations, which often involve unsatisfactory compromises – compromises that may be the source of extreme violence and failure, both practical and symbolic.

The importance of these public meetings can be shown by their growing number and the development of themes which prove that the women are working to control their conditions of entry into French society – education, training, employment, rights, housing – but at the same time, changing their position within their community and their families. The carefully organized use of a number of mediators – 'emancipated' African women, doctors, teachers, social workers, officials from local authorities, an Imam – in the presence of a large number of women, shows how acculturation and integration converge. Women also expect to change the way in which their image has been appropriated and to reinterpret the ways in which they are regarded which are not acceptable to them: representations made by African men, by the indigenous French, but also some of their own self-representations.

Conclusion

In conclusion two points can be emphasized that seem to characterize this associative movement of African women. Firstly, it manipulates its cosmopolitan origins using secularism and ethnic references. It spreads itself across different origins, using them as resources and frameworks to constitute social bonds. The overlapping and entanglement of associative life makes it possible for the women to become more open, and redefine themselves rather than to become involved in conflict. Secondly, associations are not limited to work in the space between families and institutions. They intervene within institutions to change the traditional way they approach and look at African women. They intervene within families, particularly with family heads to help them to accept, even unwillingly to recognize the new status of women that is already a reality because of their public interventions and their new responsibilities. Their activities come out of a social fabric where solidarities between women enable them to move towards a new identity based on an active citizenship, able to assert their rights with established authority but also with their families and their communities. As long as these forms of 'informal politics' are fully valued, the meaning of African women's presence in France can be reconstructed.'

Translated by Jane Freedman

Notes

1. Insee 1990.
2. An area in the suburbs of Paris.
3. A suburb of Paris.
4. For more details on these laws see Chapter 1.
5. Women speaking at a meeting organized by AFAVO, August 1998.

Maghrebi Families in France
Camille Lacoste-Dujardin

The major problems within Maghrebi families in France, problems that often spill out of the family circle and become a primary topic for the media, concern the young and above all adolescents. In effect, adolescence is a critical time in a person's life, already difficult to live through in families with a solely French culture, and much more so in families whose cultural references are at least dual, if not plural, and are in reality highly complex. The dichotomy habitually drawn between, on one hand, the private family space with Maghrebi cultural references, and on the other, the public social space dominated by French culture, is not in practice as clear as this. In reality, the two cultures cross over, interpenetrate and compete with one another on many occasions in time and in space. Moreover, there are a large number of possible arrangements and compromises that may be put into action from one family to another, depending on a wide range of variables such as the social background of the parents in their country of origin and the social status they have acquired in France, their educational level, their age, the profession of the father, the length of their residence in France, etc. For these reasons, any schematization must be reductive, as will be the model presented here. I will, however, try to nuance this model in attempting to introduce at least several of the various categories of differentiation that exist.

The Patriarchal System in Question

Whatever the many differences in the lived realities of Maghrebi families of immigrant origin in France, it is nonetheless true to say that their familial model of reference is the product of a patriarchal system. This system has been in existence from Morocco to Japan, and its traces are still visible in northern Mediterranean societies, although they are weaker in these areas. Today in the Maghreb the influence of patriarchal ideology is concretized in many different areas of life including State laws, as is evidenced by the codes of family law. The importance of the patriarchal system within the Muslim religion, a system that assigns women in priority to the role of motherhood, is reinforced today by the action of fundamentalists who play on issues of identity and the opposition to Western culture, and who use religion towards political ends. Finally the patriarchal system is influential in representations, systems of thought and patterns of behaviour, not only in the Maghreb but also amongst immigrants into France, particularly the men.

Today, however, there are many currents in opposition to this patriarchal system because the widening of communications, migratory movements and the global media make people aware of other models and engender other aspirations. Also because the changes in family composition provoked by urbanization, education and medical progress lead to different projects and modes of behaviour in children and transform their role. These changes, which put patriarchal ideology into question, play a certain role in the current situation of crisis in the Maghreb, but they are much more widely developed in France and affect immigrants of Maghrebi origin with much more force.

The Immigrant Family

Within Maghrebi families parents and children do not have the same norms or modes of behaviour. In the parents' case, these have been acquired essentially in the Maghreb, and in the childrens' case, essentially in France. For the parents, references to Maghrebi culture constitute a grid through which they filter all their later experiences and acquisitions. These references are made up of an ensemble of representations, norms and values inculcated from birth through adolescence to adulthood in the Maghreb, both within their families and outside through school and other forms of socialization. Today, in France, Maghrebi parents are conscious of being a minority and thus whilst participating in their society of residence in all their activities outside of the home – and even in part inside the home due to the infiltration of the media – these same parents are all the more conservative in their family culture. As for the children, whilst being permeated with Maghrebi culture, which is inculcated by their parental education at home, they participate to a much greater extent than their parents in their society of residence. Since childhood they have acquired knowledge of this society, they share its activities and pursuits, they engage in social relations and are thus socialized into French society and adhere to its values and norms. This determines their aspirations and projects, which are in reality very close to those of French children.

Moreover, many of them, having been born in France, are themselves French by virtue of the *droit du sol* (right of territory).

In reality, this ambivalence in the habits of children of Maghrebi immigrants, this different experience of two different systems of representations, values and cultural norms, is aggravated by the functional inequality between the two cultures themselves. The two cultures do not differ merely in their mode of transmission: the Maghrebi culture of the parents and the home on one hand, the French culture of school, socialization and aspirations on the other. More seriously, in most cases they do not carry the same weight. In effect, the parents are often of a relatively low social class and educational level and the mothers, particularly, are frequently illiterate. The culture they have transmitted to their children is an oral, popular and often rural Maghrebi culture. This culture cannot compete with the culture of the society of residence, a culture that is learned at school, which is written, knowing, urban, even internationalist, and in reality dominant. From this unequal clash of cultures spring the conflicts during the period of crisis and questioning that is adolescence. These conflicts are even more severe today in the new relations between generations, as adolescence is becoming increasingly prolonged.[1] And in the personal relations of young people within the French society they inhabit, only Western culture is operative. As for the Maghrebi culture of the parents, it is more often than not, for young people of both sexes, merely a component of their identity, at best an 'added extra', which is contained within the private domain.[2]

Troubled Parents

Objectively, therefore, the parents have a longer road than their children to travel, between the two different ways of life that they have known, and between two cultures. For them, compromises are more difficult to negotiate and it may even be the case that they cannot assume the changes in their lives, and remain unable to move forward. The fact that these same parents took the initiative and accomplished a migratory project is, for the father especially who was often the initiator of the project, a sign of their willingness to change. This willingness may, however, exist only in relation to the society from which they departed, because they could not be fully aware of the depth of the changes they would be faced with once they and their families became immigrants. Without a doubt, they did not realize that they would be forced to abandon many of their habits and customs. Nor did they predict that their children would not only not reproduce their own models of conduct and behaviour but would actually move significantly away from these models and, in their parents' opinion, even come to betray them (Lacoste-Dujardin, 1988). Finally they could not have foreseen that the social rules in France, in this other society in which they had come to live, were not the same as those in the Maghreb, and that they would have such difficulty in overcoming the profound changes with which they would be confronted.

If certain of their children do try to understand the considerable difficulties that their parents experience, others misunderstand them to the point of reproaching them for these same difficulties. A young girl expresses this feeling in harsh terms: 'They knew very well that in coming to France they would be confronted with all these problems that Maghrebi families face, that they would lose their children because the children don't want to follow their parents' traditions as they know another way of life'[3] (Lacoste-Dujardin, 1992, p. 14). The demands of their children are in effect completely new to the parents. Their childrens' more developed intellectual demands and aspirations are something unknown, even more so in the case of girls than of boys.

The Family

In Maghrebi culture on the one hand, and French culture on the other, what is understood by 'family', this basic circle of social organization, differs profoundly. In individualist French society, the family is 'founded' by a man and a woman who, on the basis of ties of affection, build it from the basis of an autonomous couple who keep up more or less distant ties with their other relations. In contrast, in holistic Maghrebi societies the sentiment of belonging to a community is still so strong that, as Boucebi argues: 'The individual is crushed by the force of the collective ego'[4] (Boucebi, 1982, p. 36). Identity cannot be other than collective. When one meets a stranger one does not ask, 'who are you?' but 'who are you from?' – in other words 'from which family?' The family is in this case a large patrilinear ensemble composed of the forefathers and all their male descendants in a long continuum, to which women are joined in function of their role in preserving and expanding the patrilineage.

The parents' family of reference is thus this large patrilinear family that provides them with their identity and within which they must assume the fixed roles imposed upon them. The weight of this reference is reinforced by the guilt the fathers feel towards this family because in their departure from their community they have taken away from it a wife and children.[5] Furthermore, far from the control of this community these fathers feel as though they are exposing their wife and children to other transgressions which risk compromising the honour of the family name.[6] This honour is guarded, and thus also threatened, by women and in particular by young women, who are perceived as the most vulnerable link in the family chain. Thus Maghrebi families in France often attempt to exercise a very strict control over their children, particularly the girls, and this is all the more so because they feel that they have been reduced to a fragment of a family. A strong demand is placed on the young to conform to the Maghrebi family model.

Young people of Maghrebi origin in France are sometimes aware of this different conception of the family. Young girls express their astonishment at the way that, 'over there they all live in a big community'. For them, the 'family' is the one that lives in France, a nuclear immigrant family composed of a father, mother and children. They scarcely make reference to the extended family that has stayed in the Maghreb. In fact, if this extended family does make any kind of intervention in their affairs this is often perceived by the children as an intrusion. This is especially true when the superior authority of one of the elders (male or female) of this extended family is invoked by the parents to sort out difficulties and differences between them and their daughters. In the same way, when parents send a girl back to the Maghreb they see it as a 'return' to the honour of the extended family, whereas for the girl concerned it is more often considered an exile. More than their parents, the young have a tendency to identify themselves as individuals and have more resolutely personal aspirations. The patrilinear model is thus inoperative when it comes to the insertion of the young into French society. This insertion can only be an individual experience. The young, and especially the girls, do not appreciate their ambitions being limited by the priority given to a rigorous and to them outdated conception of the patrilinear family. They share to a much greater extent the French conception of the family, that is of a family founded on an affective relationship between a couple, a partnership where the roles and gender relations are on a seemingly much more egalitarian footing than those laid down in the Maghrebi patriarchal order.

This issue of the relations between the sexes is a decisive one in immigrant families of Maghrebi origin. The crucial problem is that of the place of women in society because women's roles in the two different cultures appear to be highly incompatible. Further, the daughters of Maghrebi immigrants in France almost unanimously reject the position of women in Maghrebi societies (Lacoste-Dujardin, 1992). Within the large extended families in the Maghreb, the distribution of roles between men and women imposed a segregation (*infiçal*) between them, a segregation which was necessary to comply with the rules of decency (*hachouma*).[7] These same masculine and feminine roles are assumed collectively within each sex and each age group so that no man or woman is isolated. If the father and mother are recognized biologically as such, it is nevertheless true that, in sociological terms, the maternal and paternal roles are assumed collectively with other members of the extended family. The bringing up of children, for example, is undertaken in a multi-maternal fashion by all the women of a certain age, and numerous other tasks such as agriculture and construction for men and cooking, cleaning and shopping for women, are undertaken collectively. This division of roles is not only effective in ensuring the collective undertaking of work, but in addition the solidarity within each gender group, a solidarity tempered by the hierarchy of age, facilitates both mutual control and mediation in case of conflicts.

In France, however, the situation is no longer the same. Immigration from the Maghreb was originally an immigration for work, a period during which the extended family delegated certain of their male members to take it in turns to go and work temporarily in France. This was followed by a period in which immigration became a more permanent phenomenon, albeit still one of single men now practising the 'profession of immigrant' (Sayad, 1977). From 1974 onwards this immigration of single men was outlawed by the French government, but on the other hand from this same date the authorization of family regroupment incited immigrant Maghrebi workers to bring their wives and children to France. Thus in the process of immigration small families were formed, restricted to a nuclear form of family life which was traditionally proscribed, where the inter-personal relationships are deprived of any recourse to a family group of the same sex. The parents thus find themselves faced with a new relationship, reduced to an unforeseen duality which is difficult for them to manage in the absence of any ideology of the couple and of the nuclear family project.

Differences between Boys and Girls

The parents thus have huge difficulties in admitting any changes in a hierarchical ordering of the relations between men and women and in gender roles established in their patriarchal society of origin. These roles are ones that they themselves have up until now respected and carried out and that they wish to see their children reproduce. In reality, however, the preoccupations of the parents are very different concerning their male and female children.[8] Most parents show little anxiety for their sons whose mere existence satisfies the demands of the reproduction of the family genealogy. These young men, by virtue of the pre-eminent status accorded to the male, satisfy their parents in the symbolic order. These same young men have the privilege of a great amount of freedom of movement, without having to give any account of their activities outside the household. This household is abandoned to the women and traditionally, like all men, sons have no tasks to fulfil within the house. Moreover, as a Kabyle saying goes: 'men know what they are doing'. However, in contrast with the Maghreb, where these same boys, whether in villages or urban areas, find themselves under the control of the men of the community or neighbourhood, in France the 'unknown' and 'foreign' street is at the door of their apartment with all its temptations, its dangers and its possibilities for deviance of all kinds. Thus, conscious of their masculine authority and encouraged in the expression of their virility, comforted by a close relationship with their mothers and strengthened by their communal masculine identity, but without a paternal role model as that of their fathers has been devalued, many of these young men resort to joining gangs, which rival each other for the domination of their territory.

Whilst parents do not keep a close watch on their sons, this is not at all the case for their daughters. It is expected that these daughters should reproduce the essentially maternal role that is assigned to women above all other social roles, especially over any role that takes them outside of the home. Girls have very few chances to go out and establish relationships outside of the home even though they wish to participate in society through outside activities. There is a huge disparity between the parents' representations of an ideal woman who conforms to community norms, and the reality of their daughters' aspirations which are composed of more individualist goals. Many of these daughters can eventually overcome these conflicts through economic autonomy gained as they leave adolescence. And this autonomy is usually accepted by their mothers because in France the law and the French references concerning the relations between men and women encourage both daughters and mothers to shake off masculine domination. However, a brake on this search for autonomy amongst the daughters is provided by a respect for their parents and a desire to promote their parents' status, especially that of their mothers. They appreciate how these mothers have been cheated as they fell between two forms of family, deprived both of the real life of a couple in France and of the solidarity of their gender group in the extended family in the Maghreb. This attachment to their mothers is often the cause of a strong interdependence between mothers and daughters, particularly the oldest daughters (Lacoste-Dujardin, 1988, 1994).

In their immigrant situation, the mothers are sometimes aware of the upheaval, if not the total inversion, of their relationships with their sons and daughters. In effect, the freedom accorded to their sons may incite them to leave home earlier, whilst their daughters, especially the older ones, tend to stay with their parents for longer. They are kept in the family home by the long negotiation of a relative autonomy, by their prolonged celibacy and deferred marriage, and through solidarity or interdependence with their mothers. 'Here it's the reverse of how it is in our home country, it's the boys who leave and the girls who stay', comments one mother. The reinforcement and the prolongation of mother–daughter relations compensates for the weakening of the mother–son tie which up until now sufficed to satisfy Maghrebi mothers, as well as all Maghrebi men, for whom the influence of their mother was more important than that of any other woman (Lacoste-Dujardin, 1996).

The Internal Functioning of Families

Immigrant Maghrebi parents thus often encounter difficulties in achieving conformity to the hierarchical order of the patrilinear extended family and this is the source of psycho-social problems. The reduction of the family to a nuclear household consisting of a father, a mother and their children, has created a new family configuration to which the parents, who were usually married by their elders without any choice over their partner, have had to adapt. In this reduced family unit they still seek to reproduce the rules of behaviour which are the norm in the extended family. In doing so they are confronted – sometimes violently – with an unexpected one-to-one relationship with their children, a relationship unmediated by other members of the extended family. The traditional double hierarchic segregation: a gendered segregation between men and women and a generational segregation between parents and children leads to precise sets of relationships between the members of the reduced nuclear family. Their positioning within these sets of relationships can be expressed by a combination of positive and negative factors.

The father is clearly dominant through the combination of his supremacy in terms of gender and generation. As for the mother and the son, each compensates an inferiority in one hierarchic category – that of gender for the mother, that of generation for the son – by a superiority in the other category. This would mean that they were in a relationship of quasi-equality were it not for the fact that the hierarchy of gender takes priority over the hierarchy of generation, which gives the son a tangible advantage over his mother. Finally, in contrast to the father, the daughter combines the two disadvantages, and is thus doubly dominated because of her gender and her generation. When conflictual relationships develop between the members of the family they are likely to be more conflictual the greater the hierarchical separation – and the linked *hachouma* – between the two protagonists. Thus it is essentially between fathers and daughters that tensions can be the strongest. In addition daughters aspire to break down the barriers imposed by their parents. They want to break the barrier of generation, and thus advocate a close relationship between parents and children. Similarly, they aim to break the gender barrier because they want to live in a couple with a husband they choose for reasons of personal affinity. This is contrary to the model offered by their parents' household, a model that they do not wish to reproduce.

In reality, each member of the family has specific problems in adapting to the situation of life as an immigrant, and these problems arise in function of their position in the family. The weight of their position in the family is a particular problem for the fathers who through their authority and their responsibilities as head of the family orient the destiny of the whole family. It is not without trauma that these fathers see their authority as the oldest man contested within their family, this family which is a refuge and the only place where they can find compensation for their social frustrations. Many behavioural reactions from fathers are possible in response to this new situation and these can be schematically grouped into three large categories. These categories, which are not without variations, have an important weight in determining family situations. These situations also vary according to other factors such as where the family lives. The grouping together of Maghrebi families in a community can, in effect, encourage the exercise of a social control which strengthens and reinforces patriarchal authority, whereas, those families who are more isolated from the Maghrebi immigrant community and in a more French environment may find it easier to adapt to French norms.

Three Large Categories

The chances of familial adaptation to change or on the contrary of the development of psychological problems, thus depend to a great extent on the behaviour of the father. Although however dominant paternal authority may be, it can be differently received by the mother, sometimes docilely accepted, sometimes supported, sometimes opposed or even rejected, particularly when this authority is enforced by excessive violence on the father's part. Three basic categories of paternal behaviour can be described. In the first case, paternal authority is transformed into authoritarianism. This authoritarianism is sometimes supported by the other men in the family, the sons, and reveals tensions regarding values considered as Maghrebi. The fathers' reaction to acculturation into French society is to oppose any changes by a counter-culturation, or an attempted enforcement of Maghrebi culture. It is within these families that the most serious psycho-social problems may develop. Revolt by the most oppressed people in the family – the mothers and daughters – may lead to them running away, which then leads to rupture with the family. This is always a bad experience and may lead to several possible outcomes. A remarkable force of character is needed for personal survival and individual achievement. If this does not occur the woman concerned may be left in a permanent state of rebellion against all forms of social authority, or worse, she may slide into delinquency, prostitution or drug addiction. But even if family conflicts do not reach this stage, continual and exacerbated family conflicts may lead to a psycho-pathological family state that is difficult to overcome. Crises occur over what the children believe to be abuses of paternal power such as fathers' threats to stop their daughters' education, to send them back to the extended family in the Maghreb or to force them into a marriage that they do not want. On other occasions both daughters and sons may jointly rebel at excessively violent behaviour from their father, violence of which their mother is often the victim. This type of behaviour is not specific to Maghrebi families but is often a result of underprivileged social conditions, for example when the father is unemployed or of a very low socio-cultural standing.

After such a crisis which ends in rebellion, the resulting case is that of a faltering or discredited father who resigns his paternal authority, and may sometimes turn to drink, gambling, etc. As soon as patriarchal authority gives way, the women in the family gain a certain autonomy and the transmission of traditional roles does not survive this new feminine independence for long. This may also be the case when an immigrant mother becomes a widow. Young Maghrebi women of immigrant origin whose fathers have died comment on the freedom they have obtained and argue that they would not have this freedom were their fathers still alive (Lacoste-Dujardin, 1992). This emancipation is more relevant to daughters and especially the older daughters in a family, although even the younger children, both boys and girls, may benefit by being brought up by an emancipated mother, more able to stimulate them in their studies and to incite them to social success. For this to be the case, however, the mother must not be too indulgent to her sons, as many Maghrebi mothers are, and must learn how to be as demanding with them as she is with her daughters. On the other hand, it seems that with an autonomous mother, whether she be separated, divorced or widowed, the daughters, and especially the eldest daughters, have some difficulty in gaining their own autonomy. The binds of a close inter-generational solidarity between women can thus be seen as the price women pay for their freedom from masculine domination within the family. The maternal influence is, in this case, determinant, since if the mother has permitted the socio-economic independence of her daughters, she has contributed at the same time to the persistence of their unmarried state. Not only can these daughters remain dependent on their mother, but they rarely dare to break the final prohibition that is still maintained by their parents. To ignore this prohibition is for their parents a betrayal of their identity. It is the prohibition of marriage with a French man, judged as exogamic, outside of the community. This ultimate restriction, which applies only to daughters and not sons, puts their familial destiny in jeopardy and poses an obstacle to the realization of the life in a couple to which they aspire.

The third case, on the other hand, is one of successful adaptation, which occurs when the father himself accepts changes. This type of behaviour is often found in men of a reasonably well-off social background who accept the breaking of barriers of gender and generation, and favour communication between parents and children, men and women. In this case change can be negotiated and agreed between parents and children as severity and conformism are absent from the relations between them. This type of relationship is found in families where social privileges – even fairly modest ones – have more importance than the maintenance of 'traditional' and strictly patriarchal representations. Most of these families have a relatively high socio-economic and cultural status – either within French or Maghrebi society – and are part of an extended family that in the Maghreb as well as in France has shown evidence of deviating from the strict community norms in order to adopt more innovative and individual interpretations of their culture. In contrast to the authoritarian models that are often found in working-class families, models of negotiation within families seem all the more successful where there is a strong professional and cultural tradition. In fact, as in all families everywhere, nothing can replace communication between parents and children. It is this willingness to communicate that is a break with the strict interpretation of the Maghrebi tradition of *hachouma*, a tradition that blocks communication. But the willingness to break with this tradition and establish communication between men and women and between generations appears to be the determining factor in arriving at a familial consensus that allows for the individual fulfilment of the children of Maghrebi immigrants in France.

Translated by Jane Freedman

Notes

1. The Algerian psychiatrist, Mahfoud Boucebi, stresses the very brief duration of adolescence in the traditional socio-cultural system, where, he adds, all the beginnings of adolescent rebellion were contained by a strong communal control (Boucebi, 1982).
2. This Maghrebi identity is operative in the public domain when it is manipulated for political ends, but this is still a relatively marginal occurrence.
3. 'Ils savaient bien, en venant en France, qu'ils seraient confrontés à tous les problèmes que rencontrent les familles maghrébines qui perdent leurs enfants qui, eux, justement, ne veulent pas suivre leur tradition parce qu'ils connaissent d'autres modèles de vie.'
4. 'L'individu est ecrasé par la force du moi collectif.'
5. In 1995 I met a couple whose decision to marry out of love and to try to gain their autonomy was punished by their exclusion from the local Kabyle community.
6. It is common today in the Maghreb to hear the comment: 'It's shameful to take one's wife to a foreign country.'
7. *Hachouma* is a notion that is rich in meaning and thus difficult to translate. It is a notion that includes chastity, modesty and decency, and that imposes restrictions on speech, communication and contact not only between the sexes but between different generations.
8. 'A boy enriches his parents' house, a girl enriches that of others', is a common saying in Algeria.

−5−

The Issue of the Islamic Headscarf
Sonia Dayan-Herzbrun

The issue of the Islamic headscarf has become a public affair since the Autumn of 1989 when the headmaster of the Lycée Gabriel Havez in Creil[1] proclaimed to the media his decision to exclude four pupils from his school for wearing a headscarf. The appearance of these 'veiled' young women in educational establishments provoked a polemic that has resurfaced periodically ever since, each time that a teacher refuses to allow into the classroom a pupil wearing the *hijab*. The conflict has been worsened on two occasions: in the Autumn of 1994, and then again at the beginning of 1999 when the extreme-Right tried to pick up the issue. This is a question that concerns only a few individuals: it is estimated that about four hundred girls are currently wearing a headscarf to school, and of those only about one hundred are in a situation where no compromise can be found between them, their families and their teachers. Despite this, however, the crisis provoked has been severe enough to necessitate several interventions by the Conseil d'État, the highest judicial body in France, as well as the publication of a ministerial paper. To understand the depth of the phenomenon and the debate surrounding it, one must resituate this issue in the specific context of France and ask why so many French people, and particularly the large majority of school teachers, feel so violently threatened by the adoption of this particular piece of clothing. In addition we need to analyse the meaning for these young women of their choice, even momentary, to wear a headscarf.

Schools and Headscarves

It is in the educational context that the wearing of the Islamic headscarf provokes a scandal. The headscarf itself is not new in France. Since the first waves of women's immigration from the Maghreb, headscarves have been visible. A sign of foreignness and exoticism, the French were not disturbed whilst the headscarves covered silent and discreet heads. The headscarf is now plunging French society into disarray because it has appeared in a public space: that of the Republican school. More precisely in the secondary educational establishments (*collèges* and *lycées*) of small towns or suburbs hit by poverty: either communities in the suburbs of Paris which once survived on agricultural activity (the production of fruit and vegetables) and small industry, or small towns which were once relatively prosperous but where factories have closed one after another. Thus the two most recent 'affairs' which relaunched the debate over the Islamic headscarf happened in January 1999 at Flers, in the Orne region, and in La Grande-Combe in the Gard region. La Grande-Combe was once a centre for coal production whilst Flers prospered from cattle and horse rearing and from a small textile and electrical goods industry. The industrial development in these towns favoured the implantation of families of workers from Muslim countries (North Africa and Turkey). It was a few of their daughters who provoked the anger of teachers or headteachers by refusing to take off their headscarves inside the school premises. The fact that these girls' mothers also had their heads covered was either completely ignored or else perceived and designated as a sign of social and cultural inferiority. In the context of the French school system, as in the case of Muslim countries where women decide to re-cover their heads, it is the conjunction between the headscarf and modernity that appears unbearable.

Three types of argument are regularly invoked in discussions concerning the Islamic headscarf. Each goes back to fundamental aspects of what can be called French political culture, a product of French history since the beginning of the nineteenth century. These three arguments concern secularism, integration, and equality between men and women. The principle of *laïcité* (secularism), which has ensured the separation of Church and state since 1905, makes religious convictions and practices an entirely private matter. The Conseil d'État's statement of November 1989 was made in regard to this secular principle. The Islamic headscarf is not mentioned as such in this statement. The question asked is that of the compatibility of 'signes d'appartenances à une communauté religieuse' (signs of belonging to a religious community) with the 'principe de laïcité' (principle of secularism). According to this principle, a Republican and secular France should assure the equality before the law of all its citizens, regardless of origin, race or religion, and as article 10 of the *Déclaration des droits de l'homme et du citoyen* (Declaration of the Rights of Man and Citizen) of 1789 proclaimed: 'nul ne doit être inquiété pour ses opinions, même religieuses, pourvu que leur manifestation ne trouble pas l'ordre public établi par la loi' (no one should be troubled for their opinions, even religious opinions, as long as the manifestation of these opinions does not disturb the public order created by the law). The Conseil d'État thus went back to the source of secularism that was designed to ensure the freedom of belief of minority groups within French society. It is well known that in the history of France, which under the Ancien Régime had been known as the 'elder daughter of the Church', the principle of secularism was employed to protect civil society and the political sphere from the grasp of the Catholic Church. Invoked with regard to young Muslim women, this principle of secularism is therefore stripped of its primary meaning and now invoked against rather than for a minority group. Applied to public education, which is one of the cornerstones of the French Republic, this principle obliges both academic programmes and teachers to be 'neutral', in other words not to impose their religious convictions on students. Pupils should be left free to express and demonstrate their religious beliefs within schools, whilst respecting pluralism and the freedom of others.

Thus conceived, school has always been held up in France as the paradigm of integration. The highly ideological notion of integration has no legal status and is not easy to define. It goes back to the idea of an attachment to a collective, and more precisely, in the case at hand, to the fusion of individuals into a national community, the only one which is recognized in France. French political culture with its inheritance not only from the 1789 Revolution but also from the politics of annexation and homogenization (religious, linguistic, and so forth) carried out by the monarchy, is based on a direct link between the individual and the nation state. Public schools have always been perceived as an instrument and an expression of this policy of detaching individuals from their particular groups and moulding them into a vast collective community. It is on these grounds that the institution of the public school has been defended during the recurrent conflicts that have occurred when the granting of privileges to private schools seemed to threaten the existence and principle of public education. These conflicts have given rise to massive protest movements, strikes and demonstrations. Integration, however, has never taken the form of cultural cross-fertilization. For the individuals who had to integrate themselves it has always been a question of adopting the social practices, codes and norms of the society into which they were entering. In return for which they acceded to French citizenship, despite the persistence of inequalities of class, gender, or skin colour. It is striking to consider that the headmaster of the school at Creil who, in 1989, started the whole *affaire des foulards* (headscarf affair), and who has since made a career in the Rassemblement pour la République or

RPR,[2] is originally from the French West Indies,[3] and has thus himself adopted the means of integration that he wished to impose in his turn on his pupils, daughters of an immigrant Moroccan worker. The model of integration-homogenization started to crack at the beginning of the 1980s under the combined effects of what was both an economic crisis and an ideological crisis. Racism and xenophobia began to be expressed openly, whereas they had appeared only in oblique forms since the end of the colonial conflicts. To such an extent that a law of August 1989 concerning the conditions of entry and residence of foreigners in France had to include a reminder that: 'Discriminatory acts by holders of public authority, groups or private individuals, incitement to discrimination, hatred or violence, defamation and abuse, for reasons of belonging or non belonging to an ethnic group, a nation or a religion, are forbidden.'[4] And that: 'School should teach pupils respect for the individual, his [sic] origins and his differences.'[5] As with secularism, however, this law was destined to be invoked against those it was supposed to protect.

It has been the teachers, headteachers, school managers and Trade Union leaders who have reacted most violently to the wearing of Islamic headscarves. The first argument they invoke to justify or to demand disciplinary measures against the girls wearing a headscarf is always that of secularism. The spokesperson for the teachers mobilized to take strike action over the issue of the headscarf in Flers in 1999 declared to the press:

> We have always fought with dignity and with respect for the convictions of the foreign communities in this town. Today we would like to stress again that our movement is only here in order to support a fundamental principle: that of the secularism of public schools.[6] (*Le Monde*, 10 January 1999)

All the legal argument centres around the notion of the *caractère ostentatoire* (ostentatious character) of the headscarf which it is argued is, by virtue of this, an instrument of proselytism. In September 1994, the Minister for Education, François Bayrou, interpreting a clause of the ruling of the Conseil d'État,[7] published a circular that, in an appendix, authorized the refusal of admission to pupils wearing 'ostentatious signs' of religious belief. A semiological debate over the ostentatious or discreet character of the headscarf was thus introduced. From this polemic, a more-or-less general discourse of rejection was arrived at. The deliberate ambiguity of this text authorized the heads of secondary schools to attempt to rival each other in their severity. In a France in the process of dechristianization, where the dominant religion is that of the market economy, the wearing of a headscarf that contravenes the rules of fashion is very visible, and so, if one so wishes, ostentatious. The accusation of proselytism, in other words of propaganda that is both religious and political and that puts educational neutrality in danger, is more difficult to understand. However, this is the argument invoked by the Fédération de l'Education Nationale, FEN, the teachers' union with close ties to the Socialist Party:

> Proselytism constitutes a restriction to the freedom of thought necessary for the development of critical thinking in young people, which is a necessary condition for access to autonomy which is one of the chief missions of the public service of secular education.[8] (*Le Monde*, 10 January 1999).

This violation of neutrality was also denounced by the Right-wing unions. The *voilées* ('veiled women') are sometimes even accused of aiming to establish an Islamic Republic in France (declaration of the ex-headteacher of the secondary school in Creil in March 1999). In all of these cases, without having to talk as Bruno Mégret, an extreme-Right leader, does of *colonisation à rebours* ('colonisation in reverse'), these women are always blamed for bringing Republican values into question.

The Right-wing parties and trades unions have even taken up the argument according to which the wearing of the headscarf is a sign of submission of women to men.[9] The adversaries of the headscarf argue that they are in fact defending young women against the authoritarianism of their fathers or their brothers. The realization that a lot of these young women have chosen freely and for themselves this dress code, often as a way of distancing themselves from their elders, particularly their parents, puts into question this essentialist idea of a return to Islam.[10] In this essentialist view of Islam represented in most of the media reports on Algeria and Iran, women are necessarily inferiorized, dominated by men, and kept in the home.[11] The origins of the young women wearing headscarves is never taken into account: relations of dependence on their fathers are not at all the same in the case of those whose parents originate from Turkey and those whose parents originate from the Maghreb (Goldberg-Salinas and Zaidman, 1998). Hanifa Cherifi, who has been a national mediator for questions related to the headscarf since 1994, expressed her surprise when on the first occasion she was called upon to mediate in an incident, young women of Moroccan origin told her that in wearing headscarves they were disobeying their parents but obeying God and the Koran.[12]

The headscarf is also accused of making women ugly and making them ashamed of their femininity. This aesthetic argument is also political.

Certainly the headscarf marks a form of sexual differentiation in an academic environment, which has only recently (since 1968) become mixed. But the images of the demonstrations of 1994 against Bayrou's circular show girls and boys marching together, the girls wearing headscarves and not in the least hidden or self-effacing. On the contrary, they can be seen climbing on top of cars to shout their indignation and attract the attention of passers-by. An opinion poll in the Autumn of 1994 estimated that 85 per cent of the French population was hostile to the wearing of the headscarf in schools, but those rare French men and women who expressed an opinion in favour, did so in the name of sexual equality, arguing that this equality would be better supported by the reintegration of girls wearing headscarves into schools than by educating them in separate rooms or by correspondence, and thus excluding them.

These discourses hide a profound unease. The wearing of the headscarf can be perceived, though few dare to say it, as a gesture of defiance by adolescents towards an institution whose values and virtues are no longer completely credible but that remains the *raison d'être* for those in the teaching profession. This dress code is one that contests the universal value of contemporary Western practices. There is a form of bodily marking of the opposition between the West and the Muslim world which occurs around the beard for men, and around the veiling or unveiling of hair for women. It will be useful at this point to analyse the meaning of this by way of an anthropological detour. This bodily marking is valid both as a designation by the other and a designation of the self.

Elements of an Anthropology of the Headscarf

The bodily marking of the opposition between the West and the Muslim world has, since its beginnings, occurred around the different treatment of hair, firstly men's hair. Observations concerning women originally concerned more their general condition and status than a precise point of their bodily aesthetic. It is a completely different story today when it is through the headscarf which covers (some or all of) women's hair that this opposition is manifested. The passions aroused by the wearing or absence of this piece of cloth suggest that what is at stake here is not banal. Everyone knows the story of Samson, recounted in the Book of Judges of the Old Testament, the extraordinary strength that resided in his long hair untouched by scissors, and his unfortunate taste for his enemy, the Philistines', wives. He revealed his secret to the last of these women, the famous Delila, and she was the cause of his downfall, succeeding in cutting off his hair whilst he was asleep and thus being able to deliver him, defenceless, to the warrior Philistines.[13] This myth is based on a widespread belief in a number of societies, according to which life, the soul, strength and fertility, come from the head, and are particularly present in the hair and the beard.[14] This belief is without doubt connected to the fact that the growth of hair is similar to that of vegetation. The hair thus appears as the site of virile power in men and reproductive power in women. The marking of the difference between masculine and feminine occurs in the opposition between the beard and other bodily hair, because whilst both men and women have pubic hair, only men grow beards. Thus the Ancient Greeks had the custom of cutting a boy's hair when he reached puberty and his beard began to grow. And if signs of virility (and all the political and social power attached to it) are concentrated in the beard, then women's hair is, on the contrary, perceived as the site of reproductive power, and is both sacred and dangerous. The headscarf must thus be understood as a screen to the reproductive power which shines from the hair.

For women the headscarf has always functioned as a social code. As with all clothing, the headscarf is a marker of time: individual time in that it marks the end of childhood, social time in that it is subject to fashions, interpretations, and that through it collective memories and meanings take meaning. It also marks (as is apparent in the infinite diversity of its forms) an attachment to a group, common to both sexes: community, ethnic group, nation, religion, locality, social class. In the West it is often not realized that women's headscarves are, in Islam, a mark of privilege: at once a privilege of religious status (of Muslims over non-Muslims), a privilege of citizenship, and a privilege of class, because women of the poorest groups in society, particularly peasants, do not wear a headscarf. This privilege, however, is obtained at the cost of a barrier to freedom of movement and autonomy. Women's headscarves are part of a complex vestimentary code and cannot be interpreted in an unequivocal manner. The headscarf has always been the object of different customs and permanent negotiations. It is certainly the mark of women's exclusion from the public space, but at the same time it is a way in which they are able to circulate within this public space. It is an instrument of social control but also a manifestation of self-control. This interpretation has never been widely accepted in the West and especially in France where a post-colonial vision persists according to which women of dominated peoples can only be completely submissive and dominated figures.

A Political Issue

Through the headscarf, and the way in which it is worn or not worn, a whole range of fashions, evolutions in taste and aesthetic judgements are expressed (Baron, 1989). From the beginning of the twentieth century, however, the headscarf has become a stake in a political debate over modernity. The modernization of the large Muslim countries close to Europe, Iran and Turkey, took place through the imposition from above, by highly authoritarian powers, of Western models, particularly Western models of clothing. Mustapha Kemal declared that: 'A civilized and international form of dress is one that is suitable for our valiant people.'[15] From 1925, men's faces were to be shaven and Western hats were to replace the fez and the headscarf. The 'unveiling' of Turkish women does not seem to have been accompanied by the same violence as that in Iran, where working-class and peasant women often had their headscarves removed with brutality. This may perhaps be explained by Turkey's greater popular desire for Westernization. When the wave of Kemalizm reached Tunisia and Morocco in 1947, Sultan Mohamed V took the decision to unveil his own daughter, and instructed her to give an official speech without a headscarf. Besides these models imposed from above by a patriarchal power, there were also initiatives from more and more numerous women trying to gain their independence and autonomy either in their own countries or, in the case of immigrant women, in their host countries. Thus the young women wearing headscarves today sometimes have mothers who stopped wearing their own headscarves to adopt the fashions of the West. This 'modernization' in the presentation of self was also linked in some cases to the anti-colonial struggle, notably in Egypt, Palestine and Algeria. This political 'unveiling' made efforts not to contravene the rules of modesty and propriety.

In the eyes of the ancient rules, the young women wearing their *hijab* are themselves unveiled. The headscarves that they wear are in reality a compromise between traditional customs and codes, passed down from their histories (and according to which women's head and sometimes their whole face was covered), and new rules of behaviour and new aspirations to autonomy, work and education. Thus, the young women of Flers proposed in January 1999 to swap their headscarves for a hat in class. This final compromise that would have allowed them to preserve a symbolic head covering was refused to them. It is clear, therefore, that the wearing of the headscarf does not mark a return to the past but rather the adoption of new vestimentary codes that are closely attached to political and social aspirations. The surface discourse of these young women is religious in nature, but this hides profoundly political attitudes. This highly publicized entry of Muslim women onto the public stage has given them a visibility seemingly at odds with the connotations of modesty linked to the wearing of the Islamic headscarf. The significance attached to the headscarf is thus inversed. Various studies carried out in countries such as Turkey, Algeria, Egypt have shown that the girls and women who adopt one of the new forms of the Islamic headscarf demonstrate by this their aspiration to education, to a professional activity, to more autonomy with regard to patriarchal power (Dayan-Herzbrun, 1995). An Algerian Muslim woman, brought up like many others in a family whose practice of Islam was no more than traditional, explains herself in these terms:

> The idea of the headscarf first came into my head in 1982 when I started to ask myself about the relationship between men and women, and about women's equality and freedom. I arrived at the conclusion that the headscarf was the best means for me to acquire my freedom . . . In covering my body, I present myself in such a way that men are only interested in my character and my behaviour, in short they consider me as a human being. In freeing myself from the male gaze I affirm my liberty.[16] (Taarji, 1990, pp.277–8)

It is, of course, desirable that this liberty should also be respected in the case of women who wish to dress in a Western fashion. However, the refusal by many European analysts to take into account this discourse, and numerous others of the same type, demonstrates a misogynist Eurocentrism hidden beneath a supposed woman friendly stance. This type of attitude is incompatible with a proper sociological analysis. This choice of a specifically Muslim entry into modernity is shown by the public behaviour of these women, to be seen in Muslim countries, but also in Europe where a striking juxtaposition of accessories is visible in the example of a young Swiss student wearing a headscarf, a walkman, a multicoloured jacket, trousers and a backpack.[17]

It is easy to object that these women could have found another means to affirm their desire for autonomy. For example, in adopting or imitating Western codes as older generations did. In support of this argument it must be recognized that the headscarf is an extremely ambiguous means of affirming autonomy, and one which can be turned against women as an instrument of oppression, as has been seen for a long period in Iran. This type of argument is recurrent in France but it does not take into account the way in which the headscarf is also a symbol of opposition to dominant powers or in any case of non-submission to the rules imposed by dominant powers. This phenomenon was already clearly visible in Algeria during the war of national liberation where the wearing of headscarves by women militants allowed them to hide tracts or arms and was at the same time a challenge to the French authorities and their assimilationist attitudes which included an attempt to unveil Algerian women. This was particularly true after the 13 May 1958 when various partisans of a French Algeria organized public unveilings of Algerian women in town squares in order to demonstrate their approval of the colonial power. The wearing of the headscarf thus took on the significance of a rejection of this power (Tahon, 1998).

It is in this light that the wearing of headscarves by women today must be interpreted. The difficulty arises in that, as with all symbols which mobilize the social imagination, the headscarf does not have one simple sense but is invested with different meanings by those who wear it. It may be the sign of a return to religious belief as an antidote to the ills of modern society: in particular drugs and delinquency. This is the goal of an organization like the Union des Jeunes Musulmans de France (Union of Young French Muslims) which declares itself hostile to assimilation and proclaims that young Muslims should have Islam as their sole identity. Their message is transmitted from person to person, from 'brother' to 'brother', as was that of the Algerian resistance in France. But the goal is different. The young converts start by conforming to the ritual of Ramadan and then go on to the practice of daily prayer, before imposing on themselves a new lifestyle which for them constitutes a 'means of redemption'. This type of journey can be seen as the result of a search for identity. But only a small minority of the young women who decide to wear a headscarf have followed such a path. In fact the wearing of the headscarf is sometimes only a temporary decision and may correspond to what has been called the spiritual crisis of adolescence. Often, however, the reasons for wearing a headscarf are multiple and varied, and it may be seen as a French way of affirming Arab identity as well as sign of Islam (Rio, 1998).

The supremely political nature of the headscarf is even more evident when women are not made to wear it but choose themselves to do so. In today's Turkey, for example, the wearing of the headscarf indicates a freely chosen adherence to one or other of the Islamic political parties. The wearing of headscarves by young women from Turkish families living in France clearly signals their belonging to one or other of these parties' French organizations. It is interesting to note that the programmes of the two organizations are widely divergent, illustrating the plural nature of political Islam. In fact political Islam is just as diverse as political Christianity with a discourse which mixes political and religious references and which is not easy to categorize. In connection with this manifestation of political Islam, there is an obvious relationship between the 'affair of the headscarves' in France and events in Algeria. In October 1988 a revolt of young people in Algeria was bloodily repressed and led to the formation of the Front Islamique de Salut (Islamic Saviour Front) or FIS as the largest opposition party. In January 1992 the electoral process was interrupted and the FIS outlawed, which did not end Islamic agitation but merely criminalized it. The first 'headscarf affair' occurred, as discussed, in 1989, which in France was the period of the Pasqua laws,[18] of random police checks and expulsions of 'illegal' immigrants, as well as of the growth in strength of the Front National. The social situation and general standards of living were worsening. Nothing improved when the Socialists regained control of government. Young Muslims, even those born and educated in France, are continually reminded of their foreign origins. Suffering discriminations in employment and realizing that neither the law, nor justice, nor the police, nor access to work, nor even school is equal for all, they often describe themselves as second class citizens. Their living conditions have often caused old solidarities and traditional forms of social control such as those of the family to disappear. To the lack of a collective memory due to the silence of their parents concerning their past and the wearing down of social ties, has been added an absence of employment prospects. Because of the current crisis in political references two types of response to this conflictual situation have developed: either a continuation of the cycle of repression and violence, or a behaviour which can be described as one of 'counter-stigmatization'. The headscarf is a sign of this second type of behaviour by which young women intend to reclaim in a positive way the Islamic identity for which they are discriminated against. Both young men and young women participate in what is above all a generational phenomenon. However, the classic sexist stereotypes intervene in their perceptions, assigning the young men to the side of activity and violence whilst young women are designated to passivity and submission. It is also expected that girls and young women should conform to the dominant rules of fashion and of seduction, and it is also this that the young women in headscarves are rebelling against.

Solutions that Do Not Work

The whole issue of the headscarves has revealed a Jacobin and Christian France which cannot resolve the problems posed by the presence in its territory of a large Muslim minority (about four million people). A minority which is colourful, divided and unstructured by any kind of religious hierarchy which could have provided an interlocutor for the

French state. The solutions proposed by different political leaders risk accentuating this same emphasis on ethnic communities that they denounce and that they claim they are avoiding. These solutions also threaten to widen the internal conflicts within the population of Muslim origin. Beneath the pretext, or a true belief, that they are protecting young girls, political leaders refuse to listen to them and exclude them from school. And all too often the Muslims who declare publicly that they are against the wearing of headscarves in schools and argue for an Islam 'adapted to contemporary needs', or who condemn the headscarf for its 'inferiorization' of women, are merely the spokespeople of political regimes adopting the language of Islam. They do nothing more than express the divisions that are tearing apart the countries from which they originate and import these post-colonial divisions into France. As Islam, and particularly the Sunnite branch of Islam which is most common in France, is based on the re-reading and re-interpretation of texts, it does not recognize the authority of one religious body. The religious law invoked by the young women wearing headscarves is that of one particular country.

The appointment in 1994, on the initiative of Simone Veil, of a Muslim woman mediator, who was given the responsibility of pacifying the relationships between girls in headscarves and heads of educational establishments, follows from the same logic as that of the appointment of 'big brothers' in troubled suburbs. These intermediaries whose good faith, lucidity and devotion should not be questioned, are of the 'same origin' as the young people to whom they are supposed to be speaking. Their competence is recognized in function of this 'origin' and not in function of their human and professional qualities which they may share with many other people. Thus the ethnicization of marginality and delinquence is reinforced and instead of being treated as social or generational problems they are implicitly considered as ethnic or community problems.

The young women in headscarves thus pose questions that are certainly closely connected to issues of gender but that are also historical, political and social, with both national and international dimensions. They cannot be reduced to a problematic of ethnic difference or of multiculturalism, which is so foreign to French society with its particular history and institutions. These problems reveal the deep structures of this society which must quickly invent for itself policies which take account the diversity of its members.

Translated by Jane Freedman

Notes

1. A suburb near Paris.
2. The Right-wing party of Jacques Chirac, the President of the Republic at the time of writing.
3. The two departments of Martinique and Guadeloupe are definitely part of France. However, the poor economic conditions and the diverse forms of social discrimination suffered by their non-white inhabitants (descendants of ex-slaves) have led to a chronic discontent, which can go so far as claims for independence.
4. 'Les agissements discriminatoires des détenteurs de l'autorité publique, des groupements ou des personnes privées, la provocation à la discrimination, à la haine ou à la violence, la diffamation et l'injure au motif de l'appartenance ou de la non appartenance à une ethnie, une nation ou une religion sont interdits.'
5. 'L'école doit inculquer aux élèves le respect de l'individu, de ses origines et de ses différences.'
6. 'Nous nous sommes toujours battus dans la dignité et dans le respect des convictions des communautés étrangères de la ville. Aujourd'hui encore, nous rappelons que notre mouvement n'est là que pour soutenir un principe fondamental: la laïcité de l'école publique.'
7. 'Le port par les élèves de signes par lesquels ils entendent manifester leur appartenance à une religion n'est pas par lui-même incompatible avec le principe de laïcité, dans la mesure où il constitue l'exercice de la liberté d'expression et de manifestation de croyances religieuses, mais cette liberté ne saurait permettre aux élèves d'arborer des signes d'appartenance religieuse qui, par leur nature, par les conditions dans lesquelles ils seraient portés individuellement ou collectivement, ou par leur caractère ostentatoire ou revendicatif, constitueraient un acte de pression, de provocation, de prosélytisme ou de propagande, porteraient atteinte à la dignité ou à la liberté de l'élève ou d'autres membres de la communauté éducative.' ('Pupils wearing signs by which they intend to demonstrate their belonging to a particular religion is not in itself incompatible with the principle of secularism, in so far as it constitutes an exercise of the freedom of expression and of demonstration of religious beliefs. But this freedom should not permit pupils to adopt signs of religious belonging which, by their nature, or by the conditions in which they are worn, individually or collectively, or by their ostentatious or protestatary character, constitute an act of pressure, provocation, proselytism or propaganda, and attack

the dignity or the freedom of any other pupil or other members of the educative community.')
8. 'Le prosélytisme constitue une entrave à la liberté de conscience nécessaire au développement de l'esprit critique du jeune, condition de l'accès à l'autonomie qui est une des missions premières du service public laïc d'éducation.'
9. Press release by the SNALC-CSEN, 4 May 1999.
10. For a critique of this essentialist conception of Islam see Kandiyoti, D. (1991), 'Islam and Patriarchy', in N. Keddie and B. Baron (eds), *Women in Middle Eastern History,* New Haven.
11. For a discussion of these prejudices see Gaspard, F. and Khosrokhavar, F. (1995), *Le foulard et la République,* Paris: La Découverte.
12. Interview in *Le Monde*, 10 January 1999.
13. Judges, chapters XIII to XVI. The argument concerning this point is developed in Dayan-Herzbrun, S. (1995), 'Cheveux coupés, cheveux voilés', *Communications*, 60: 165–84.
14. For a fuller discussion of this point see Onian, R. B. (1973), *The Origins of European Thought,* New York University Press.
15. Cited in Göle, N. (1993), *Musulmanes et modernes*, Paris: La Découverte, p. 56.
16. 'L'idée du hijab a germé dans mon esprit en 1982 quand j'ai commencé à m'interroger sur les questions du rapport hommes-femmes, de leur égalité et de la liberté de la femme. Je suis arrivée à la conclusion que le hijab était le meilleur moyen pour moi d'acquérir ma liberté ... En couvrant mon corps je me présente à l'homme de manière à ce qu'il ne s'intéresse qu'à mon esprit, à mon comportement, bref, à ce qu'il me considère comme un être humain. En me libérant de son regard, j'affirme ma liberté.'
17. Seen on French television in March 1999.
18. For a more detailed explanation of these laws see Chapter 1.

Part II
Representations and Identities

−6−

The Representation of Ethnic Minority Women in Comic Books[1]

Mark McKinney

The status of French-language comic books as commodities in a rapidly changing youth culture market means that, of necessity, cartoonists and comics publishers are keenly attuned to developments affecting and of interest to young people, including such diverse but interrelated phenomena as the 'Beur' movement of the early 1980s, the fight against racism and the Front National (FN), and the importing and adaptation of hip-hop culture. Cartoonists have not passively reflected these developments, but have actively participated in their shaping, sometimes directly. Their representations of ethnic minority and immigrant women, therefore, provide significant insights into the ways in which gender and ethnicity have been constructed in popular culture since the early 1980s.[2] In fact, the history of these representations stretches back to the colonial period and earlier (cf. Nederveen Pieterse, 1992; Pigeon, 1996), allowing useful comparisons to be made between colonial and contemporary representations.

In what follows, I analyse a body of works, some mainstream and others more marginal, whose primarily realist depictions of contemporary history and everyday life, set in France,[3] include women from France's former colonies.[4] My research is based on the assumption that the production, circulation and consumption of representations of ethnic minority women in comic books are normally part of an 'othering' process, through which dominant forms of collective and personal identity are constructed – as national, post-colonial, French and male. Nonetheless, these representations often mediate conflicting ideologies and are sometimes the site of resistance to oppressive identity constructions.

My results are based on a sample of approximately seventy-five comics featuring ethnic minority women characters. For the purposes of this study, they can be grouped into three periods across an approximately twenty-year span (1977–99):[5] the interval extending from the late-1970s through the early 1980s, during which immigration became an openly contested stake of French politics and a theme not only in comics, but also in fiction; the mid-to-late 1980s, marked by the rise and fall of the 'Beur' movement; and the late 1980s to the present, over the course of which the existence of a diverse, multi-ethnic population and an accompanying innovative, multicultural artistic production have increasingly become an unavoidable part of France's cultural landscape. During the first period, minority women were very rarely depicted, and then usually as fleeting symbols of a Third-World demographic potential and adjuncts to the archetypal male immigrant worker, as in Enki Bilal and Pierre Christin's *La Ville qui n'existait pas* (*The City That Didn't Exist*) (1994), and/or victims of racism and sexism, for example in Chantal Montellier's *Andy Gang et le tueur de la Marne* (*Andy Gang and the Marne Killer*) (1980).

Comic-book representation of minority women only really took off during the mid- to late-1980s, thanks mainly to two factors. First, political activism by the 'second generation' helped bring about a partial shift in dominant perceptions – ethnic minority groups, especially those of Maghrebi origin, were increasingly perceived as being permanently settled in France and less as strangers living there temporarily (Wihtol de Wenden, 1990, p. 395). Women's participation in and leadership of events such as the 1983 'March for equality and against racism' left a legible, if rare trace in some comics. For example in 'Marche ou crève' ('March or die'), a short story in *Les Beurs* (*The Beurs*) (1985) by Larbi Mechkour and Farid Boudjellal, cartoonists of Algerian origin, Nadia goes off to join the marchers, leaving her father grumbling: 'Samia, your kids want to colonize France!!!', an ironic twist on French racist rhetoric. The story represents the generation gap between mother and daughter through differences in dress, roles and space: Nadia, wearing a bright red jacket and bare-headed, goes out to occupy public space, leaving her mother behind in the home, wearing more traditional dress, including a headscarf, and serving tea to Nadia's seated father (cf. Douglas and Malti-Douglas, 1994, pp. 206–7). A second factor was the cultural production of minority artists in the comics industry, like Spanish-French cartoonist and publisher José Jover and Caribbean-French artist Roland Monpierre, as well as Maghrebi-French artists such as Boudjellal and Mechkour (McKinney, 1998). As a result, many of the comic book character types with wide currency today were tried out during this period, often initially in the work of minority cartoonists, including the runaway (McKinney, forthcoming), the *métisse* (McKinney, 1997b), the sexy 'Beurette' (young French Arab woman), and the studious 'Beurette'.

The third period, from the late 1980s to the present, has seen a limited diversification of character types, most being of North African (usually Algerian) origin or from France's and England's former colonies in West Africa (though occasionally from the French Caribbean and, even more rarely, from Vietnam and China), but generally in secondary roles. The relative paucity of such representations is due in part to the fact that a single artist, Farid Boudjellal, produced many of the comics in which minority women and girl characters appear. Moreover, since 1990 his work has been published almost exclusively by a major comics company run by an ethnic minority publisher (Mourad Boudjellal, his brother). Other artists of Maghrebi origin who published during the early-to-mid 1980s left the field during the slump that had hit the industry by the end of the 1980s.

The gender skew in the pool of artists is at least as troubling as the ethnic imbalance: the success of a Claire Bretécher should not obscure the fact that only a small proportion of French and Belgian cartoonists are women, and generally their work is not well-known (Pilloy, 1994, p. 16). Of the works analysed here, only four were drawn by women (though women coloured several others): *Mouler, démouler* (*Mould, Extract*) (Bretécher, 1995), *La Voyageuse de petite ceinture* (*The Woman Travelling on the Small Loop*)[6] (Christin and Goetzinger, 1985), *Bye-bye grisaille* (*Bye-Bye Grey Skies*) (Duvivier, 1997) and *Andy Gang et le tueur de la Marne*; and the second of these was scripted by a man. Moreover, I have not yet succeeded in locating a single ethnic minority woman cartoonist. This imbalance has undoubtedly had a significant impact on the manner in which ethnic minority women and girls are depicted. In most comic books they are regularly relegated to the margins of the stories where they appear and are very often the object of heterosexist voyeurism, thereby reproducing a dominant colonial relationship to colonized women (Savarese, 1995). According to Annie Pilloy (1994, p. 16) 90 per cent of the comic books published by Lombard and Dupuis, two of the largest publishing houses, had a male as the main protagonist, and among these, women and girls serve mainly as a foil for the males, often as sex objects, and are rarely depicted as the equals of men and boys.

Multiple Marginalization

Among the works analysed here, only a handful give equal space to ethnic minority women or girls: a young Algerian-French woman is the central character of *La Voyageuse de petite ceinture*, an early comic about a 'Beurette' runaway; and the Moroccan-Belgian Leïla, another young runaway, is a main character in Stassen and Lapière's dyptich, *Le Bar du vieux Français* (*The Old Frenchman's Bar*) (1992, 1993), along with a black youth who flees to Belgium from an unnamed African country.[7] Even in these books, and the more recent *Bye-bye grisaille*, the portrayal of female runaways who are alienated from their families and communities of origin dovetails with the dominant assimilationist perspective, inherited from colonial times, that second-generation Maghrebi women are cultural lynchpins who do or should abandon their foreign cultural heritage in order to help align their group with mainstream cultural norms. Their detachment from their Maghrebi cultural roots may also render runaway women more attractive to white male readers, but in each case the women are shown criticizing the predatory sexual behavior of white men or eluding their unwanted advances. In these instances, the cartoonists appear to be aware of the eroticizing and exoticizing dimensions in contemporary comic-book representations of sexually liberated ethnic minority women (cf. Bloul, 1994).

On the other hand, a significant number of comics give a substantial role to one or more women or girls as part of a sexually and often ethnically mixed group of characters, with a more or less equal focus on both genders – *Les Beurs*, which focuses on 'Beur' and 'Beurette' characters, even satirically thematizes 'Beurette' (and other minority) demands for equal representation in autonomous cultural productions. Unlike the all-male multi-ethnic groups inspired by the 'Black-Blanc-Beur' (black-white-Arab) trio in Mathieu Kassovitz's film *La Haine* (1995), as in Boudjellal and Jollet's comic book *Ethnik ta mère* (1996), multi-ethnic groups of both girls and boys are to be found in several recent works, some of which are volumes in ongoing series: *Aventures en Megahertz* (*Adventures in Megahertz*) (Ridel and Lelièvre, 1997), *Bye-bye grisaille, Malika secouss* (*Malika Rocks*) (Tehem, 1998, 1999), *L'Ombre du triangle* (*The Shadow of the Triangle*) (Christin and Aymond, 1999) and *Paris-trottoir* (*Paris-Sidewalk*) (Constant and Vandam, 1999). This may indicate a trend towards more empowering representations of ethnic minority women and girls, specifically those of Maghrebi origin. However, although in each of these cases the girl has an Arabic name, virtually no other sign of her cultural specificity is included in *Aventures en Megahertz*, *Bye-bye grisaille* and *Malika secouss*, leaving the multi-ethnic peer group to substitute for the non-existent representation of the minority community. The result is more a paint-by-numbers version of republican assimilationism than a form of multiculturalism able to negotiate between different ethnicities.

To take one example, Tehem, an artist from Reunion Island, has published two volumes of a series of humour-based comics, collectively entitled *Malika secouss*, whose title character is a feisty, sexy Maghrebi adolescent. In many of the vignettes where Malika appears, she tries to find an outlet for her prodigious, pent-up energy in her rather dull *banlieue*, the 'cité des Pâquerettes' (*'The Daisies Estate'*). Although Malika spends most of her time with two male adolescent friends, Jeff (white) and Dooley (black), she occasionally agrees, with great reluctance, to spare a moment for an unnamed white boy who remains completely enamoured of her, despite her obvious disinterest and repeated attempts to shrug him off. Whereas white male desire is textually represented through paedophilia in *Bye-bye grisaille*, mixed-race prostitution and revanchist colonial sadism in *La Voyageuse de petite ceinture*, and delusional paternalism in *Le Bar du vieux Français,* in *Malika secouss* it is thematized from Malika's point of view mostly as an annoyance, although the series still plays significantly on heterosexual male voyeurism.

An analysis of some specific roles and situations can also be revealing. Ethnic minority women are usually at the bottom of the socio-economic hierarchy: for example, black women work as cleaners for exploitative institutions in *La Nuit des clandestins* (*The Night of the Illegal Aliens*) (Ceppi and Christin, 1992), although by the end of the story they have helped to overthrow the unjust world order that feeds off cheap Third World labour in France and abroad (cf. McKinney, 1997a). In Boudjellal's *L'Oud: la trilogie* (*The Oud/Arab Lute: The Trilogy*) (1996), Djamila Slimani is an Algerian-French woman who works as a cashier in a grocery store. Her lack of socially-valued job skills means that she is destined to remain a member of the working class, like her immigrant parents. However, Djamila attributes her professional situation to an inability to learn, and strongly advises her sister Ratiba, a studious 'Beurette', to study hard and do well in school in order to avoid ending up in a similar job. Only a few comics show ethnic minority women higher up the socio-economic ladder: for example, in Yvan Alagbé's *Nègres jaunes* (*Yellow Negroes*) (1995) the daughter of a *harki*-officer-turned-French-policeman[8] works as a gynaecologist. Her privileged position stands in stark contrast to that of Martine, a so-called *sans-papiers* (illegal alien) from Benin, who is hired to clean the policeman's home. By contrasting the differing ways whereby the two women entered the French economy, Alagbé illustrates the discriminating effects of colonial history and neo-colonial imperialism on women of colour and, consequently, the widely divergent positions that they may occupy in the contemporary hierarchy of social classes. *Dyaa* (1997), Alagbé's subsequent comic with Martine, re-named Martinah, is narrated by Ibrahima, a Soninké taxi-driver working in France. Although Ibrahima and Martinah are of different religions

(Muslim and Christian), the alienation caused by their exile in France brings them briefly together. Both are lonely and isolated in part because they are separated from their partners: Auguste, Martinah's husband, brought her to France but then abandoned her and returned to Africa; and Ibrahima had to leave his wife and child at home in Africa when he went to look for work in France. Despite their bleak tone, *Nègres jaunes* and *Dyaa* inject some welcome complexity into homogenizing media portrayals of black Africans in France, and are the first comics to devote sustained, sympathetic attention to the plight of African *sans-papiers* women in France.

Marginality is also represented in spatial terms. Ethnic minority women and girls are often shown living in poor city centre neighbourhoods, as in Boudjellal's *Le Gourbi* (*L'Oud: la trilogie*, 1996, pp. 66–111), whose title, meaning 'a hovel', refers to the Slimani family's cramped Parisian living quarters (cf. Douglas and Malti-Douglas, 1994, pp. 204–5). Elsewhere, in Boudjellal's satirical *Le Beurgeois* (1997), African women are among the squatters who risk being evicted from a dilapidated building in an urban area undergoing renovation. Alternatively, cartoonists place ethnic minority women and girls in the working-class high-rises in the *banlieues*, sometimes in squalid and violent conditions, as in Jean-Christophe Chauzy's *Béton armé* (*Armed/Reinforced Concrete*) (1997), whose punning title refers both to the concrete of the run-down apartment buildings and to the estate's division into hostile camps that engage in armed conflict.

In comics with an anti-racist edge ethnic minority women are regularly shown to be the victims of prejudice, mistreatment and racist attacks, including violence instigated by the racist Front National. Luz's *Les Mégret gèrent la ville* (*The Mégrets Manage the City*) (1998) is a satirical send-up of Catherine and Bruno Mégret's mis-management of Vitrolles, a city near Marseilles whose mayoral position was won by the FN in the municipal elections of February 1997. In Luz's comic book, women of colour (men too) are often targets of the Mégrets, and serve to highlight the grotesque contradictions in the ideology and politics of the FN. In one episode Catherine Mégret noisily leads a group of anti-choice demonstrators in a take-over of an abortion clinic, only to freeze in her tracks when she realizes that the patient she has barged in on is black. Many of the comic's French readers would be aware that the Mégrets are militantly anti-choice and that in January 1998 the Mégret-controlled city council of Vitrolles passed a municipal ordinance promising 5,000 francs to families with at least one parent who was French or European, a measure with obvious xenophobic and racist connotations.

The Persistence and Contestation of Neo-colonial Representations

Many of the interlocking forms of marginalization described above – racism, nationalist exclusion, class oppression and economic disenfranchizement – are shown by comics to affect ethnic minority men as well as women. It is through the sexualization and sexual objectification of ethnic minority women that the sexist dimension of France's eurocentric colonial heritage is most clearly evident. Such representations derive from a tradition that dates back to the height of the colonial era, when black women and girls in French comics were usually portrayed as 'friends, mistresses, pseudo-queens, and concubines' (Pigeon, 1996, p. 146), and, like their male counterparts, served the white supremacist 'purpose of demonstrating the absurd inferiority of the objectified Black' (p. 142).

In the case of French Caribbean women, some character types can be traced back to the specific colonial-era representations of the 'doudou', the mulatto and the white creole.[9] In two comics, *La Nuit des clandestins* and *La Variante du dragon* (*The Dragon Chess Move*) (Golo and Frank, 1989), a 'doudou' figure adds an exotic touch to the drab Parisian scenery, though she is desexualized such that she resembles the black 'mammy' in US culture. However, Caribbean woman are represented in this and a few other cases as able to manipulate cultural codes (like voodoo and creole) hermetic to most metropolitan French readers. A late twentieth-century version of the dangerously seductive creole woman[10] can be found in *La Variante du dragon*, a comic book *polar* (or crime novel) about a Parisian criminal underworld filled with immigrants and people of colour (such as Chinese, Caribbeans, Russians, Maghrebis). In this book, Catherine Sainte-Croix, a *béké* (a white Caribbean of settler descent), is a drug-dealing femme fatale reminiscent of exotic female villains in the *Steve Canyon* comic-strip series by American artist Milton Caniff.

Highly eroticized representations of the sexually charged 'black Venus' (Nederveen Pieterse, 1992, pp. 142–3, 182–7) can still be found today in comic books set in the Caribbean (cf. Bachollet, Debost, Lelieur and Peyrière, 1994; Savarese, 1995). In *Lettres d'outremer* (*Overseas Letters*) (1996), set mainly in Guadeloupe, Warnauts and Raives explicitly raise questions about colonialism and political repression in the French Caribbean today and grant the black Caribbean women a certain degree of automony. Nevertheless, their black women characters are also eroticized and exoticized. Typed representations of Caribbean women can also be found in the art of Caribbean artists, such as *Kreyon noir* (*Black Pencil*) (n.d.) and *Coco Clip* (1995), a magazine directed at the bilingual creole/French community in mainland France. However, their exoticism is relativized by that fact that they appear side by side with typed depictions of Caribbean men, gullible tourists and ridiculous bureaucrats.

If the shift from colonial to post-colonial attitudes and desires (Bloul, 1994) often includes a measure of critique or revision, this cannot always be attributed to a clearly defined anti-colonialist position. Rather, it derives from a range of often complex and contradictory perspectives, which, in the case of cartoonists, includes the colonial-era comics tradition. A good illustration of this tension can be found in the recurrent depiction of ethnic minority women as prostitutes, like the Asian, black and Maghrebi women working in a neo-colonial bordello in *La Voyageuse de petite ceinture*, and Ling-Ling, a Chinese woman working in a Parisian opium den in the Chinese neighborhood of Paris's thirteenth *arrondissement*, who has sex with Catherine Sainte-Croix in *La Variante du dragon*. In Baru's *Bonne année* (*Happy New Year*) (1998), Djemila is pimped by her brother, Ali, a drug addict dependent on his sister's earnings who is using his image as a 'barbu' (a bearded man – a Muslim neo-traditionalist or revivalist) as a mask. Baru's cautionary tale uses prostitution to dramatize the abject conditions faced by Maghrebi women in those *banlieues* where poverty is endemic. However, the preponderance of sexualized representations of Maghrebi women suggests that they function primarily as objects of post-colonial male desire.

In the case of North Africa, the similarity between colonial and post-colonial comic-book imagery has led one critic to characterize the difference between the two as simply 'change within continuity' (Basfao, 1990, p. 332). The seductions of the harem and its female occupants have long been a ubiquitous feature of orientalist French cartoon and comic book treatments of North Africans and Muslims, reaching back at least to images printed at the time of France's invasion of Algiers in 1830 (Porterfield, 1998, pp. 138–40). Neo-orientalist harem imagery exists in recently-published comics depicting North African and Muslim minorities in France like *La Variante du dragon*. By the end of this book, however, Djamilah, first glimpsed in a harem-like setting in a Paris apartment, is anything but a docile sex object. Instead, she takes part in a shoot-out with a leader of a rival drug distribution gang to exact revenge for her brother's death. Harem imagery can even serve a critical function. For example, in *La Voyageuse de petite ceinture*, the harem imagery is obviously meant to be read as one of Naïma's escapist fantasies, replaced at the end of the comic by concrete action that might lead to a better life, though at the price of increasing the distance between her and her parents.

In 'Love Story Beur', in *Les Beurs*, similar imagery affirms the liberated sexual attitudes of young people of Maghrebi origin. At the story's conclusion Kamel still loves Naïma, a sexy 'Beurette', despite the fact that she has been entrapped, raped and relegated to a harem-like setting by an older magician (cf. Douglas and Malti-Douglas, 1994, pp. 213–14).

It is often difficult to disentangle neo-colonial ideology from legitimate critiques of patriarchal authority in representations of North African families in France. In part this is because North African fathers and brothers have long been viewed as domestic variants of the oriental despot presiding over his harem. Moreover, French calls for gender equality within North African family structures have historically been made in terms of the supposed need for assimilation into dominant French culture, a perspective that is often predicated on the suppression of any substantive Arabo-Muslim cultural differences. The Islamic religion is sometimes presented as rigid and intransigent or even extremist, and a reinforcing factor in the patriarchal oppression of women, as in *Bonne année*, although a few depictions of a more moderate, less menacing Islamic faith and religious practice do exist, most notably in Boudjellal's *Ramadân* (*L'oud: la trilogie*, 1996, pp. 113–59). In 'Orientalism, occidentalism and the control of women', Laura Nader argued that 'male control structures' on both sides of the Occident/Orient divide are maintained through differential 'strategies of positional superiority', which are articulated around representations of women's roles. In the West, the orientalist depiction of Muslim women as more oppressed than Western women serves to buttress structures that oppress the latter (as well as Muslim women in the West), while a similar, though less institutionalized mirror process of occidentalism is observable in the East. In representations of 'non-Western' others, an 'absence of explicit comparison is a controlling process' (Nader, 1989, p. 330). This type of control structure or process may be found at work in *Le Bar du vieux Français*, in which a critique of traditionalism, especially patriarchy, associated with Islam, in a Moroccan-Belgium family is not extended to the surrounding Euro-Belgian society, which by implication is uncritically equated with women's liberation.

On the other hand, in *Ramadân*, Boudjellal takes great pains to contest the representation of the Maghrebi man as domestic despot by establishing an explicit comparison between a Maghrebi-French and a Euro-French couple that works to dissolve the controlling process described by Nader. When Nourredine Barouche slaps his sister Nadia, she responds angrily by critiquing his offensive behaviour which replicates and reinforces their father's patriarchal control and which, she explains, is what had forced her to leave home in the first place. Boudjellal makes a telling comparison between the Maghrebi-French pair (Nourredine and Nadia) who proceed to mend their fences (Nourredine apologizes for his violent behaviour), and a divorced Euro-French couple who observe them. Boudjellal's dual critique, of patriarchal violence and widespread constructions of Maghrebis and Muslims as inferior, is reinforced later in the book, when we learn that the father of a Euro-French girl beats his wife, just as the immigrant Algerian patriarch does in a fit of rage. In both Euro-French and Maghrebi-French cases the book presents violence against women as reprehensible.

Ramadân also offers a gently humorous presentation of the holy month's observances and of women's role in the maintenance and modification of family structures and Islam (cf. Douglas and Malti-Douglas, 1994, p. 215). The book illustrates the process of secularization and presents the immigrant Algerian mother as the anchor for a set of observances that are fast disappearing in the context of daily life in France.[11] At the end of the month of Ramadan, Salima Slimani is the only character still observing the required fast, one of Islam's five pillars of faith. Her daughter Ratiba quits fasting temporarily because she has her period and then definitively so that she will have enough energy to study for her *bac* (the competitive exam at the end of French secondary-school studies). Meanwhile, Djamila, Ratiba's depressed older sister, is told by Salima to stop fasting because she has stopped eating altogether after breaking off her engagement to a man with patriarchal views and an expressed desire to return to Algeria. These examples show how the observance of religious rituals is modified under the pressures of the community's hopes for social advancement, embodied in Ratiba, the studious 'Beurette'. It also shows second-generation women refusing patriarchal values, represented by the sustained resistance to male coercion and control put up by Nadia and by Djamila, an example of the sexy 'Beurette' (her name means 'pretty'). On the other hand, a striking feature of the comics studied here is the almost complete absence of explicit references to Islamic revivalism's relationship to women, except as evoked in *Bonne année*, *Paris-trottoir* and *Les 4x4*, a new series scripted by Christin.

New Representations

Some of the more innovative tendencies discernible in contemporary comics portraying ethnic minority women are to be found either in their use of female voices and viewpoints, or in particular tropes like the runaway, the forming of mixed couples, and the *métisse*. In several comics, women and girls narrate or focalize their stories. For example, in *La*

Voyageuse de petite ceinture, almost a third of the book is given over to depicting Naïma's memories and dreams, most of which are narrated in her voice. At the end of *Le Bar du vieux Français*, Leïla's story is narrated verbally through her journal entries, which replace – to a limited extent – the earlier narration of her story provided by a colonial-era character, the old Frenchman (cf. Halen, 1993, pp. 379–80). However, giving women and girls a narrative voice or the ability to focalize is by no means a guarantee of a clean break with the colonial tradition of representation or with sexist objectifications of women, and both these books are problematic in this respect. On the other hand, in *Ce qui me donne envie de mourir (What Makes Me Want to Die)*, Alagbé (1996) uses a tryptich structure to open up a space for his character Leïla to express herself in terms that contest neo-colonial representations and the sexual exploitation of women of Maghrebi origin. The section she narrates is sandwiched between two others, in which Euro-Frenchmen who buy sex from her tell their sordid tales. In the middle section, Leïla tells the simple but poignant story of her activities one day. She decides to walk down to the port to look at the sea, but her walk is spoiled when the man who had been her client the previous day accosts her. She brushes him off, but the encounter deepens her feeling of alienation and brings her to tears. Leïla wonders why she feels like dying, but the answer is as clear to the reader as the harsh sunlight beating down on the young woman. A moment later, as Leïla hurries along, sobbing, through Marseilles's streets, a fish vendor kindly calls out to her, offering comforting words and a fresh fish as a gift. By giving expression to the woman's perspective, Alagbé sets up a powerful dialogical relationship between Leïla's story and the sections narrated by male characters, who attempt to reduce her to a disposable sexual commodity.

Cultural difference and hybridity are often figured through mixed heterosexual couples and liaisons between characters of different ethnicities, whether negatively – as prostitution, in *Ce qui me donne envie de mourir* – or more positively, for example in the mixed black/Maghrebi couples found in *Paris-trottoir*, *Le Bar du vieux Français* and *Jambon-Beur: les couples mixtes (Ham-Beur/Butter: Mixed Couples)* (Boudjellal, 1995), which all feature black African men in positively marked relationships with Maghrebi-European women. In fact, whereas there has been a 'continuing structuring absence in French cinema of the stable mixed-race white/Beur couple' (Tarr, 1997a, p. 79), it has been accurately observed that in Boudjellal's *L'Oud: la trilogie*, 'the smoothest romantic relationships are between mixed couples' (Douglas and Malti-Douglas, 1994, p. 205). Nonetheless, if the most common type of mixed couple is composed of a Maghrebi and a white European, this is because it allows cartoonists to engage with some of the most highly charged areas of interaction between majority and minority cultures in post-colonial France. Indications that large or increasing numbers of mixed couples have formed are often seen by majority commentators as positive signs that a minority group is dissolving into mainstream French society. On the other hand, Rabia Abdelkrim-Chikh (1988, pp. 243–6) interprets 'the *marginal* use of exogamy by Muslim women' in France (my emphasis), as a means of destabilizing two cultural systems with pretensions to exclusivity and wholeness (Muslim/Christian, or Maghrebi/French), and thereby creating a hybrid space of greater freedom and autonomy. This sheds light on the significance of the mixed couples and the runaway in *L'oud: la trilogie* (the first comic-book reference to a Maghrebi-French runaway, to my knowledge). Nadia Barouche's elopement with a French boyfriend, leaving Toulon for Paris, opens up a space of freedom, allowing her to escape from the control of her father and her brother, Nourredine. In Paris, Nadia is aided by her cousin, Djamila, who keeps her where-abouts secret from Nourredine, even though she is perfectly aware that the young man is scouring Paris in search of his sister. Boudjellal depicts other forms of female solidarity in the series, including healthy friendships between Maghrebi-French and Euro-French women and girls, which provide mutual support for women who are having difficulties in sorting out their relationships with men and their families.

When Nourredine finally finds his sister, she is working in the office of J'Y Suis, J'Y Reste (I'm Here, I'm Staying), an anti-racist organization where he has gone to lodge a complaint after having been the target of racial discrimination. This episode points to a crucial feature in Boudjellal's negotiation of cultural change. In his comics, cultural adaptation resembles the 'conflictual' model of integration advocated by Moroccan-born sociologist Adil Jazouli (1985, p. 52) – it involves making legitimate demands on French society and requires a fair exchange between majority and minority ethnic groups. In her discussion of mixed couples, Abdelkrim-Chikh (1988, p. 240) provides a complementary definition of integration as a collective process undertaken by a cohesive community instead of by atomized individuals. *L'Oud: la trilogie* ends with the reunion of the entire Maghrebi family, when Nadia, her new-born *métisse* baby daughter, Linda, and Nourredine all return to Toulon to celebrate the end of Ramadan. The tropes of the runaway and the mixed couple allow the Maghrebi community as a whole to be integrated into French society by introducing flexibility into the family structure, thereby enabling it to adapt to new conditions and avoid being destroyed. At the same time, the

Maghrebi community's cultural integrity is symbolically restored by the *temporary* elimination of Nadia's boyfriend Jacques, the interloper, who is nowhere to be seen at the family reunion and religious feast. In addition, the family's regained unity is mirrored by the almost fantastic reappearance of a previously disbanded North African musical group, which shows up to serenade the family. At home in Toulon the reunited family – paradoxically, despite all sorts of transformations – celebrates a cultural wholeness that they appeared to have lost (cf. Douglas and Malti-Douglas, 1994, pp. 204, 216).

Some of the first *métisse* characters in post-colonial French comics date from the early 1980s, when *métissage* came (back) into fashion and appeared (again) as a theme in prose fiction,[12] as well as in film (cf. Sherzer, 1998). The rise to prominence in the French public sphere of real-life *métis/ses* – such as writer Leïla Sebbar, anti-racist activist Harlem Désir, and tennis champion Yannick Noah – must have had some influence on the portrayal of *métis/ses* in comics. For example, the hagiographic *Il était une fois . . . Yannick Noah (Once Upon A Time . . . Yannick Noah)* (Gendrot and Chéret, 1984) features Yannick as the star, although his *métisse* sisters, Nathalie and Isabelle, appear in ancillary roles. The earliest comic-book *métisse* character I have found is in José Jover's gritty *polar*, *Sale temps. Pierrot la caravane (Nasty Weather. Pierrot the Camper)* (1983), where the sexy sixteen-year-old daughter of Samira and Léo, Zahia, is prostituted by a French mechanic to immigrant Arabs. Here ethnic hybridity is figured as debased but titillating sexual promiscuity.

Métissage was a social fact and a cultural theme produced by European colonization, so it is significant that some of the more complex and innovative French comics use *métis/ses* to embody post-colonialism's contradictions and the suppressed memories of colonial antagonisms. For example, in *Les Oubliés d'Annam (The Forgotten Ones from Annam)* (Lax and Giroud, 1990, 1991), Kim-Chi, the daughter of a renegade French soldier and a Vietnamese woman, goes to France where she meets her French grandmother for the first time. Kim-Chi and her reconciliatory voyage represent a hidden counter-history of French anti-colonialism as well as a hope that colonial-era differences may be resolved (cf. McKinney, 1997b). In Boudjellal's *Jambon-Beur: les couples mixtes* a similar ethno-nationalist cleavage is mediated through the treatment of an Algerian-French *métisse* character, Charlotte-Badia, born to Mahmoud Slimani and Patricia Barto. She embodies what Etienne Balibar (1998, p. 76) has called the 'frontière non-entière' (un-whole frontier) between France and Algeria: what appear to be two nations in fact add up to one and a half, so tight are the bonds between them, because of arrested decolonization, neo-colonialism and migrations.[13] In *Jambon-Beur: Les couples mixtes* the refusal to recognize the hybrid nature of this frontier produces a schizophrenic condition in Charlotte-Badia, who hears voices in her head. In order to dissipate the conflict between the antagonistic pressures on and within her, she splits fantastically into identical twins, two physically indistinguishable but culturally different characters, Charlotte and Badia. The violent energy thus released threatens to break apart the mixed couple, Mahmoud and Patricia, and can only be diffused by an open airing of and negotiation between painful memories of the Algerian War (1954–62) and immigration on the part of both Algerian and French families.

Whereas in the earlier *Ramadân,* Boudjellal had envisioned a future less fraught with obstacles for Linda, the *métisse* child, the confrontation with the colonial rift foregrounded through Charlotte-Badia in *Jambon-Beur: les couples mixtes* is linked to the reappearance of the spectre of the Algerian War in French public consciousness, largely due to the outbreak of civil war in Algeria after 1992. Boudjellal's comic book is a memorial project that resembles Yamina Benguigui's (1997) documentary *Mémoires d'immigrés (Immigrants' Memories/Memoirs).* Both create a hermeneutic that encourages the reader/viewer to search the submerged histories of colonization and emigration/immigration for the root causes of divisive conflicts in contemporary French society, and for clues to their solutions. In their search for common ground, both attempt to mediate between the perspectives of the ethnic majority and France's Maghrebi ethnic minority, and do so through texts which challenge dominant representations of ethnic minority women and girls. More of these creative interventions are needed to help make definitive and lasting changes in the field of representation, which is a crucial step towards full equality for ethnic minority women.[14]

Notes

1. Some of the research for this chapter was made possible by funding from the Department of French and Italian, the Philip and Elaina Hampton Fund for Faculty International Initiatives and the Alumni Travel Fund, all at Miami University (Ohio).

2. Although a few female characters from other ethnic minority and
   immigrant groups can be found (such as gypsy, Portuguese, Romanian,
   Spanish), I am primarily concerned here with the representation of
   post-colonial immigrant women and their daughters in Europe. My
   use of 'ethnic minority women' should be understood in this restricted
   sense. For the same reason, I am mostly setting aside here the larger
   body of comics set in (the former) French and Belgian colonies.
3. Although my focus here is primarily on French comics it is often
   difficult to distinguish between Belgian, French and Swiss French-
   language comics, because their traditions cross-fertilize each other,
   the three national markets are closely linked, and various shared
   suppressions and other distortions in Belgian and Swiss cultural frames
   of reference are induced by the industry's bias in favour of the
   dominant reading public in France. Limited space keeps me from
   making much in the way of distinctions between different national
   perspectives, so with regret I will generally refer to the works cited
   here as 'French'. For the record, at least five of the cartoonists whose
   work is discussed here are Belgian (Duvivier, Lapière, Raives, Stassen
   and Warnauts) and one is Swiss (Ceppi). Halen (1993) provides an
   insightful analysis of post-colonialism in Belgian comics.
4. One exception is *Bonne année*, a dystopian political fiction by Baru
   (1998) set in the future, which I include here because some of the
   conditions it depicts are arguably not too far removed from those one
   can find today in some French *banlieues*.
5. My temporal categories draw on two articles by Wihtol de Wenden
   (1988, 1990), which usefully summarize and sketch out the French
   imagery surrounding Maghrebis in France. See also Douglas and
   Malti-Douglas (1994, pp. 198–9).
6. The 'petite ceinture' is an old, disused and partially dismantled train
   track formerly used to circumnavigate Paris.
7. *Le Bar du vieux Français* provides a good example of how European
   national references are muted when they are not French. Although
   Stassen (1996, personal interview) confirmed that part of the story is
   set in Belgium, specifically in his hometown of Liège, this would not
   necessarily be obvious to French readers, who might assume the
   European setting to be northern France. Nevertheless, specific national
   elements are also important. The attribution of Moroccan roots to the
   character Leïla is undoubtedly due to the relative importance of
   Moroccan immigration to Belgium, whereas Maghrebi women in
   comics by French artists are almost uniformly of Algerian origin.
   At the same time, the elaboration of a shared European, generally

eurocentric, post-colonial vision in French-language comics is discernable in the integration of Belgian and French elements, for example, through the title character, an old Frenchman (cf. Halen, 1993).

8. *Harki(s)* refers to Algerian auxiliary colonial soldiers who fought for the French during the Algerian War.
9. On the 'doudou,' see Bachollet, Debost, Lelieur and Peyrière (1994, p. 113), and Chamoiseau and Confiant (1991, pp. 88–92).
10. As in Eugène Sue's popular novel *Les Mystères de Paris* (serialized 1842–3). See Savarese (1995, p. 116).
11. My argument is based on the symbolic significance of the fact that, with the exception of Salima, every single adult member of the family, including the father and eldest son, breaks the fast before the end of Ramadan.
12. See *Le Chinois vert d'Afrique* (*The Green Chinese Boy from Africa*) by Algerian-French author and minority rights activist Leïla Sebbar (1984).
13. Balibar's variation on the figure of the frontier is an attempt to take into account the particularly conflictual nature of Franco-Algerian relations (he opposes his 'frontier' to René Gallissot's concept of the 'mixte franco-algérien' (Franco-Algerian mixing), which Balibar deems insufficiently conflictual and dialectical).
14. The comics analysed in this chapter are sold in a variety of speciality comics shops in Brussels (Brusel, Le Dépôt, Sans titre, Slumberland), Paris (Boulinier), Lille (L'Atlantide, Librairie Favereaux) and Geneva (Papiers gras). Those in print may also be found in the comics sections of book superstores, including the FNAC and the Furet du Nord (in northern France).

Comics cited

Alagbé, Y. (1995), *Nègres jaunes*, Wissous (France): Amok.
— (1996), 'Ce qui me donne envie de mourir,' *Atteindre Marseille*, vol. 2 of *Le cheval sans tête*, September, 67–72.
— (1997), *Dyaa*, Wissous (France): Amok.
Baru (pseud. Barulea, H.) (1998), *Bonne année*, Tournai: Casterman.

Bilal, E. (art) and Christin, P. (scenario) (1994), *La Ville qui n'existait pas*, Geneva: Les Humanoïdes Associés, first edition 1977.

Boudjellal, F. (1995), *Jambon-Beur: les couples mixtes*, articles by M. Lagardette, colours by S. Balland, Toulon: Soleil Productions.

— (1996), *L'Oud: la trilogie*, Toulon: Soleil Productions.

— (1997), *Le Beurgeois*, colours by J. Schipper, Toulon: Soleil Productions.

— and Jollet, T. (1996), *Ethnik ta mère*, colours by S. Balland, Toulon: Soleil Productions.

Bretécher, C. (1995), *Mouler, démouler*, Paris: Bretécher.

Ceppi, D. (art) and Christin, P. (scenario) (1992), *La Nuit des clandestins*, Geneva: Les Humanoïdes Associés.

Chauzy, J.-C. (1997), *Béton armé: un monde merveilleux*, Tournai: Casterman.

Christin, P. (scenario) and Aymond (art) (1999), *Les 4x4*, vol. 3: *L'Ombre du triangle*, colours by Chagnaud, Paris: Dargaud.

Christin, P. (scenario) and Goetzinger, A. (art) (1985), *La Voyageuse de petite ceinture*, Paris: Dargaud.

Coco Clip (1995), no. 2, July–September.

Constant and Vandam (1999), *Bitume*, vol. 4: *Paris-trottoir*, colours by B. Constant, Tournai: Casterman.

Duvivier, M. (1997), *Mauvaise graine*, vol. 2: *Bye-bye grisaille*, colours by J. Gale, Tournai: Casterman.

Gendrot, C. (scenario) and Chéret, A. (art) (1984), *Il était une fois . . . Yannick Noah*, with Y. Noah, colours by Chéret, C., Paris: Hachette.

Golo (pseud. Nadeau, G.) (art) and Frank (pseud. Reichert, F.) (scenario) (1989), *La Variante du dragon*, Tournai: Casterman.

Jover, J. (1983), *Sale temps. Pierrot la caravane*, Grenoble: Glénat.

Kreyon noir (n.d. (1995?)), no. 1.

Lax (pseud. Lacroix, C.) (art) and Giroud, F. (scenario) (1990), *Les Oubliés d'Annam*, vol. 1, Marcinelle: Dupuis.

— (1991), *Les Oubliés d'Annam*, vol. 2, Marcinelle: Dupuis.

Luz (pseud. Luzier, R.) (1998), *Les Mégret gèrent la ville*, pref. by Cavanna, special issue no. 5 of *Charlie Hebdo*.

Mechkour, L. (art) and Boudjellal, F. (scenario) (1985), *Les Beurs*, Paris: L'Echo des Savanes/Albin Michel.

Montellier, C. (1980), *Andy Gang et le tueur de la Marne*, Paris: Les Humanoïdes Associés.

Ridel, C. (art) and Lelièvre, J. (scenario) (1997), *Radio kids*, vol. 5: *Aventures en megahertz*, colours by A.-M. Ducasse and G. Penloup, N.p.: Coeur de loup.

Stassen, J.-P. (art) and Lapière, D. (scenario) (1992), *Le Bar du vieux Français*, vol. 1, Marcinelle: Dupuis.

— (1993), *Le Bar du vieux Français*, vol. 2, Marcinelle: Dupuis.

Tehem (1998), *Malika secouss*, vol. 1: *Rêves partis*, Grenoble: Glénat.

— (1999), *Malika secouss*, vol. 2: *Crise de têtes*, Grenoble: Glénat.

Warnauts (E.) and Raives (pseud. Servais, G.) (1996), *Lettres d'outremer*, Tournai: Casterman.

7

Constructing Spaces of Transition: 'Beur' Women Writers and the Question of Representation
Anissa Talahite

France in the 1980s saw the emergence of a generation of 'Beur' writers,[1] young writers of North African immigrant origin who exchanged 'their fathers' hammer and spade for a pen that attempts to write a precarious present and problematic future' (Djeghloul, 1989, p. 80). Among them, women's voices played a significant role.[2] At a time when anti-racist demonstrations and marches were highlighting the pressing issue of racial discrimination, 'Beur' women writers started to explore the intersections of ethnicity and gender. For example, Sakinna Boukhedenna's *Journal: 'Nationalité: immigré(e)'* (1987), Farida Kessas's *Beur's Story* (1990) and Soraya Nini's *Ils disent que je suis une beurette . . .* (1993) explore the tensions between conflicting constructions of gender as defined by different cultures, as well as the impact of the disempowering process of migration on the relationship between the sexes. With a tendency to adopt the autobiographical genre traditionally associated with women's writing, these texts generally express a need to document aspects of 'Beur' women's lives which have been underrepresented. However, the ethnographic dimension that characterizes these texts is often counterbalanced by the use of irony, narrative distance and a problematized speaking 'I'. This tendency is particularly apparent in novels that directly challenge linear autobiographical narratives and question unified modes of representation. This chapter focuses on this latter category through the examples of Farida Belghoul's *Georgette!* (1986), Tassadit Imache's *Une fille sans histoire* (1989) and Leïla Houari's *Zeida de nulle part* (1985). The aesthetic search which characterizes these three novels is informed by a common desire to construct alternative discourses of identity based on a challenge to essentialist definitions of ethnicity and gender.

The world of the unconscious, the imaginary and the subjective has often been the site of expression for the subject constructed as 'Other' in

Western society. As Julia Kristeva argues, the questioning of patriarchal notions of history by post-1968 French feminists coincided with the desire to explore the domain of the repressed and to inhabit the space of subjectivity (Kristeva, 1986, pp. 187–213). Writing constitutes one of the ways in which women have attempted to construct spaces of expression outside patriarchal control represented by linearity, rationality and objectivity. In the case of ethnic minority authors such as Belghoul, Imache and Houari, this quest for self-expression is double-fold in the sense that their novels interrogate patriarchy and at the same time challenge ethnocentric notions of self. Furthermore, it is a quest complicated by the fact that, while writing can be seen as providing the marginalized subject with a site of self-expression, the process becomes at other times a source of alienation. The complex and interrelated ways in which notions of ethnicity and gender have been constructed in history mean that finding a voice for the racialized female 'Other' is never an unproblematic task. The quest for a voice to express the double exile of race and gender in contemporary French society is often presented as a perilous journey through images and iconographies inherited from the past. Patriarchal and colonial histories as colluding forces leading to the protagonist's sense of disintegration are central elements in the three novels considered here. This chapter examines the various strategies used by the three novelists to deconstruct the signifying practices responsible for constructing notions of self based on dominant discourses of ethnicity and gender: the role of language in Belghoul's *Georgette!*, the construction of history in Imache's *Une fille sans histoire* and the search for memory in Houari's *Zeida de nulle part*.

Georgette! and the Question of Language

Farida Belghoul's *Georgette!* was published in the aftermath of the early 1980s anti-racist campaign with which the author was directly involved.[3] According to Alec Hargreaves, writing a novel was for Belghoul, 'A kind of retreat from the manipulative forces which, the author had become convinced, were at work everywhere in the political arena; literary expression alone seemed to offer the possibility of personal authenticity' (Hargreaves, 1997b, p. 86). Thus, Belghoul's first and only published novel to date marks a departure from the world of 'real' politics and a retreat away from the pressures of male and white dominated society. However, it could also be regarded as a continuation of the writer's political struggle as it indirectly addresses some fundamental issues about ethnicity, racism and the construction of 'otherness'.

One of its key themes is the difficulty for the subject speaking from a position of 'otherness' to articulate a voice. This is reflected through the anxieties of the narrator, a seven-year-old girl who is learning to write. The novel depicts the little girl's struggle to make sense of the 'otherness' imposed by others: by the school that is associated with experiences of alienation but also by her family, in particular her illiterate immigrant father, whom the daughter sees partly through the lenses of the dominant culture. The voice of the young protagonist, which is still in the process of shaping itself, is shown as being constantly under threat. However, this is counterbalanced by the fact that she is in many ways a particularly vigilant and critical character (Rosello, 1993, p. 36). Although inwardly confident and defiant, her voice is, nevertheless, never free of contradictions. While she is often able to interpret the world around her on her own, often idiosyncratic terms, the little girl is constantly threatened by dominant voices perceived as more articulate. For example, references are made to her father's ability to sing in Arabic and recite verses from the Koran in a voice described as 'as beautiful as a horse rising to the sky' (Belghoul, 1986, p. 108). In contrast, the little girl who has no original culture to resort to is 'always mute' or 'talks nonsense', and is forever confronted with what she describes as 'dryness of the voice' (p. 108). Her struggle goes beyond the process of integrating new notions of correct French grammar at school. Linguistic creations such as 'peluches d'orange' or 'boule-d'ogre' (mispronunciations of the words for 'orange peel' and 'bulldog' which also contain the words 'cuddly toy' and 'ogre'), or the famous inversion in the opening sentence: 'La sonne cloche. . . Non, la cloche sonne' ('The ring is belling. . . No, the bell is ringing') (p. 9), are both signs of her difficulty with the French language and self-conscious acts of subversion of a dominant language seen as an imposition.[4]

Georgette! explores the intricate relationship between language and constructions of the self through the voice of a child who is not entirely socialized. To enter language – and in particular writing – means a certain loss and a sense of self-fragmentation or 'a separation of the subject from its self-image' (Kristeva, 1984, p. 42). According to post-Lacanian feminist theory, a sense of self as distinct from the 'Other' appears with the acquisition of language which is associated with the 'law of the father':

> [t]he child must now resign itself to the fact that it can never have direct access to reality, in particular to the now prohibited body of the mother. It has been banished from this 'full', imaginary possession into the 'empty' world of language. Language is 'empty' because it is just an endless process of difference and absence: instead of being able to possess anything in its fullness,

the child will now simply move from one signifier to another, along a linguistic chain which is potentially infinite. (Eagleton, 1983, p. 167)

In the novel, there is a tension between the 'law of the father' manifest in the role of the girl's teacher and the 'law of the father' incarnated by the girl's father, an immigrant worker whose authority is undermined by the position which he occupies in society as an ethnic 'Other'. For example, the father offers to help his daughter with her homework by advising her to start writing on the last page of her exercise book, as one would do if writing in Arabic. The next day, the school teacher looks for the homework on the first page of the book, only to find a blank page. This image encapsulates how the little girl's sense of self is related to her experience of language and self-representation, since her writing remains 'invisible' to those with the power to ascribe meaning to her reality. Besides, the father uses the exercise book himself to write what presumably are words from the Koran which he refers to as 'words from God' (Belghoul, 1986, p. 46). His writing, which is intended to show his daughter that he is not totally illiterate, is immediately devalued in the eyes of others: he is reprimanded by his wife who asks him not to 'dirty' the girl's book, while the daughter refers to his writing as 'a child's scribble' (p. 58). The traditional authoritarian father figure is therefore brought down to the level of a child, with a reversal of the traditional relationship between father and daughter:

> Why did I let him play with my exercise book, my God, why? Tonight, I'll tell my mother everything. She'll drop an atom bomb on his idiotic face. His scribble writing is just rubbish. There's no such thing as writing backwards! The truth is that he can't write and he's telling me fibs. This chap is completely cracked! He lies like a kid. Thank God, he made a mistake, thank God! He picked my exercise book up the wrong way round, what a stroke of luck.[5] (p. 58)

This role reversal (echoed in the novel by other symbolic reversals such as word inversions or 'writing backwards') enables the girl to re-work the relationship of power between the child who is outside language and the adult who defines meaning.

Later in the novel, the girl attempts to rehabilitate the image of the father by likening him to an 'Indian chief', a metaphor sustained throughout the novel and constructed around the idea of ethnic difference. This metaphor begins with a racist comment made by the girl's school mate who calls her a 'red skin'. Later, having internalized the stereotype, she herself sees her own mother as 'the Cheyenne woman' and is embarrassed by her 'long multicoloured dress [which] shows underneath the coat' (p. 96). However, at other times, she is able to subvert the stereotype to create a positive self-image:

> I stick a red skin on my face. I walk to school, my red face is magnificent. It shines like a gold jewel. People are jealous of my beauty. They do not guess it is a trick. Behind, I'm hiding an ugly little one with claws full of blood, like the teacher's fingernails.[6] (pp. 76–7)

The mask or 'red skin' which she places on her face is in fact a strategy of survival learned from the native Americans' 'war secret' (p. 72), which consists in smearing one's face with red earth so as not to be recognized by the cowboys.[7] The identification with the way another ethnic 'Other' (the native American) is constructed enables the heroine to construct another reality for herself. Thus, she is able to understand her own sense of a fluid and unlocatable identity and to subvert the fixed notions of ethnicity which have been imposed on her and her family.

The fantasized name 'Georgette', 'adopted' by the girl (and the title of the novel), encapsulates the idea of an undefinable and unspeakable identity. The name 'Georgette' is introduced during an episode between the girl and a presumably imaginary, lonely old lady in a park. During this strange encounter, situated between reality and fantasy, the old lady asks the little girl whether she would be willing to write letters pretending to come from her sons. The old woman would then show her neighbours the letters to prove that her sons have not completely abandoned her. The girl refuses on the grounds that her father would disown her if he were to discover that his daughter could impersonate others: 'Suppose I write "Dear Mum" to an old woman who is new in my life. And I sign Pierre, Paul or Jean. And suppose my father hears about it, he'll kill me immediately. He wont even bury me . . . '[8] (p. 147). The fact that the persons whose identity she is expected to endorse are male and French is also significant. The girl is aware of the rigidity of race and gender identities and of the taboo associated with any attempt to shift or challenge their boundaries. It is at this moment that she fantasizes her father calling her 'Georgette!' in a disapproving gesture. 'I thought, she is intelligent like her father. I thought, she is proud. And look at that: she calls herself "Georgette"!'[9] (p. 148). The name 'Georgette' (emphasized by the exclamation mark also present in the title of the novel) represents the idea of 'otherness' in a society marked by ethnic division.[10] The fact that the girl's 'real' name is never revealed refers to her difficulty in naming herself, as names are imposed by others. At the same time 'Georgette' highlights the fact that names are inventions or fictions created to produce the illusion of an identity. The way ethnic difference is contained and represented in names and other cultural artefacts is placed within a context involving the complex interplay of self and other, therefore suggesting that identities are not pre-given but are, above all, the product of interactions. The fact that the protagonist has her double or alter-ego, 'Georgette', superimposed as it were upon her, explores, re-enacts and interrogates what Mohamed calls 'the fundamental ontological opposition between self and other' (Mohamed, 1983, p. 264), which characterizes societies based on ethnic division.

By highlighting names, language and other cultural representations as sites of tension within the subject, the text of *Georgette!* problematizes the very means through which it aims to create meaning. In this respect, the death of the little girl (who, at the end of the novel, is knocked over by a car on her way home) reflects the struggle of the novelist at pains to establish a sense of identity through writing. The last sentence of the novel, 'I am choking at the bottom of an ink pot' (Belghoul, 1986, p. 163), establishes a clear link between the voice of the protagonist and that of the writer and places the process of writing at the centre of the narrative.

Une fille sans histoire and the Construction of 'History'

Like Farida Belghoul's *Georgette!*, Tassadit Imache's first novel, *Une fille sans histoire*, draws on the experiences of a 'Beur' female protagonist and her struggle to establish a sense of a self in a society riddled with racial tensions.[11] The story opens with the voice of the narrator, Lil, who, as a young adult, is attempting to write and reclaim her own story and history, both being understood as one and the same project. The word 'histoire' (history) in the title acts in the novel as a multi-referent, pointing to the unwritten history of the North African immigrant community, the 'his-story' within which the female protagonist, as a woman, cannot completely inscribe herself, and 'history' as a narrative constantly being reconstructed. A family photograph found in her father's wallet after his death is the starting point for a journey back into Lil's childhood in the 1960s, against the background of the Algerian war. Using a first person narrative voice (with the third person taking over the narration at times), the novel tells the story of the little girl in the photograph, following the pattern of an autobiographical narrative. It centres on the female protagonist – who, like the author, is of mixed Algerian and French parentage – and her attempts to construct her own story against the complex and conflicting personal histories that she has inherited from her parents. Her

name, Lil, short for 'Leïla', is imposed by her French mother in the hope
that it will be taken for the French name 'Liliane'. The two antagonistic
figures of the French mother and the Algerian father embody the ethnic
duality inherited from colonial history which Lil has to confront:

> So many times she had shivered at the thought that she could break into two
> pieces eager to fight one another: France and Algeria. For a time, she thought
> she had found refuge in school, on the other side of the estate, where History,
> when it is unbearable, is not found in school textbooks . . . She had heard
> nothing there about almost a century and a half of colonialism.[12] (Imache,
> 1989, pp. 123–4)

Lil's task is then to reconstruct a story in order to fill in the silences and
gaps which dominate the conflictual history of France and Algeria.

The alternation between first and third person narratives suggests a
conflict between Lil's self-perception and the ways in which others
perceive her, constantly highlighting the question of who is writing Lil's
story. The idea of a dominant text being imposed on the narrator's story
is expressed through the interference of external onlookers. For example,
the figure of the photographer introduced through the discovery of the
family photograph becomes a prime metaphor in the novel. Lil encounters
another photographer at the children's home where she is placed into
care with her sisters and brother. The photographer who is visiting the
home to compile pictures of children for a calendar selects Lil as his
model. For a moment, Lil dreams of being contained in his gaze: 'This is
what Lil had imagined: the photographer was carrying her off in his gaze
and transporting her, intact and invulnerable, far away from this bloody
history'[13] (p. 61). The sense that the external gaze can reunify the
fragmented parts of Lil's history is destroyed when the little girl discovers
with dismay that her image is not a reflection of her 'real' self as she had
perceived it: 'Then he had shown her the photo he had selected for the
calendar. On it, her eyes were bluer, her hair blonder. No trace of the
wound under her right eye could be seen. Lil had burst into tears'[14] (p.
60). Lil discovers that the photographer has the power to edit her image
and remove all signs of her Arab identity. Beside changing the colour of
her hair and eyes, he had also removed the scar under her eye, the result
of a racist attack. She had told the photographer about it while posing for
the picture, hoping for a sympathetic response:

> Suddenly she felt the pain. The pain which the arrow had planted, burning
> her skin, radiating through the wing of her nose. She had wanted to cry out and
> give vent to her fear. But the photographer had said: 'Don't move! Keep still!'

So she had stammered, while passing a dirty finger over the fine scar.
'Look! Look!'
And to him, she had told the story.[15] (pp. 58–9)

The discrepancy between Lil's experiences (the painful and burning scar)
and the image produced by others (the photograph where the scar does
not feature) point once again to her erasure from history. The children's
re-enactment of the adults' war in the children's home echoes another
scene in the novel which takes place in a police station where Lil's father,
along with other Algerians suspected of helping the FLN, is arrested and
tortured. The memory of the agony of a child violently beaten by the
police stays with the father after he returns home. The image of the scar
is also used to place the economic exploitation of Algerian immigrants
within the wider context of the violence of the Algerian war. A victim
of a night shift accident in a factory, Lil's father is left with an injured
hand. His children gather to look at his injury, which is described at
length in a Zolaesque passage where the physical takes on symbolic
meanings:

> With the back of the hand placed on the plastic-coated tablecloth, the fingers
> seemed paralysed in a comic, obscene, begging posture. The overly square
> phalanges covered with calluses, the broken, dirty fingernails, and the swollen
> flesh coated with iodine had made them vaguely sick. A worrying, persistent
> black thread ran from one finger to the other, more fragile and improbable
> than the throbbing lattice of veins on his wrist.[16] (p. 112)

By placing Lil's 'invisible' scar in parallel with other physical and
metaphorical scars, the reader is able to construct a continuity in the images,
which counteracts the humiliating, reifying gaze of the photographer.

Just as 'the teacher's eye', which threatens to reduce the protagonist
of *Georgette!* to silence, is neutralized by the narrator's ability to voice
her despair, so the photographer's gaze is challenged by Lil's attempts to
demystify the images around her. This task is not without difficulties and
self-contradictions. It includes revisiting the past with the aim of reclaim-
ing her history. Towards the end of the novel, Lil is tempted to join her
father buried in his homeland of Algeria. Going back to him would mean
claiming a land and a history hitherto denied her: 'The truth was that she
had to make this journey alone. Crossing the sea. Without turning around,
finally reaching . . . Him'[17] (p. 124). Thus, at this point the dead father
seems to embody Lil's longing for permanent meaning, as when she had
wished to remain 'intact' and 'invulnerable' within the photographer's
gaze (p. 61). At the same time, Lil is aware of the utopian nature of this

desire for, unlike her father, she has no 'homeland' to go back to. Going 'back' to Algeria where her father is buried is a fiction, ironically expressed by Lil's brother when he tells the family, *'Lil goes to Algeria'* (p. 125), an italicized phrase that suggests the title of a children's adventure story or, perhaps more significantly, the title of a colonial travel journey. Lil herself recognizes that the 'return' is a fiction: 'She knows that she is going there not so much to get to know Algeria as to renounce it. It is the last thing left for her to lose'[18] (pp. 127–8). Lil's longing for her father represents the mourning for an identity which she is progressively renouncing, and could be interpreted in many respects as 'an unconscious strategy to dissimulate the rupture' (Mokkadem, 1995, p. 182). The father, a figure strongly associated with the 'homeland' of Algeria, offers the protagonist a space which she can occupy temporarily on her journey towards self-knowledge. As Helen Tiffin has argued, in deconstructing such concepts as 'homeland' and 'identity', post-colonial writers often adopt a 'provisionally authoritative perspective, but one which is deliberately constructed as provisional' (Tiffin, 1987, p. 23). Thus, the father figure and the construction of 'home' in *Une fille sans histoire* could be seen as offering provisional perspectives that the narrator endorses but also disclaims. At the end of the novel, Lil does not undertake the journey to the father's hometown of Tizi Ouzou that she had planned. Thus, the possible meaning of Algeria as 'home' is one which is consciously deferred: 'You know, I will go to Tizi Ouzou . . . tomorrow or the day after, or next summer'[19] (Imache, 1989, p. 142). As in *Georgette!*, it is the father who embodies the heroine's longing for permanent meanings while the latter's own identity remains within the realm of the unlocatable.[20] This ambivalence, whereby the subject searches for a definable identity while being aware of the illusory nature of such a quest, is present in both Belghoul's and Imache's novels.

Zeida de nulle part and the Search for a Collective Memory

Leïla Houari's first novel, *Zeida de nulle part*, was published in France alongside other emerging writers of North African immigrant origin in the early 1980s.[21] Although she is from Belgium, and of Moroccan origin, and there are undoubtedly elements in Houari's novel (and in her other writings) that are specific to the experiences of the Moroccan immigrant community in Belgium, the commonality of experiences shared by North African communities in Belgium and in France means that she is generally treated as a 'Beur' writer (Hargreaves, 1997b, p. 5). Furthermore, Houari's treatment of gender also links her to the generation of female writers of

North African immigrant origin who started writing in the 1980s. Like *Georgette!* and *Une fille sans histoire*, *Zeida de nulle part* explores the tensions and conflicts facing a female protagonist at pains to find a space in a world that denies her existence. Using the theme of the return to the 'homeland', Houari examines questions of belonging and identity within the context of the double alienation of cultural and gender displacement.

The central protagonist is a young woman called Zeida whose name, meaning 'birth' in Arabic, encapsulates the quest for origins. Born into a Moroccan family having immigrated to Brussels, Zeida is preoccupied with recreating a link with her past and ancestry in Morocco, and decides to return to the Moroccan village which her parents had left years before. The first part of the novel is set in Brussels where Zeida, as a young woman, is in conflict with her family and with a society which perceives her as an outsider. She is described leaving her parents' home temporarily and having a relationship with a man who, like her, is of Arab origin. Both experiences, however, contribute to alienating her further. Unable to relate to her environment, Zeida is overwhelmed with feelings of uncertainty about her identity, declaring: 'No I am not an Arab, I am nothing, I am myself.'[22] (Houari, 1985, p. 15). At the same time she longs to be reunited with her culture of origin and her past, which she fantasizes through imagining the land of Morocco evoked by a sensuous male body:

> she was looking for the body that would tell her about its sun, the heart that would only beat to the rythm of the 'gnaouas' [percussion musicians], she wanted to taste the salt on a mouth smelling of olive oil, this time she would go to the end, to find the black horseman of her dreams, to appease the sand wind blowing in the desert of her heart.[23] (p. 16)

These sensual images encapsulate Zeida's desire for the 'Other' which she later materializes through her decision to leave Brussels and live with an aunt in Morocco. As in *Une fille sans histoire*, Zeida's efforts to establish continuity with her past are dominated by nostalgia for a way of life which has been lost through the disempowering effects of exile:

> the coldness of exile has pushed your past back into the distance, father, has wounded your pride, you were a horseman, you used to hunt in the green plains of the Atlas mountains, you spent whole nights in a tent with the shepherds, the smell of mint tea mingled with that of the animals, you tell me, I was young once, yet you never tell me about it . . . I am looking for your youth and my own becomes hesitant[24] (p. 17)

The incestuous figure of the horseman, which is central to Zeida's fantasies, embodies the glory of a past now lost to both father and daughter, partly because of cultural displacement but mainly because the father is unable to tell his daughter about it. To recreate the past, Zeida can only reinvent it through dream images which are often clichéd representations of a North Africa of barren landscapes, shepherds and horsemen. Thus, Zeida's decision to return to the parents' homeland can be interpreted as an attempt to confirm and reinstate the father's lost image, epitomized here by the mythic representation of the mysterious 'black horseman'. Like Lil's journey in *Une fille sans histoire*, Zeida's 'return' represents a longing for cultural meanings which cannot be entirely disassociated from patriarchal images.

If the father 'never tells' his daughter about his past, Zeida's mother, in contrast, is mainly depicted recounting her life prior to emigrating to Belgium. The mother speaks of a life dominated by hardship, the frustration of not being able to get an education, and her marriage to a man whom she had not chosen. In fact, the mother's voice takes over the narrative for a while in a long passage where she relates in detail her arranged marriage.[25] The fact that the narrative voice shifts from Zeida's perceptions recounted in the third person to the mother's direct speech is not without significance, especially in the context of Zeida's quest, and it can be understood as part of the novel's attempt to re-establish links with the past. Given that in traditional North African culture the past is often transmitted through the voice of mothers and grandmothers and the oral tradition of story telling, the fact that the voices of Zeida's mother and her aunt are given particular space in the novel can be read as an attempt to re-establish a genealogy through female voices. This is exemplified when Zeida's dead grandmother addresses her grand-daughter in one of her dreams to recount her own death:

> Zeida, I am your grandmother . . . a black turbaned man appeared and called out to me . . . he was handing me a shroud and smiling, then everything stopped around me[26] (p. 43)

The grandmother's use of the image of the 'black turbaned man' echoes the figure of the 'black turbaned horseman' which haunts Zeida's dreams, thus establishing a continuity between the two women and linking Zeida's dream fantasy with death (p. 39).

The gesture of the man giving the grandmother a shroud is to be found in another of Zeida's dreams, where the black horseman enters a palace suspended in the sky and then stops with his horse to throw a scarlet cloth over a golden cage inside which is 'a woman with no eyes and no navel' (p. 65). The image of the woman with no eyes and no navel clearly relates to Zeida's quest for origins, but the meaning of the covering of the cage is ambiguous. On the one hand, it suggests the stifling of the female subject by the masculine figure of the horseman, and can be read as a warning that Zeida's dreams of Morocco as 'home' do not have a future. On the other hand, it could also mean that Zeida, like her grandmother, has completed her journey. It is of course difficult to ascribe specific meanings to these dreams without confining the novel to single interpretations. However, it is relevant to note how the dream images function within the narrative. Rather than forming a decodable sequence, they punctuate Zeida's linear story (her life in Brussels, her stay with her aunt and her relationships with the people in the village, and finally her decision to 'return' to Europe) with mysterious and indecipherable figures. As in *Georgette!* and *Une fille sans histoire*, the borderline between dreams and reality is problematized in an attempt to articulate the protagonist's history from the point of view of the unconscious. In this respect, the novel can be seen as part of a larger body of post-colonial texts addressing questions of cultural displacement, which attempt to rewrite history from the point of view of suppressed and repressed narratives, using archetypal images and the idea of a psychic collective memory.[27]

The idealized image of Morocco seen through the protagonist's eyes is very close to a utopian vision. The place occupied by dreams and the emphasis on symbolic images – the moon, the darkness, the landscape – convey a world of cosmic elements that corresponds to the protagonist's subconscious desires. Thus, the Moroccan countryside is fantasized as an archetypal landscape where the psyche can finally be reconciled with the world. The fact that Zeida is treated as a 'foreigner' by the villagers who perceive her as being 'European' does not stop her from identifying to some extent with the people and the land around her. This identification is very much informed by Zeida's idealized and nostalgic vision of the land, conveyed through pastoral descriptions of the rural landscape and of the simplicity of peasant life. The detailed descriptions of Zeida's aunt cooking, kneading the bread and making a fire, and of her husband drinking mint tea and telling the family religious stories or legends about the village, are endowed with the sense of individuals at one with the world. These images are dominated by the protagonist's unconditional admiration for the rural way of life. As a child, she used to marvel at everything she saw when on holiday in her parents' village:

How she loved the people she saw riding donkeys! She had been touched by the women moving slowly forward with enormous bundles of fine wood on their backs, bent in half, with sweat on their brow; when cars passed by, they would stop and smile.
Her father would hoot his horn at anything and everything. Zeida was happy![28]
(p. 27)

The child's subjective perspective is sustained throughout the novel, even when Zeida as an adult returns to Morocco. The transfixed, idealized images used to depict the country situate it outside history, creating a utopian vision.

Utopia in literature has traditionally represented a means of escaping the pressures of a society riddled with the tensions of history.[29] For Houari, it seems to offer a way of reflecting on her vision of a society where the displaced subject can live at peace with her/himself and where the self cannot be colonized. However, this does not mean that conflict and tension are done away with completely. Even though the land is a source of solace for Zeida, it only represents a temporary solution to her conflicts. The end of the novel shows her leaving Morocco as she realizes that her future lies in Europe. Both her experiences in the village where, as an outsider, Zeida feels alienated, and her dreams, which make her progressively realize the utopian nature of her quest to belong, contribute to this decision. As in *Une fille sans histoire*, the dream of a lost homeland serves as an insight into the condition of exile without, however, offering solutions.

The study of these three novels reveals that ethnic and gender identities are far from being trans-historical and immutable positions. Instead, they are presented as places of transition that are constantly being revisited and transformed. The foregrounding of marginal voices in *Georgette!*, repressed sub-texts of personal and collective history in *Une fille sans histoire* and the interference of dream images in *Zeida de nulle part* are examples of ways in which notions of linearity, centricity and narrative authority can be problematized. In each case, dominant definitions of identity based on ethnicity, culture, gender or other pre-existing 'texts' which contain the 'Other' are brought into question by the use of textual strategies that remain outside the reach of social control.

Thus, one important task that these novels perform is to construct a space of transition where the marginalized female and ethnic 'Other' can find a voice. As they interrogate the relationship between self and representation, these novels engage with a self-reflective narrative process which attempts to answer the question: how can one represent that which is outside representation? Speaking as 'Other' is a task riddled with self-contradictions that the novels leave open and unresolved; clearly any imposition of closure would stand in direct contradiction with the temporary and unstable nature of the voices that speak through these texts. In other words, the greatest challenge for Belghoul, Imache, Houari and other women writers, speaking with the voice of the marginalized ethnic and gendered 'Other', is to speak from a particular history and a particular experience without, however, being confined and contained within those categories.

Notes

1. The term 'Beur' is placed here between inverted commas in the light of recent reservations about its suitability in the late 1990s and beyond. See for example Hargreaves (1997a).
2. The presence of 'Beur' women has not been felt only in literature but in other cultural domains such as cinema and music.
3. Belghoul is also the author of an unpublished novel, *La Passion de Rémi*, an unpublished short story, *L'Enigme,* which developed into the novel *Georgette!* and two films, *C'est Madame la France que tu préfères?* (1981) and *Le Départ du père* (1983).
4. This translation misses out the play on the verb 'clocher' ('to be faulty'). (Note that all English translations in the text are by the author unless stated otherwise. The page numbers are those of the original texts in French.)
5. 'Pourquoi je l'ai laissé jouer avec mon cahier, mon Dieu, pourquoi? Ce soir, je raconte tout à ma mère. Elle lui enverra l'bombe atomique sur sa gueule d'idiot. Son écriture pourrie c'est des gribouillages. L'écriture à l'envers n'existe pas! En vérité, il sait pas écrire et il me raconte des histoires debout. Il est complètement marteau, ce bonhomme! Il ment comme un gosse. Heureusement qu'il s'est trompé, mon Dieu, heureusement! Il a pris mon cahier à l'envers, c'est un coup de chance.'
6. ' . . . je me colle une peau rouge sur le visage. Je marche vers l'école, mon visage rouge est magnifique. Il brille comme un bijou en or. Les gens sont jaloux de ma beauté. Ils devinent pas que c'est une ruse. Derrière, je cache un petit affreux avec des griffes pleines de sang, comme les ongles de la maîtresse.'

7. In *Peau noire, masques blancs*, Frantz Fanon describes the colonized subject as the product of tensions between identities and masks, thus emphasizing the fluid and changeable nature of racial identity. It is possible to see *Georgette!* as a novel that likewise explores the ambiguity between perceived racial identity and re-enacted racial identity, which is developed at length in Fanon's analysis.

8. 'Et j'écris "chère maman" à une vieille toute nouvelle dans ma vie. Et je signe Pierre, Paul ou Jean. Et si mon père l'apprend, il me tue immédiatement. Il ne m'enterre même pas . . .'

9. 'J'croyais elle est intelligente comme son père. J'croyais elle est fière. Et r'garde-moi ça: elle s'appelle Georgette!'

10. Belghoul admitted that 'she had deliberately chosen the name "Georgette" as the most alien she could think of in Arab ears' (Hargreaves, 1997b, p. 38).

11. Tassadit Imache has since published two novels: *Le Dromadaire de Bonaparte* (1995) and *Je veux rentrer* (1998). She is also the author of two children's books: *Le Rouge à lèvres* (1988) and *Algérie: filles et garçons* (1991).

12. 'Tant de fois elle avait tremblé à l'idée qu'elle pût se fendre en deux morceaux avides d'en découdre. La France et l'Algérie. Un temps, elle avait cru trouver refuge à l'Ecole, de l'autre côté de la cité. Là où l'Histoire, quand elle est insoutenable, n'est pas écrite dans les manuels . . . Elle n'y avait rien entendu sur presque un siècle et demi de colonialisme.'

13. 'Ce que Lil avait imaginé: le photographe l'emportait dans ses yeux, et la promenait intacte, invulnérable, très loin de cette foutue histoire.'

14. 'Puis il lui avait montré la photo qu'il avait retenue pour le calendrier. Elle y avait les yeux plus bleus, le cheveu plus blond. On ne voyait plus trace de la blessure sous l'oeil droit. Lil avait éclaté en sanglots.'

15. 'La douleur était là, soudain. Celle que la flèche avait plantée, brûlant la peau, irradiant l'aile du nez, enflammant son visage. Elle avait voulu crier, hurler sa peur. Mais le photographe avait dit: "Ne bouge plus! tiens-toi tranquille!"
'Alors elle avait balbutié en passant un doigt sale sur la fine cicatrice. '"T'as vu? t'as vu?"
'Et à lui, elle avait raconté.'

16. 'Le dos de la main posé sur la nappe plastifiée, les doigts semblaient paralysés dans une pose comique, obsène, de mendicité. Ces phalanges trop carrées, couvertes de callosités, ces ongles cassés, sales, ces chairs boursouflées enduites de teinture d'iode, les avaient vaguement écoeurés. Inquiétant, obstiné, un fil noir courait d'un doigt

à l'autre, plus fragile, plus improbable que le réseau battant des veines de son poignet.'

17. 'La vérité, c'est qu'il allait falloir faire seule ce voyage. Traverser la mer. Sans se retourner, arriver enfin . . . jusqu'à Lui.'

18. 'Elle sait qu'elle va là-bas non pas tant pour la connaître que pour renoncer à elle, l'Algérie. C'est la dernière chose qu'il lui reste à perdre.'

19. '"Tu sais, j'irai à Tizi Ouzou . . . demain ou après-demain, ou l'été prochain."'

20. The father figure in these novels deserves a study in its own right particularly within the context of the discourse on 'multiple masculinities' as opposed to 'hegemonic masculinity' (Hearn and Collinson, 1994; Morgan, 1992).

21. The author of another novel, *Quand tu verras la mer . . .* (1988), Leïla Houari has also explored different genres, such as theatre with *Les Cases Basses* (1993) and poetry with *Poème-fleuve pour noyer le temps présent* (1995). She has been particularly active in community youth projects and has published *Et de la ville je t'en parle* (1995), poems written as part of workshops conducted with young poets of Moroccan origin in Brussels, and *Femmes aux milles portes, portraits, mémoire* (1996), an illustrated collection of portraits of women of North African immigrant background from France and Belgium.

22. 'Non je ne suis pas arabe, je ne suis rien, je suis moi.'

23. '. . . elle cherchait le corps qui lui apprendrait son soleil, le coeur qui ne battait qu'au rythme des gnaouas [musiciens-percussion], elle voulait goûter le sel sur une bouche qui sentait l'huile d'olive, cette fois elle irait jusqu'au bout, pour trouver le cavalier noir de ses rêves, apaiser ce vent de sable qui souffle dans le désert de ses entrailles.'

24. '. . . le froid de l'exil a reculé ton passé, mon père, a meutri ta fierté, tu étais cavalier, tu chassais dans les plaines vertes de l'Atlas, tu restais des nuits entières sous la tente avec les bergers, l'odeur du thé à la menthe se mélangeait à l'odeur des bêtes, tu me dis j'ai été jeune mais tu ne me racontes jamais . . . je cherche ta jeunesse et la mienne se fait hésitante . . .'

25. Alec Hargreaves describes Zeida's mother as a 'secondary narrator' who enables the narrative to establish an 'affective bond between the mother and the reader' as well as allowing the latter to 'participate more fully in the protagonist's own divided emotions' (Hargreaves, 1997b, p. 98).

26. 'Zeida je suis ta grand-mère . . . un homme noir en turban blanc m'apparut, il m'appela . . . il me tendait un linceul et me souriait, c'est alors que tout s'est arrêté autour de moi . . . '

27. Examples of writers who have written narratives exploring the idea of a hybrid self through a mythic journey through the collective unconscious include Wilson Harris' *Palace of the Peacock* (1960), Assia Djebar's *Vaste est la prison* (1995) and Toni Morrison's *Beloved* (1987), to name but a few.
28. 'Comme elle aimait ces gens qu'elle voyait sur des ânes. Ce qui l'avait touchée, c'était les femmes qui avançaient avec, sur le dos, des fagots énormes de bois fins, elles se déplaçaient lentement pliées en deux, la sueur au front; quand les voitures passaient, elles s'arrêtaient et souriaient.
'Le père klaxonnait pour n'importe quoi. Zeida était heureuse!'
29. Critics have analysed how women writers often create a 'green world' of archetypal images where the female self can express itself fully as a way of escaping the pressures of a male-dominated society. Annis Pratt argues, for example, that 'the only possible abrogation of sexual politics is to project other worlds of being (extrasocietal solutions)' (Pratt, 1981, p.70).

'Beur' Texts Cited

Belghoul, F. (1986), *Georgette!*, Paris: Barrault.
Boukhedenna, S. (1987), *Journal: 'Nationalité: immigré(e)'*, Paris: L'Harmattan.
Houari, L. (1996), *Femmes aux milles portes, portraits, mémoire*, Paris: Syros.
— (1995), *Et de la ville je t'en parle*, Brussels: EPO/IDI.
— (1995), *Poème-fleuve pour noyer le temps présent*, Paris: L'Harmattan.
— (1993), *Les cases basses*, Paris: L'Harmattan.
— (1988), *Quand tu verras la mer. . .*, Paris: L'Harmattan.
— (1985), *Zeida de nulle part*, Paris: L'Harmattan.
Imache, T. (1998), *Je veux rentrer*, Arles: Actes Sud.
— (1995), *Le Dromadaire de Bonaparte*, Arles: Actes Sud.
— (1991), *Algérie: filles et garçons*, Paris: Albin Michel Jeunesse.
— (1989), *Une fille sans histoire*, Paris: Calmann.
— (1988), *Le rouge à lèvres*, Paris: Syros.
Kessas, F. (1990), *Beur's story,* Paris: L'Harmattan.
Nini, S. (1993), *Ils disent que je suis une beurette. . .*, Paris: Fixot.

8

Close Encounters: French Women of Vietnamese Origin and the Homeland in *Retour à la saison des pluies* and *Les Trois Parques*

Emily Roberts

How might Vietnamese women of the diaspora carry with them their association with their homeland? As a stranger might carry an orphan, 'for whom he seeks nothing but a tomb?' (Lê, 1995, p. 58). As the monstrous dead foetus of an unborn twin? Or as a rancorous child, sealed under a veneer of Westernization, that cracks under internal and external pressure as time goes on? These disturbing images are evoked in the works of two women authors of Vietnamese origin, Kim Lefèvre and Linda Lê, both of whom are French citizens who have spent a large proportion of their lives in France. Lefèvre, a Eurasian, left Vietnam for educational reasons in 1960, while Lê fled the Vietnamese Communist régime as a child in 1975. This article will compare Kim Lefèvre's second autobiographical novel, *Retour à la saison des pluies* (1995) and Linda Lê's more recent novel, *Les Trois Parques* (1997), with a view to analysing how these texts construct the attitude of women of Vietnamese origin towards their Vietnamese identity.

Retour à la saison des pluies

A Catholic, educated Eurasian, Kim Lefèvre left Vietnam in 1960, when she was in her twenties, emigrating to France for educational and professional reasons. She has written two autobiographical novels focusing on her identity as a Eurasian and her memories of the 'old country' from her position as a mature, Westernized French citizen. The first, *Métisse blanche* (1989), provides an account of her peripatetic existence in Vietnam during her youth, during which her identity as a *métisse* (a Eurasian) remains a constant source of alienation and confusion.

She is rejected as a *métisse blanche* (white Eurasian) by Vietnamese society, on the basis of her whiteness, and as a *métisse jaune* (yellow Eurasian) by French expatriate society and even by Westernized Eurasian society, on the basis of her social and cultural affiliation with the Vietnamese.

In *Métisse blanche,* and in subsequent interviews, Lefèvre invoked what she refers to as 'nostalgic' memories of Vietnam, that is, an internalized mental construct that is not related to contemporary reality (Lefèvre, 1995, p. 23). However, her mediated, controlled narrative of personal reminiscence was followed by a resurgence of the past, which led to the genesis of a sequel, *Retour à la saison des pluies.* In the opening pages of this second novel, whose first person narrator can be taken to represent Lefèvre herself, remnants of her Vietnamese past have risen to the surface, partly through chance, partly because she has decided to resume contact with a long-denied aspect of herself. In her own words: 'Vietnam started to erupt into my life'[1] (p. 21). The first section of the novel follows her encounters with people, particularly women, from her past, leading her to re-establish contact with the Vietnamese community in Paris, her own Vietnamese past and her family.

The narrator explains that she has avoided contact with other people of Vietnamese origin over the past thirty odd years. Although she is aware of the existence of Vietnamese areas of Paris, it is obvious from her description that she is not familiar with the Asian 13th *arrondissement.*[2] Indeed, as a Eurasian, she has never been fully integrated into the Vietnamese community, which continues to isolate and exclude Eurasians in France, as in Vietnam (Le Huu Khoa, 1993, p. 93). This ostracism is compounded by her lack of family ties with members of the Vietnamese community and her own family's atypical, un-Confucian attitudes to familial relations (Lefèvre, 1995, p. 165). (The Confucian emphasis upon family relations and community still prevails in the Vietnamese community in France, although it is increasingly questioned by younger generations.)[3]

Another source of the narrator's isolation is the degree of her accultura-tion, and the familiarity with the Vietnamese language that she has forfeited as a result. She experiences this exclusion in a large Asian supermarket in the 13th. When she asks the name of a fruit she vaguely remembers from her childhood, she encounters the following reaction:

'We call it "Gac", but we don't know the French name.'
She says "we" when she speaks to me; I am therefore "the other".[4] (p. 40)

This positioning of the narrator as 'Other' can be attributed to her appearance as a *métisse*, and her faltering Vietnamese. A female friend from her youth criticizes the standard of her Vietnamese, 'stuffed with French expressions'[5] (p. 57). The position of her Vietnamese identity in relation to her French identity is embodied in her difficulties with the Vietnamese language, which is now filtered through her knowledge of French.

The narrator's encounters with people from her Vietnamese past make her simultaneously more receptive to her memories, and more desperate to control them through the fear of yet more trauma. One day she runs into Bach Tha, one of her former students. Although she views this meeting as a stroke of good fortune, she is also annoyed that she has been denied the opportunity to prepare herself for it. This meeting clarifies the division between the experiences of pre- and post-1975 immigrants. Bach Tha celebrates her good fortune at having arrived in France in 1970, before the great exodus of 1975 (p. 26). The narrator learns that another acquaintance from Vietnam, Nam, is also in Paris. Nam was formerly employed as a lawyer in Vietnam, but now works as a canteen supervisor. When she expresses shock at her friend's fate, her interlocutor matter-of-factly observes: 'Yes. But they arrived after 1975, with the boat people'[6] (p. 24). Other women have experienced a discreet form of discrimination (p. 33), or simply found it difficult to settle due to homesickness. The women the narrator knows from Vietnam are from a privileged background, educated in an élite Franco-Annamite school. In the majority of cases, there is a stark contrast between their comfortable Vietnamese past, and their difficult French present. Their experiences of life in France and Vietnam are an inversion of the narrator's own experiences, because she herself enjoys a contented, wealthy lifestyle. However, she does so by actively repressing memories of her Vietnamese past.

The suffering of the discontented women is related partly to the moment of their arrival, partly to the racism they then encountered and, the novel implies, partly to their inability to shed their Vietnamese attitudes and fatalism. Female stoicism and fatalism are enshrined in the founding tenets of Confucianism, which teaches women to bow to their destiny, even if it is contrary to their own deeply held aspirations (Le Huu Khoa, 1996, p. 54). The narrator's mother, Kieu, still resident in Vietnam, also conforms to this mould, despite her youthful affair with a French soldier which left her pregnant and abandoned. Lefèvre's attitude towards her mother (and hence her Vietnamese identity) is ambivalent. Firstly, she sees her as a tragic figure, reiterating the comparison made in *Métisse blanche* between her mother and the tragic heroine of a Vietnamese classic epic poem, *Kim-Van-Kieu* (Lefèvre, 1995, p. 85). Despite the cruel reversals of fortune she undergoes, Kieu, the model of female Confucianist behaviour, always accepts her lot and exercises her Confucian duties. The narrator also views her mother as a character in a melodrama, melodrama being: 'The product of traditional societies where everyone has their preordained place'[7] (p. 88). The heroine of a melodrama lacks the grand, dignified stature of a tragic heroine. She commands pity, but not necessarily respect and awe. The narrator is not sure whether Confucian women such as her mother should be admired for their endurance and strength, as tragic heroines shouldering the burden of their fate, or scorned for their passivity and acceptance of subjugation, as actors in some banal, maudlin melodrama.

The duality in the narrator's character, the constant tension between her Asian and French identities, is embodied in the way she alternately identifies with and objectifies her mother. On the one hand, she claims: 'I have continually considered her destiny as my own'[8] (p. 72). On the other, her mother's life seems excessively sensational: 'I would smile derisively if it wasn't for the fact that my own mother's fate were involved'[9] (p. 88). Lefèvre attributes her own change in attitude to her adaptation to French society, which expects the individual to struggle for improvement, rather than stoically accept one's condition. Whereas her long-suffering exiled acquaintances do not alter their behaviour to fit into a French context, she keeps this aspect of her identity locked away, privileging her Western façade. She fears the reincorporation of her Vietnamese past into her French present, because it might destroy the carefully constructed Westernized persona that has protected her from trauma:

> Over the course of the long years I have spent in France I have secreted a resinous forgetfulness. With time, it has hardened, and become a second skin, harder and more resistant.
>
> The thought that this skin could crack and flake off like dead bark, leaving me fragile and unprotected, alarms me. I feel like a warrior who is being sent to battle without armour.[10] (p. 120)

Up to the moment of the televized interview in which she publicly states her intention to return to Vietnam, the narrator may have claimed to wish to return, but an inner voice always contradicted her: 'And while my mouth pronounced this categorical affirmation, another voice, coming from the depths of my being, very faint and very far away, a little voice, childlike and bitter, shouted: "Never!"'[11] (p. 15). The past is thus clearly differentiated from the present. Her Vietnamese identity, associated with the past, is expressed through the childish inner voice, synonymous with a 'melodramatic' or 'tragic' lack of control over events. In contrast, the capable, Westernized veneer that speaks out in the interview in the present is associated with power, social acceptance and maturity, thanks to Lefèvre's familiarity with French culture as a French-educated Eurasian.

The separation between her Western and Asian identities can be related to Lefèvre's understanding of her own genesis, as the product of the ephemeral union of a man and a woman brought together by little besides physical attraction. Her parents' cultural differences are such that they do not even appear to issue from the same humanity: 'In my eyes, it was perfectly understandable; they were of different races, their characters and cultures were mysteries one to the other. Basically, they weren't members of the same human race'[12] (p. 80). As the product of the union of two distinct species, Lefèvre is tacitly positioning herself as a hybrid.[13] In *Métis*, the Eurasian writer Philip Franchini draws a clear distinction between the 'hybrid' and the *métis*: 'In botany and zoology, it [the *métis*] denotes [the product of] different varieties of the same species. It can be distinguished from the hybrid, which issues from two distinct species'[14] (Franchini, 1993, p. 11).

As a 'hybrid', the narrator is a combination of two incompatible genetic structures, intertwined but not mixed, rather than a *métis*, whose genetic information is combined, enmeshed. *Retour à la saison des pluies* constitutes an attempt to move the narrator beyond the status of the random issue of two incompatible cultures and societies, towards an identity that would reintegrate the two cultural aspects of her character into a more harmonious whole. To achieve this, the narrator releases and confronts her Vietnamese identity, through encounters first with the Vietnamese community in France, then, in the second half of the book, with Vietnam and her family.

Through her return to Vietnam, a logical progression from the gradual reintegration of her Vietnamese past into the present, the narrator rediscovers her love for her mother and sisters. Her renewed encounter with Vietnam allows her to recapture good memories, and to lay uncomfortable recollections to rest. She is also forced to recognize that the landscape of her memories bears little relation to what she sees and experiences. This combination of experience and observations leads to the exorcism of her internalized Vietnamese double. The narrator is able to definitively abandon her former Vietnamese self on Vietnamese shores, an act represented by the final scene of the novel, in which she watches the traces of her presence in Vietnam being washed away, as her Vietnamese past has been:

Some children up to their waists in pond water are trying to catch earth crabs or snails in the mud. A little girl stands alone on the bank. Seeing her, I feel as if I am staring into murky waters where I can make out the reflection of my former face, like that of the child, both close and foreign, a face that belonged to me on a different river bank.

There is a common Vietnamese saying: 'Life is like a mirror: it sends back your own image when you are close, and it forgets you when you are far away.'

So it is with the mirror of my past life. It restores a few reflections when I am present, but when I leave this country my image will fade away and I will leave no more trace on this watery countryside, where it is beginning to rain once more.[15] (Lefèvre, 1995, p. 222)

The little girl stands in a state of isolation, frightened to plunge in and join the others. She represents both the social ostracism that the author experienced as a Eurasian child, and the author's distance from her Vietnamese past. The child is at once near and far, familiar and unfamiliar. The past that she embodies cannot be recaptured or reconstituted through an encounter with contemporary Vietnam, for it only exists in its original state within the narrator. Thirty years of change, both in herself and in Vietnam, flow between the narrator and her former Vietnamese self.

The narrator's return to the homeland acts as a return to her origins and ends with a resolution of her dual identity through a series of paradoxes. She feels that she has returned to: 'The womb that gave birth to me'[16] (p. 143). When there, she confronts the inner child, who has become her double, her mirror image, and is reborn by expelling it into the uterine warmth of Vietnam. Her recognition of the fact that the Vietnam of the present has little in common with that of the past allows her to exorcize her internalized Vietnamese double, and to redefine herself as a French citizen of Vietnamese origin through choice rather than fear. When the internalized double is abandoned, the narrator's 'hybrid' duality is resolved. In this novel, then, Lefèvre does not so much 'find' a 'lost' identity, as Yeager claims in his assessment of the novel (Yeager, 1993, p. 48), as retrieve, confront and finally transcend a repressed sense of self.

Les Trois Parques

The conundrum at the centre of the narrator's cultural identity in *Retour à la saison des pluies* – how to reconcile the Vietnamese with the French aspects of her identity – also dominates Linda Lê's *Les Trois Parques*. Whereas Lefèvre draws a distinction between pre- and post-1975 immigrants, and exhibits sympathy for all the boat people, Lê shows a knowledge of the different waves of the 1975 exodus and uses the acerbic narrative voice of *Les Trois Parques* to demonstrate a dry disdain for the wealthy first wave boat people, whose tragedy is made to appear banal and slightly distasteful.[17] The Vietnamese community as a whole is also shown in a disparaging light, due to its exploitative relationship with the homeland. Lê's greater awareness of the politics of the Vietnamese community in France contrasts with Lefèvre's 'outsider' view. The narrative of *Les Trois Parques,* in which the author wrestles with the dilemma of the cultural identity of her French heroines of Vietnamese origin, is suffused with heavy irony and a sense of impending doom. The exuberance of Lê's language, coupled with her striking use of imagery and metaphor, illustrate her own identity as a writer fluent in both the language and culture of France and the folklore and traditions of Vietnam.

Jack Yeager interprets Linda Lê's novels as an attempt to create an imaginary space that can become her homeland, 'Lê carves out a linguistic space, appropriates and reinvents language and the French novel, makes a linguistic and literary field in French her own state and nation and declares herself its citizen. Writing from this invented space she creates a homeland' (Yeager, 1997, p. 265). This claim that Lê is creating a place to call her own seems a rather rosy interpretation of her darkly pessimistic literary endeavour. In *Les Trois Parques*, Lê's bleak vision appears to preclude the possibility of a harmonious encounter between the home-lander and the Vietnamese resident in France.

Les Trois Parques centres on the preparations of three unnamed Parisian women of Vietnamese origin for the impending visit of their Vietnamese father/uncle, nicknamed Le Roi Lear (King Lear). The two sisters, the heavily pregnant L'Aînée (The Eldest), and the recently pregnant younger Belles Gambettes (Good Legs), left Vietnam as very young children with the first wave of boat people, escorted by their previously estranged grandmother. Their maternal cousin, La Manchote (The One-Armed Woman), was sent to France after being discovered having sex with her twin brother. The two sisters and cousin represent metaphorically both the three states of the French Indochinese Union during the French colonialist period (Annam, Tonkin and Cochinchina), and different attitudes of the Vietnamese living in France towards the homeland.

The older sister, L'Aînée, represents Annam, the former imperial centre of Vietnam and epicentre of traditional Vietnamese society. As a woman of Vietnamese origin, she also ostensibly represents the 'ideal' of the culturally integrated immigrant who has adapted to life in France, while retaining her homeland identity. She is married to a white European husband who respects Eastern cultures. She retains her links to Vietnamese language and Vietnamese culture, and writes to her father in Vietnam regularly. Her perception of Vietnam is nonetheless coloured by propaganda disseminated by the Vietnamese community in France. Like her grandmother, Lady Chacal (Lady Jackal), a typical first generation *Viêt kieu* (Vietnamese in exile) who contributed to bogus anti-communist schemes supporting the regeneration of Vietnam (Lê, 1997, pp. 69–70), L'Aînée falls prey to the anti-communist politics of the Vietnamese community. She avidly reads an anti-Hanoi scandal sheet which rails against the communists, describing them as 'les saigneurs du pays' ('the bleeders of the country', a pun on the word 'seigneurs', meaning 'lords') (p. 144). Even her decision to invite her father to France is based upon the hysterical, sensationalist information provided by this organ (p. 157).

Like other members of the Vietnamese community, L'Aînée prides herself on her material assets, especially her new house with its modern conveniences and constantly full refrigerator. The depiction of the elder sister conforms to Lê's portrayal of the majority of the Vietnamese in France, who feel the need to parade their relative wealth in front of the homelanders.[18] This phenomenon is an inversion of the Confucian prestige economy, based upon a definition of self-worth hinging on the respect one is accorded by others.[19] The desire to flaunt her wealth lies behind L'Aînée's decision to finance her father's visit to France. While she is ostensibly fulfilling her filial duties, she is more concerned with making an impression on her father, before sending him back to the homeland. She also corrupts another traditional source of Confucianist female identity, her role as the vessel of the life of a male. Her self-importance, which derives from the life growing within her, eclipses her Confucianist respect for her elders and for other males in her family: 'The coming of Le Roi Lear presented itself as the crowning glory of her respectable career. Was my cousin going to refuse herself the eloquent spectacle of the greeting between the two generations, the old man bowing before the little prince whose apparition would send him raving to his tomb?'[20] (p. 25).

L'Aînée decides when Le Roi Lear should visit, expecting him to prostrate himself symbolically in front of the new generation, born in the West. This is symptomatic of the rather patronizing stance towards the homelanders adopted by the Vietnamese community in France, which is derided in this novel. The *Viet kieu* are shown to manipulate and rework traditional Confucian values to fit in with the Western ethos of rights rather than responsibilities, and so enhance their sense of superiority. L'Aînée's relationship with the homeland is thus affected by the prejudices of the

Vietnamese community, as well as her own exposure to Western society. The younger sister, Belles Gambettes, is in the process of extricating herself from a relationship with her parasitic French lover, Théo. Her name (Good Legs) functions as a metonym for South Vietnam, the lower part of the Vietnamese body politic. Saigon, the capital of what was in colonial times Cochinchina, has long been associated with decadent sexuality and hedonism. Belles Gambettes is correspondingly narcissistic, fully aware of her sexual attractiveness, in contravention of the rules of Confucianist female behaviour which dictate self-effacing modesty of dress, comportment and attitude. The younger sister's selfish attitude towards her two female relatives – she is there for the free food and to beg money for an abortion from La Manchote – is in keeping with Saigon's perceived ethos of mercenary self-interest. Yet Belles Gambettes' attitude belies a traumatic past that has effectively cauterized her emotions. As a child, she was isolated during a period of intense aerial bombardment. Just as Saigon's brashness and amoral pragmatism obscure a troubled past, so Belles Gambettes has buried her Vietnamese past in her subconscious, immersing herself in Western culture and practices.

However, Lê's sustained use of the parable of King Lear suggests that the character who seems to have abandoned her Vietnamese roots the most definitively, namely the youngest, Westernized daughter, is actually the least treacherous of the three women in her relations with the father, who represents the homeland. If she is read as representing Saigon, then it is notable that the capital of Cochinchina was the seat of Southern resistance to the Northern communist regime, consistently opposed to communist rule and affiliating itself with Western powers that feared the scourge of communism. The reference to the King Lear parable, along with the use of the principal protagonists as metaphors for the French Indochinese Union, suggests that the true enemy of traditional Vietnam is communism, rather than Westernization. As a young woman of Vietnamese origin, Belles Gambettes has the fewest ulterior motives in her desire for reconciliation with the father. Although she shows no overt interest in cultivating her Vietnamese identity, she does not defile it by scorning the homeland, as L'Aînée does. Nor is she drawn to the reunion by its potential for disaster and misery, like her cousin, La Manchote.

The two sisters are both pregnant, the elder rejoicing in her pregnancy and the chance to perpetuate the Vietnamese family line, the younger wishing to retain her independence and autonomy through a termination, in keeping with her Western acculturation. But they are both bearing Eurasian children, symbolic both of the legacy of the colonial embrace, and of the degree of their integration into the host country. Yet both women also carry their Vietnamese identity around within them. For L'Aînée, it is conceptualized through a combination of childhood memories and the effects of the propaganda produced by the French context in which she lives. In contrast, Belles Gambettes keeps her memories of Vietnam sealed away within her, avoiding immersion in the French Vietnamese community, just as the narrator of *Retour à la saison des pluies* locks away her memories of the homeland. Instead, she privileges the Westernized, sexually assured, independent persona that she wears on the outside.

The third central protagonist, La Manchote, is the novel's first person narrator, and has privileged insights into the thoughts of others. She represents Tonkin, the focal point of communist foment. As a Vietnamese woman living in France, part of La Manchote, her hand, will symbolically remain forever in the homeland, preventing her from fully integrating into French society. She chooses a different path from her two cousins. She does not deliberately repress her associations with the homeland like the younger sister, nor does she maintain and cultivate them as a benchmark of her own privileged status, as the elder does. Rather, she immerses herself in her memories, cutting herself off from the world around her. Her past trauma makes her an isolated, eccentric figure who wallows in the recollection of her own misfortunes, seeking out human company only in order to witness tragedy. She is drawn to the elder sister's house by the prospect of a doomed reunion, a re-enactment in different circumstances of her own tragedy.

La Manchote's downfall was brought about by her sexual union with her own double, her identical twin brother, causing him to be confined to a mental asylum and her to be expelled from the homeland (p. 203). Lê explains the disappearance of La Manchote's hand, her brother's madness, and her ability to predict misfortune, in a parable concerning witches. When a witch falls in love with her human counterpart, she touches his heart, losing her hand in the process. Her lover either dies or goes mad as a result (pp. 231–2). She is then condemned to living with mortals as a pariah, able to foretell catastrophe by the itching of her stump, but unable and unwilling to intervene (p. 238). The intimate encounter of like with like is thus represented as both traumatic and destructive. When this is read alongside the tragic ending of the novel, with Le Roi Lear dying before the reunion with his daughters can take place, it appears that an attempted reconciliation between the homeland and the *Viet kieu* can only court disaster. The father dies in Vietnam as a direct result of his preparations for the visit to France. L'Aînée's house, where the three women are gathered, fills with whispering, female ghouls, unleashed by the machinations of fate leading to this tragic conclusion and resonant of the supernatural world of Vietnamese legends as well as a Greek chorus. All three women, the three Fates of the title, bring about their misfortunes through their participation in ill-fated acts of union. Despite their different degrees of acculturation, the two sisters are surrounded by an ancestral chorus that underlines the impossibility of fully shedding or controlling their Vietnamese identity. The harpies rejoice in their inability to achieve a harmonious union with the land of their forebears, and La Manchote becomes one with the chorus, revelling in the tragedy set in motion by a simple invitation issued to the father. As the all-seeing, all-knowing narrator, crippled by her own close encounter with her mirror image, La Manchote both recounts and represents the danger of unnatural and dangerous unions.

In this environment, among the ghostly whisperings and the insistent ringing of the telephone, L'Aînée is further punished for her perversion of traditional beliefs and practices. She begins to double up with pains in her stomach. Given the advanced nature of her pregnancy, the reader is led to assume that she is either suffering from premature labour pains or losing her baby. The narrative of her pain and the ringing of the phone, heralding the information of the father's death, is interspersed with the description of Le Roi Lear's ascent to heaven.

The climax of the novel suggests that a reunion between the home-lander and the three Vietnamese women living in France is unthinkable. This reading is enriched by a consideration of the horror story used as a metaphor for the cancer of communism:

> The scandal sheet had made a great show of dissecting the last case of teratology:[21] some poor sod, barely twenty years old, with a slightly rounded stomach and the pains of a pregnant woman, was one day brought to the death peddlars of Hanoi. They opened him up without further ado, and took a stillborn foetus out of his stomach, scarcely two kilos in weight, with a tuft of hair on his head and all his fingers and toes. For twenty years, the poor sod had been carrying around the foetus of his twin, who should have been born at the same time as him but, thanks to the miracles and miseries of fusions/effusions, had shrunk into a tumour and, rather than seeking the light of day, had taken refuge in the stomach of his twin.[22] (pp. 221–2)

The foetus is never born and remains preserved in his twin's abdomen, bringing the latter pain and, eventually, death. At a literal level, the internalization of one's double is monstrous and mutually destructive. On a symbolic plane, this image also represents the danger of reuniting the traditional Vietnamese homelander with the *Viet kieu*. One sister cossets and nurtures a distorted Vietnamese identity that would be fundamentally challenged by such an encounter, the other seals it away under a seemingly impenetrable layer of Westernization. An encounter with a representative of the homeland would disrupt their internalized Vietnamese identities.

In both these novels, the protagonists' Vietnamese identity is distinct from that of the traditional Vietnamese. It is also challenged by an actual or planned encounter with the Vietnam of the present, which acts as a mirror image, existing independently and elsewhere. Lefèvre tentatively explores the hypothesis that an encounter with the homeland could provide a solution to her angst-ridden state as a cultural 'hybrid'. Her narrator arrives in Vietnam with an internalized 'nostalgic' Vietnamese identity, which she is able to abandon once it has been exorcized through an encounter with the homeland of the present. Her confrontation with both present-day Vietnam and the exorcized troublesome inner child culminates in an image that suggests her rebirth. She cuts her umbilical cord with the Vietnam of the past and returns to the West. Her duality is resolved through a liberating acceptance of the paradox of her cultural identity.

Lê's novel, in contrast, insists upon the tragic consequences of an attempt to effect a reconciliation between the *Viêt kieu* and the homeland. Rather than resolving the puzzle of the relationship between the three protagonists' 'nostalgic' Vietnamese identities and the present-day homeland, both plot and imagery construct the planned encounter as unnatural and grotesque. The close encounter between women of Vietnamese origin living in France and the homelander either frees them of the burden of their unresolved cultural identity, as in the case of Lefèvre, or, as in Lê's novel, reawakens a dormant and visceral horror of its nature.

Notes

1. 'Le Viêt-Nam commençait à faire irruption dans ma vie.' (All translations are by the author.)
2. For a useful introduction to the 13th *arrondissement*, consult J. Costa-Lascoux and Live Yu-Sion (1995).
3. See Jamieson (1993) for a discussion of the importance of Confucianism to traditional Vietnamese culture.
4. 'Nous, on l'appelle "Gac", mais le nom en français, on ne le connaît pas.' Elle s'addresse à moi en disant "nous", je suis donc "l'autre".

5. 'Truffé d'expressions françaises.'
6. 'Oui. Mais ils sont arrivés après 1975, avec les boat-people.'
7. 'Le produit des sociétés traditionnelles où chacun a sa place préétablie.'
8. 'J'ai continuellement considéré son destin comme le mien propre.'
9. 'Je sourirais de dérision s'il ne s'agissait pas du sort de ma propre mère.'
10. 'Durant les longues années passées en France il s'est sécrété en moi une sève d'oubli. Avec le temps, elle s'est durcie, est devenue une seconde peau, plus dure et plus résistante. La pensée que cette peau peut craquer, se détacher comme une écorce morte, me laissant démunie et fragile, m'alarme. Je me sens comme le guerrier qu'on envoie au combat sans armure.'
11. 'Et tandis que ma bouche énonçait cette affirmation catégorique, une autre voix, venue du fond de mon être, ténue et lointaine, une petite voix enfantine et rancunière criait: "Jamais!"'
12. 'A mes yeux, c'était parfaitement explicable ; ils étaient de races différentes, leurs personnalité et leur culture constituaient un mystère l'un pour l'autre; au fond, ils ne faisaient pas partie de la même humanité.'
13. I am using the term 'hybrid' in literal terms, as the product of the union of two discrete species. My use is distinct from Homi K. Bhabha's theoretical use of the term to describe the subversively productive spaces that exist within colonial discourses (Bhabha, 1994).
14. 'En botanique ou en zoologie, il est celui de variétés différentes appartenant à la même espèce. Il se distingue de l'hybride qui est issu, lui, de deux espèces distinctes.'
15. 'Dans une mare, des enfants immergés à mi-corps essaient d'attraper des crabes de terre ou des escargots dans la boue. Seule une petite fille se tient timidement sur le bord. En la voyant, j'ai le sentiment de plonger mon regard dans une eau brouillée où je devine le reflet de mon visage d'autrefois, semblable à celui de cette enfant, à la fois proche et étrangère, un visage m'ayant appartenu sur une autre rive.
'Un dicton vietnamien dit: "La vie est comme un miroir : il vous renvoie votre image quand vous êtes proche, il vous oublie quand vous êtes loin."'
'Ainsi du miroir de ma vie passée. Il m'en restitue quelques reflets tandis que je suis présente, mais lorsque je quitterai ce pays mon image s'effacera et je ne laisserai plus de trace dans ce paysage d'eau où il recommence à pleuvoir.'

16. 'Le ventre qui m'a enfanté.'
17. According to Marion Van Renterghem, Linda Lê, thirty-six when she wrote *Les Trois Parques* in 1997, left Vietnam when she was fourteen (Van Rentherghem, 1997, p. 1).
18. Le Huu Khoa also identifies this need to parade their success in the West, playing on the myth of Western wealth and consumption (Le Huu Khoa, 1996, p. 77).
19. For more information on the prestige economy, based on the principle of saving face and winning respect, see Jamieson (1993, pp. 30–3).
20. 'La venue du roi Lear s'annonçait comme le couronnement de cette respectable carrière. Ma cousine allait-elle se refuser l'éloquent spectacle du salut entre les deux générations, du veillard s'inclinant devant le petit prince dont l'apparition l'envoyait dinguer dans la tombe?'
21. Teratology is the branch of biology that is concerned with the structure and development of monsters.
22. 'La feuille de choux avait déroulé la natte des grands jours pour y disséquer le dernier cas de tératologie: un pauvre bougre, vingt ans à peine, un ventre un peu rond et des douleurs de femmes enceintes qui l'amenèrent un beau matin chez les morticoles de Hanoi. Lesquels l'ouvrirent sans plus de cérémonie et retirèrent de son ventre un foetus mort-né, deux kilos à peine, une touffe de cheveux sur le crâne et des abattis bien numérotés. Le pauvre bougre portait depuis vingt ans dans son ventre le foetus de son jumeau, qui aurait dû naître en même temps que lui mais, miracle et misère des fusions-effusions, le foetus s'était rétréci en tumeur et, au lieu de chercher à voir le jour, il s'était réfugié dans le ventre de son jumeau.'

–9–

Gender, Hospitality and Cross-Cultural Transactions in *Les Passagers du Roissy Express* and *Mémoires d'immigrés*
Mireille Rosello

Like a number of contemporary French novels, films, autobiographies and testimonies, *Les Passagers du Roissy Express* (1990) and *Mémoires d'immigrés* (1997) raise complicated theoretical issues about the significance of hospitality and its intersections with ethnicity and gender. Whenever any type of exchange between people of different cultural backgrounds occurs (be it a commercial exchange, or a gift, or a ritualized transaction), different laws of hospitality may clash, sometimes violently, especially if the situation takes place in a country where individuals are represented as belonging to separate cultures or communities. In France, French persons of European origin (who have forgotten that their ancestors were not always French), and French persons of Maghrebi origin (who are not allowed to forget that their parents or grandparents were 'Arabs') have to come to terms with at times profoundly different and incompatible expectations about how to share space or how to conceptualize hospitality.

It would be simplistic to assume that there is a simple co-existence of two modes of hospitality: the traditional French one, inherited from the Revolutionary ideal (and which, according to Fassin, Morice and Quiminal (1997), is in danger of deteriorating into principles of inhospitality); and a traditional North African one, imagined as the sophisticated and delicate art of nomads and desert people. Such generalizations mask profound discontinuities and differences. As *Les Passagers du Roissy Express* illustrates, lifestyles in Paris are as remote from those of its *banlieues* as those of the 'peasant' once were from the city-dweller. Similarly, without being anthropologists, we can guess that the lifestyle of Mauritanian nomads has little in common with that of the inhabitants of the suburbs of Algiers. At the same time, it is important not to dismiss the ways in which people construct potentially harmful, stereotypical views of their unknown neighbour's laws of hospitality, even if the laws in question are only imagined and misconstrued. As was demonstrated by Chirac's infamous statement about how the noise and smell of the immigrant neighbour drives the French worker crazy,[1] the illusory and perhaps comforting distinction between the next-door neighbour and the exotic foreigner is no longer operative. In other words, in 1990s France, it would be illusory to assume that whatever is different about even an imagined Arab hospitality and French hospitality can remain completely separate. Cohabitation has more or less ensured that each individual knows that hospitality is not universally defined, and the two sets of laws (each of which also contains differences within) cannot coexist without influencing each other, at least at the level of cultural knowledge. Nevertheless, the question of who you invite into your home, for how long, and how you treat them, varies tremendously not only from group to group but also from class to class within both majority and minority ethnic groups. A lack of understanding of the neighbour's rules of hospitality can lead to conflict. In such situations, what is the role played by women? Can they provide us with new models of inter-ethnic hospitality, with new stories and new laws?

To explore this issue, I would like to turn to two episodes from two different texts, both dealing with the conflict arising when an Algerian woman attempts to offer hospitality to white French people. *Les Passagers du Roissy Express* is a travel narrative/guide book in which French writer and former publisher François Maspéro and photographer Anaïk Frantz take a trip through the Parisian *banlieues* as if they were a foreign destination, a device that allows them to explore and critique the artificial binary opposition between exotic spaces and familiar point of origin. At one point in *Roissy Express*, an exchange between Anaïk and a woman of Algerian origin is on the verge of leading to a moment of hospitality, but their complicity is interrupted by François' decision to move on. After analysing the muffled conflict that the scene generates between the main protagonists, I will turn to another example, where the failed moment of hospitality is apparently more brutal and more ostensibly racist or at least xenophobic. In *Mémoires d'immigrés*, a collection of interviews compiled by Yamina Benguigui, the daughter of Algerian immigrants, Benguigi reminisces about her childhood and tells the story of a misunderstanding between a little girl of Algerian origin and her European neighbour, who does not recognize that the former is trying to share a ritual gift with her. By comparing these two episodes, I would like to analyse the promises and limitations of cross-cultural encounters, but also reflect on the possibilities offered by the way such episodes are narrativized and narrated. In the process of telling their tale, both Anaïk Frantz and Yamina Benguigui manage to modify the original situation and bridge cultural gaps at the same time as they denounce their existence.

Madame Zineb's Tea: Hospitality in the *banlieue*

François and Anaïk's deliberately atypical tourist destination questions simple definitions of tourists, travellers, migrants and neighbours. Their itinerary within metropolitan France is structured by encounters with different ethnic groups that neither tourism (which sometimes artificially highlights and most of the time downplays cross-cultural encounters) nor migrations promote. In a country where the politicized issue of migration leads to heated debates about who has the right to extend hospitality and how the state can police such activities, François' and Anaïk's experiences raise interesting questions by bringing to the surface discrepancies between their expectations as Parisian educated nomads and the forms of hospitality that they discover when they meet people whose ancestors or parents were Italian, Algerian or Senegalese, to name but a few of the nationalities they encounter.

One of the problems that we may encounter when we become strangers in a strange place, whether as tourists or as immigrants, is that we are not sure that our own models of hospitality are transferable. We are not sure either that they are *not* transferable. To make matters worse, because hospitality is also a form of generosity, it can or should never be reduced to the way it is prescribed by our education and unwritten rules of etiquette. In hospitality, there is always some excess, a gift that goes beyond what is strictly enforceable. But when two communities meet, or when an individual from one community finds him or herself in a different group, then the possibility that both societies define hospitality in exactly the same way is remote. Consequently, individuals are forced to compare or sometimes confront different practices of hospitality, different conceptions and expectations about what it means to be the host, the hostess or the guest.

In *Roissy Express*, the situation is complicated by three elements. First of all, because of the rather atypical form of travelling chosen here, commercial hospitality and individual hospitality are constantly interwoven, and commercial hospitality is examined through the anthropologist's lens rather than consumed as a service. Secondly, because of the almost parodic structure of the trip, no clear boundary between tourism and immigration can be established. If, for the native whose land is invaded by a tidal wave of condescending westerners, the tourist, as Jamaica

Kincaid suggests in *A Small Place*, is an ordinary man turned into a monster by virtue of the relative increase of power that displacement confers on him, 'an ugly, empty thing, a stupid thing, a piece of rubbish pausing here and there to gaze at this and taste that' (Kincaid, 1988, p. 17), then Maspéro and Frantz are not exactly tourists. Yet, they are not immigrants either. Even if they try to construct the *banlieue* as a space of difference (partly to test that stereotype), the impression that they are abroad, elsewhere, can, at any time, be relativized and rationalized. They are, after all, French Parisians, representatives of the dominant culture, who can go home whenever they wish to do so. They do, however, accept that their specific position as city dwellers diminishes their cultural competence in the far-off *banlieues*. They do not try to impose their norm, they are aware of their fragility (although the critical distance that they maintain as intellectuals sometimes betrays their generous impulse).

Thirdly, their encounters are complicated by the fact that the person who accompanies is a woman and a photographer. Frantz's gender is humorously and self-consciously problematized from the very beginning of the journey as if she knew that her presence implicitly modifies the genre of the travel-narrative-by-two-explorers. When François first calls her and asks: 'how she felt about this idea he had, yes, a rather strange and perhaps a bit foolish idea', Anaïk replies: 'I'm your man.'[2] (Maspéro, 1994, p. 10). This woman, 'Maspéro's man', is also a photographer whose pictures, according to François, are atypically non-predatory: 'They never took people by surprise, were never muggings or rapes'[3] (p. 11, modified translation). The woman as photographer is thus defined as the opposite of the stereotyped (often) male photographer who steals images from his subjects as if he were robbing them of their soul.[4] And Frantz herself also blurs national and ethnic frontiers: her identity is constantly defined as a form of movement or 'in-betweenness'. The text gives us a brief portrait of her at the beginning of the trip but this narrative résumé insists less on hard facts and figures than on her general attitude and mentality. Anaïk lives on the margins, constantly challenging the categories of a world defined in terms of class, nationalities, ethnicities and even geographical neighbourhood: 'Anaïk lived in Impasse de l'Ouest, but she spent her life on frontiers. She might go to Africa, as she did one year, but might just as easily not leave the fourteenth *arrondissement* in Paris'[5] (p. 11). Her family name (Frantz) may suggest to the reader that her ancestors were born outside of the Hexagon, but *Roissy Express* never gives us any indication about her ethnic background or personal history. And yet, the story does insist on her identity. Anaïk is a traveller, a nomad whose imagined community is constituted by: 'bizarre people mostly –

what are usually called dropouts, misfits, even tramps'[6] (p. 11). A photographer who does not know how to sell her pictures and whose professional identity is, consequently, relatively unstable and unimportant, Anaïk works on that 'contact zone' (Pratt, 1992) which makes many of her potential customers uncomfortable with her photographs: 'All too often, her photos provoked displeasure and irritation: why photograph *that*? 'That' was precisely the world right under our noses, which we never see: the frontier world that every one of us finds a bit scary, even very scary'[7] (pp. 11–12). From the very beginning, the reader is thus warned that what Anaïk will show us is not necessarily what we wish to notice and that her presence is a promise of unconventional encounters. She is a woman and a man, a French speaker who has chosen images as her language of predilection and whose own background serves as a catalyst for the reader to become aware of the identity of the photographed subject.

Just as her position as a frontier dweller challenges the very construction of national and ethnic identity, her voice is not easily perceptible within the economy of the book, and the reader is implicitly encouraged to keep in mind this oblique positioning when the time comes to interpret the various episodes that take place during the trip. While *Roissy Express* as a whole is clearly the result of a close collaboration, the separation between Maspéro's and Frantz's voice is not always obvious. Frantz is solely responsible for the photographs but the text is a braid of their perceptions, although it looks as if Maspéro was ultimately in charge of the prose. At times, it is very difficult to know who is speaking, whose opinion is expressed, because the text does not present us with a single, unified narrative voice. At times, a sentence informs us that 'François' did or said something, letting us assume that Frantz might be the narrator; but then another sentence starts with 'Anaïk' and seems to indicate that Maspéro has taken over as the narrative voice. So that when whole paragraphs or pages do not refer to either of the characters by name, it is not clear whether we should assume that the text speaks for both of them, or for one dominant narrator. An interesting textual hybridity results from this ambiguity.

More importantly, the text does not try to pretend that the two travellers always agree, and one particular scene raises interesting questions about hospitality, or more specifically about a breach of etiquette, a moment when hospitality is offered and refused. Towards the beginning of their journey, Anaïk and François find themselves in the vicinity of the famous housing estate referred to as 'Les 3000' in Aulnay, one of the northern suburbs of Paris situated on the RER B. 'Les 3000' is an archetype of what was built during the 1960s and the media tend to treat it as a symbol of all architectural and social disasters. The pair, however, carefully avoid assuming too much about the infamous *cité* and the text emphasizes its history on the one hand and personal encounters on the other. One particularly ambivalent moment occurs when Frantz meets a woman and asks her whether she can take a picture.

The woman is described as: 'a lady dressed in a long, glinting silk tunic, her head covered by a scarf'[8] (p. 34). In other words (but these words are precisely not used), here is a woman whose physical appearance usually leads the onlooker to think 'Islam, tradition, Arab, North Africa'.[9] Cultural reflexes might also make us suspect that such a traditional woman will probably resent, or at least be suspicious of, Frantz's desire to photograph her. But in this case, Madame Zineb complicates our assumptions by accepting graciously, interpreting the gesture as a mark of friendship and affection, and inviting the two travellers in to tea:

'It warms my heart, you asking to take my photograph.' She's feeling down . . . She invites them up for a cup of tea. Anaïk hesitates. François refuses because time's getting on, it's turned seven and they still have some way to go. Or, as Anaïk later complains, because he was embarrassed. They'll send the photos. They'll come back and see her. They swap addresses and telephone numbers. Madame Zineb has a sad smile.[10] (p. 34)

An informal but genuine exchange takes place between the two women from different ethnic backgrounds. Yet the moment of complicity does not last. Madame Zineb's invitation is declined, not by Anaïk but by François whose excuse seems in contradiction with the logic of the trip. The idea that they must go on, almost for the sake of going on, rather than accepting this woman's invitation, belies the original desire to meet the inhabitants of the *banlieues* that, as Parisians, they cannot associate with on a daily basis.

What I find remarkable here is that the text does not try to hide a moment of discomfort and conflict between the two travellers. Here, for a few crucial seconds, Frantz is silenced. Maspéro's reply does not take into account her desire to accept the woman's hospitality. At the same time, the disagreement is not buried and the text allows Anaïk's voice to re-emerge by spelling out the contradiction. The sentence starting with 'Or' is an unexpected supplementary version that proposes a less flattering version of François' act. What Anaïk interprets as his 'embarrassment' is not denied, it remains a working hypothesis, an accusation that he does not wish to answer, allowing the reader to suspect that he may have unconsciously accepted responsibility for Madame Zineb's 'sad smile'. Why did Anaïk want to accept, why did François refuse? The text cannot quite come to terms with the explanation but at least the tension between the two reactions is faithfully preserved, as well as the consequence of François' decision. The comment on Madame Zineb's sadness marks the space of a debt incurred by François whose refusal is poorly motivated. The passage keeps the memory of a moment of failed hospitality where two women apparently shared the same unwritten assumptions and desires, a complicity that seemed to go beyond cultural boundaries but curiously, stopped on the border of gender.

Indeed, immediately after telling us about the incident with Madame Zineb, the omniscient narrator inserts a parenthesis that has obviously been added after the completion of the book. A voice that says 'she' when talking about Anaïk tells the reader that in October 1989 – six months after the trip through the *banlieues*, the photographer returned to 'Les 3000' and was finally able to accept Mme Zineb's invitation in François's absence: 'October 1989: return to the 3000. Anaïk took Madame Zineb her photos, and this time they all had tea together'[11] (p. 34). The presence of this passage within the economy of the travel narrative metaphorically reproduces a moment of hospitality that took place in spite of François's refusal and embarrassment. After the journey is completed, a foreign element is added to the body of the text, as if hospitality were given to a stranger for a short while. The paragraph is framed by a parenthesis, as if to mark the limits of a right to visit rather than a right to stay indefinitely, but it still gives an idea of who Madame Zineb really is. Her husband, her children but also her happiness and her sadness are received into the text in the same manner as Anaïk was welcomed as a guest. François remains in the background, neither giving nor receiving hospitality but allowing the story to entertain possibilities that he cannot quite imagine, to express forms of generosity that are foreign to his instincts, to his perception of the world.

These two brief allusions to Madame Zineb could be just an isolated moment and the episode itself not worth noticing if, twenty pages later, another disagreement did not confirm that the issue of who accepts whose invitation, and who interprets behaviours as welcoming or threatening, is crucially linked to the overall goal of the trip to the *banlieues*. The temporary disagreement between Anaïk and François over whether or not to accept Madame Zineb's invitation proves to be much more significant. Their gut reaction to the presence of the unknown, what we could call their instinct towards or, rather, their unformulated appreciation of foreignness is fundamentally different. When strangers meet, each individual becomes a potential host or a potential guest, but also, in François' case, a potential enemy. In a sense, in order to extend infinite hospitality (greeting the stranger whoever he is, wherever he comes from), one must deploy infinite naiveté or perhaps a certain indifference to the possibility of seeing one's hospitality abused. Once again, François and Anaïk represent the two poles of a rhetorical and ideological spectrum. He is on the side of cautious analysis, she seems capable of that infinite positive suspicion that makes her 'hesitate', as with Madame Zineb, or makes her doubt that her interpretations are correct, but still give the stranger the benefit of the doubt. In the following passage, compare the rhetoric of opinions, likes and dislikes used by François, and the generous but tentative assumptions with which Anaïk responds to her companion's anxieties:

> He *does not like* the fact that all the time they were talking to the two young women, three or four idle youths had been circling them and discussing something. He *does not like* the fact that these boys have followed them, even walking in front of them at times, right down the avenue; that they watched Anaïk taking photos; that they called others over. *Nor does he like* the way Anaïk leaves her large bag wide open. 'Maybe,' she says, 'they want me to take their photo but daren't ask.' Maybe.[12] (p. 44, my emphasis).

At this point, François has become seized with what Anaïk calls 'vertige sécuritaire', a form of paranoia that puts him on his guard and makes him uncomfortably vulnerable. Three times he repeats that 'he does not like' something. Anaïk is apparently oblivious to the threats that he has noticed, and when she tries to interpret what is scaring her friend, she does so according to her own generous logic. The explanation may be that the stranger is shy, a shyness that is a form of reserve and not a threat, and that would easily disappear if she offered the young men the same attention and respect she gave Madame Zineb. Her 'maybe' contrasts with François' reiterated dislike and preserves the space of doubt or error. Similarly, when Madame Zineb had offered tea, she had hesitated, a space of indecision that François had rudely interrupted, upsetting a careful and delicate form of exchange between people who may not share the same rules.

In this instance, while Anaïk is ready to give the gift of her art to shy teenagers, François suspects them of inhospitality. He almost accuses them of being thieves, but he does so indirectly, via a rather authoritarian and sneaky comment on Anaïk's open bag. He implicitly suggests that she is putting them at risk, that she should obey his laws of caution. Her 'maybe', however, makes a suggestion too. She implies that more thinking and interpreting remains to be done, that the situation is not clear and that more communication is needed to ascertain everyone's real feelings. His 'maybe', on the other hand, is a grudging concession to the fact that he cannot rule out her interpretation, but stops short of crediting it with verisimilitude.

In this exchange, the reader realizes that everything is linked and that a whole system of hospitality/inhospitality is being discussed, even if the two travellers seem to be exchanging banalities. Twenty pages after the encounter with Madame Zineb, Anaïk suddenly demonstrates that François' comments on her bag are indistinguishable from an overall system of which she disapproves. Apparently out of the blue, she concludes: 'Even so,' repeats Anaïk, 'It is not good. We really should have had tea with Madame Zineb'[13] (p. 44, modified translation). Madame Zineb, already a distant memory in the reader's mind, reappears like the ghost of failed hospitality.

This time, doubts and hesitations have disappeared, replaced by a certainty: 'It is not good.' And like François, she 'repeats' her statement as if she could not forgive herself. Through her analysis of the situation, the text proposes an unwritten law of hospitality that ought to regulate the guest's conduct. According to Anaïk, the two travellers are guilty of transgressing this law, and her subsequent return underscores the less than trivial nature of this transgression. Anaïk, the woman, seems to know that the refusal of hospitality has consequences that do not easily disappear.

Cakes Offered, Refused and Buried

In *Les Passagers du Roissy Express*, the potentially devastating and lasting outcome of the refusal of hospitality remains an intuition, a vaguely formulated statement of disapproval. Other stories go even further and articulate Anaïk's intuition. In Yamina Benguigui's *Mémoires d'immigrés* another failed moment of hospitality leads to the burial of one generation's form of generosity. *Mémoires d'immigrés* is a series of interviews that also function as an autobiographical search for forgotten or uncelebrated roots. Through her questions to two generations of immigrants and children of immigrants, Benguigui elicits answers and triggers a flow of memories within herself. Those memories are then woven into a narrative that gives them meaning and re-establishes their legitimacy. In one instance, while she is interviewing Naima, who is reminiscing about the festival of Aïd, an occasion that enabled her father to recover some of his dignity, Benguigui is suddenly reminded of her own childhood and a moment of alienation, of failed hospitality, when as a little girl she had to negotiate misunderstanding and hostility:[14]

> When the time had come to celebrate Aïd, in one of those generous moments that were so typical of her, my mother asked me to go round to the neighbours' and take them a plate of little cakes that, according to the custom, is given away in memory of a dead relative. 'Go round to the lady next door and make sure to tell her that the cakes are a gift from uncle Moussah.' 'Yes mom,' I had replied, a docile thirteen-year-old little girl. And I can still see myself, petrified with fear, ringing the door bell, carefully holding the plate to avoid dropping the cakes; and to this day, I can still hear the shrill, hostile voice asking, 'Who is it, who is at the door?' 'It's me, Yamina, your neighbour's daughter, my mother told me to bring you some cakes from uncle Moussah!' 'You can tell your mother that I don't know that uncle of yours', the neighbour's voice had retorted. I remember shrugging my shoulders and thinking, 'How could you know him, he is dead.' The following year, I had tried again and knocked on another neighbour's door. This one had a house, and a beautifully tended rose garden. But I had not been any more successful. So the following year, when a similar plate was inflicted on my sister, we both agreed to bury the cakes in a vacant lot, far away from home. I can't help smiling when I remember that story.[15] (pp. 182–3)

Madame Zineb's encounter with the two travellers of *Les Passagers du Roissy Express* resulted in an increased feeling of 'depression', 'a sad smile' that haunts Maspéro like a remorse. Here, the level of communication between the two protagonists is even more rudimentary. The conversation takes place on each side of a closed door, not even on the symbolic threshold where boundaries are at least exposed as permeable. The little girl never sees the neighbour. The Medusa-like, terrifying grown-up who can 'petrify' children remains a 'voice', whose tone clearly signifies that no hospitality will be granted. The woman does not even know that she is refusing a gift. According to her, this little foreigner is transgressing a rule that everybody should know: people must be acquainted before offering each other cakes. Her simplistic analysis of a situation that she does not understand forecloses the possibility of further exchanges at the very moment when she thinks that she is communicating. She gives the little girl a new message to take back home: 'You can tell your mother that I don't know this uncle of yours.' But this pseudo-reply is meaningless. Rather than continuing a conversation, it forces the cross-cultural dialogue underground, and the girl's reaction to the message will not be formulated. The neighbour's perspective is that she had the last word.

However, the little girl does have an answer to the insulting and paternalistic lesson she has received, even if she keeps her thoughts to herself. She shrugs off the incorrect interpretation and refuses to continue to act as the misunderstood messenger, withdrawing from a place of possible mediation. The three voices are now cut off from each other, that of the mother ('make sure to tell her that the cakes are offered by uncle Moussah') that of the neighbour ('You can tell your mother that I don't know this uncle of yours') and that of the little girl, whose remark is never voiced ('How could you know him, I thought, he is dead'). The fact that the little girl talks only to herself forever excludes the neighbour from a new system that she could have learned. The gift of the cakes, that could have been followed by an explanation of a religious and cultural custom if the woman had interpreted her surprise as the result of ignorance rather than a breach of etiquette, remains incomprehensible. 'Petrified' and silenced by the woman's inhospitable misinterpretation, the messenger is reduced to a form of powerless superiority. She knows better, she is bilingual and bicultural but she but cannot educate the other woman.[16]

As a result, the gift fails. Uncle Moussah, whose memory was cele-brated by an act of generosity, is relegated to a past that cannot be commemorated. At the end of the paragraph, however, a new ritual has been invented. The cakes have been buried. Those cakes that were supposed to symbolically resurrect the uncle, or at least keep his memory alive, are returned to a grave from which they will not be able to re-emerge as long as the same complex ceremonies and counter-ceremonies continue to take place between the mother, the neighbour and the daughter-mediators. Yet, the burial cannot be reduced to the disappearance of the object or of the conflict that they symbolized. The cakes are not destroyed, eaten, or thrown away. Although we often equate the idea of burying emotions and feelings with unhealthy forms of denial, I would argue that this burial is not a metaphor for repression, rather it is a forceful and highly charged symbolic act.

If the cakes had been eaten, after all, from a purely economic perspect-ive, part of the original logic would have been respected, since the cakes were meant to be eaten. At a superficial level, the little girls waste food, a sacrilegious gesture even for those who live in the midst of abundance. At another level, eating the cakes that were supposed to be given away in memory of the uncle would be another form of sacrilegious transgression. The children do not eat the cakes because for them, they are no ordinary cakes, they continue to represent something that can only be given away, even if the gift is refused. Once the original ritual fails, once the neighbour sends them away, they do not throw the cakes away, they have to improvise. They decide to bury the uncle and his memory, but also the gift and its refusal, the failed moment of communication between the two women. The main purpose of this clandestine ceremony is not explained. Is it to shield the mother from the knowledge that her gesture of generosity missed its mark, or is it to protect the messengers from the consequences of their failed attempt at translating their own law of hospitality? Either way, the children do not want to go back home with the refused gift. Consequently, the mother will never know what happened.

The latent conflict between two laws of hospitality is never completely smoothed out, and worse still, the refusal of the gift may have killed a custom for good. We can assume that Yamina Benguigui, if she has become a mother herself, has thought twice before entrusting her own daughters with a plate of cakes to be offered to the neighbour. One word in the story suggests that the narrator does not completely forgive the mother for failing to realize that she was sending her family on an impossible mission, 'the following year . . . a similar plate was *inflicted* on my sister' (my emphasis). The responsibility of translating the untranslatable is 'inflicted' on the sisters, a burden of which the mother remains unaware.

But the encounter is not an altogether sterile misunderstanding. The spurned gift becomes or remains an object sanctified by shared customs. Even if only the two little girls participate in the improvized but serious burial ceremony, their micro-ritual replaces other types of initiation practices and bonds them as witnesses. They can remember and commemorate the event in all its complexity, in all its contradictions. They thus initiate themselves into the world of cross-cultural mediation which they already inhabit and which they will inhabit until their death. However, the ritual shared by the two mediators is not collective and not legitimized by an ethnic, religious or cultural community. The comfort of feeling that a whole society would recognize and affirm the gesture is lost. In this sense, the burial of the cakes is but a parody, or a mournful repetition of the original ritual gift, both like and unlike the death of the scapegoat, the Freudian murder of the father. Here, what is buried stands for what was already dead. Thus the ritual is both less and more efficient than the original which it replaced and is meant to unite a whole people. The two sisters create their own commemorative ceremony but they cannot share it with the rest of the community, or with the French neighbours who interpret them as foreign elements. And not only does the French woman remain ignorant, but the mother is not told that her gift was not accepted.

Conclusion: the Gift of Post-colonial Texts

Maspéro's and Benguigui's books tell stories of ambivalent moments of relative failure and relative success. In both cases, a woman tries to offer a symbolic gift across the ethnic and cultural line, but within a community of neighbours who share the same space. In both cases, that hospitality is refused, but the refusal is followed by a complex set of negotiations that the texts explore in a delicate and sophisticated way, showing how a moment of failed hospitality can lead to a complex reshuffling of positions of power and knowledge. As Marcel Mauss puts it, depending on how the gift is performed, power is gained or lost, by the recipient, or by the giver.[17]

In *Les Passagers du Roissy Express*, the text carefully documents a moment of discord between the two travellers and accepts both the resulting friction and a unilateral resolution when Anaïk returns to the scene of the crime alone and finally accepts the invitation that François had refused. The original refusal is not erased, but at least the text allows for the possibility of some sort of reparation and, more importantly, allows the situation to evolve, communication to improve and hospitality to be better understood, accepted and reciprocated, even in asymmetrical ways. Just as Madame Zineb welcomes Anaïk into her home, the story welcomes Madame Zineb into this multifaceted history of the French *banlieue* where she becomes an important character.

In *Mémoires d'immigrés*, the moment of failed hospitality is more problematic in its cruelty and violence. If Madame Zineb's invitation was declined, the little girl's gift is much more violently rejected by the neighbour who does not even agree to open her door. And the woman who refuses the gift is not offered a second chance, with the result that the cakes are finally buried. On the other hand, the narrative does not make do with an internal parenthesis and goes much further towards an imaginative form of resolution of the conflict. The final text magnifies the private ceremony between the two little girls and makes it public, shareable by a new community of readers that cuts across ethnic and religious boundaries. The children who had never told the story have become grown-ups and, as readers, can now participate in the commemoration of what has become an episode from the past.

Both texts function like a new gift, a new invitation, or perhaps, a new plate of cakes that are dug up from their symbolic grave to be offered again both to the French woman and to the mother in a gesture of reconciliation. Indeed, neither passage is intrinsically tragic in tone. In *Roissy Express*, Madame Zineb smiles, though sadly. In *Mémoires d'immigrés*, the narrator smiles too, 'I can't help smiling when I remember that story'. Their bittersweet fables of half success and half disaster manage to do the work of mediation that the little girls could not do from behind a closed door. Publication opens the door between two communities who cannot otherwise easily talk to each other or establish a meaningful relationship, because both ignore the rudiments of the other's code and no-one is capable of explaining it to them.

What *Mémoires d'immigrés* does for its readers is to put two customs in contact by explaining the meaning of the two women's behaviour. The link between the cakes and the memory of uncle Moussah is spelled out to readers who don't know anything about Aïd; and the story also warns Muslim mothers that their daughter-mediators may be incapable either of transmitting their message of generosity or of returning with a message of hostility. Readers may imagine that Benguigui's mother and other individuals occupying the same social function never find out about their daughters' sobering experiences. They may also imagine that publication of the story will not change anything for the mother. Perhaps she will not, perhaps for one reason or another she cannot read such texts. But the possibility also exists that this trio (the mother, the neighbour, the daughter) will, as readers, discover that they were involved in a complex, polyphonous dialogue and share a mental act of recognition, especially if they share the narrator's amusement. The story thus creates a new space of encounter, the space of the book where different communities are shown to cohabit, even if imperfectly and uncomfortably. As readers ourselves, we too may remember similar previous experiences and be given a chance to reinterpret the dynamics of hospitality and inhospitality between cultures. The complex reappraisal that may then take place is the ultimate gift of successful post-colonial texts which create new spaces for women of different ethnic backgrounds to experiment with and rethink cross-cultural laws of hospitality.

Notes

1. 'Imagine a French worker living with his wife on a housing estate, who sees that the neighbours packed into the next-door apartment are a family with one father, three or four wives and twenty children, who make FF50,000 in benefits without working, naturally. Add the smell and the noise. Well, the French worker will go crazy. And it is not

racist to say that.' ('Imaginez un travailleur français qui vit avec sa femme, et qui voit sur le palier de son HLM, entassés, une famille avec un père, trois ou quatre épouses et une vingtaine de gosses, qui gagne 50.000 francs de prestations sociales, sans naturellement travailler. Ajoutez à cela le bruit, et l'odeur. Eh bien le travailleur français sur le palier devient fou. Et ce n'est pas être raciste que de dire cela.') (Statement made 19 June 1991 during a dinner in Orléans, reported in *Le Monde*, 21 June 1991.)

2. The page numbers refer to the published translation, *Roissy Express*. When indicated, I have modified the translation.

3. 'Elles n'étaient jamais faites par surprise, elles n'étaient jamais agression. Ni images à la sauvette, ni images-viol' (p. 18).

4. For a particularly problematic example of such predatory photography, see Michel Tournier's novels, especially *Le Roi des Aulnes* (1970) and *La Goutte d'or* (1986).

5. 'Anaïk habitait l'impasse de l'Ouest mais elle passait sa vie aux frontières. Pour cela, elle pouvait aller en Afrique, comme elle le fit une année, mais elle pouvait aussi bien ne pas quitter le quatorzième arrondissement' (p. 17).

6. 'Des gens bizarres, la plupart du temps, de ceux qu'on appelle des marginaux, asociaux ou même clochards' (p. 8).

7. 'Trop souvent ses photos déplaisaient, irritaient: pourquoi photographier *ça*? Ca, c'était justement ce monde qu'on a sous les yeux et qu'on ne voit pas: ce monde des frontières, qui, à chacun de nous, fait un peu peur' (p. 18).

8. '[U]ne dame revêtue d'une longue tunique aux reflets de soie, la tête couverte d'un foulard' (p. 48).

9. For a refreshingly unstereotypical analysis of the different possible roles of the much maligned 'foulard' (Islamic headscarf) in the Maghreb, see Woodhull (1993a).

10. '"Cela m'a fait chaud au coeur que tu me demandes de me photographier." Elle avait le cafard [. . .] Elle leur propose de monter chez elle prendre le thé. Anaïk hésite. François refuse parce que l'heure avance, il est plus de sept heures et ils ont encore de la route à faire. Ou, comme le lui reproche ensuite Anaïk, parce qu'il est gêné. Ils enverront les photos. Ils reviendront. Adresses. Téléphones. Mme Zineb a un sourire triste.' (p. 49).

11. 'Octobre 89: retour aux 3000. Anaïk a rapporté les photos à Mme Zineb et, cette fois, elles ont pris le thé ensemble' (p. 49). Note that the English translation cannot specify that the man was not present. The 'all' even implies otherwise.

12. '*Il n'aime pas* que tout le temps qu'ils ont parlé aux deux jeunes femmes trois ou quatre jeunes gens désoeuvrés aient tourné autour d'eux, se soient concertés. *Il n'aime pas* que ces garçons les aient suivis, et même observés, pendant qu'Anaïk prenait ses photos. En aient appelé d'autres. *Il n'aime pas non plus* qu'Anaïk garde toujours son sac grand ouvert, béant. "Peut-être, dit-elle, qu'ils veulent me demander de prendre leur portrait et qu'ils n'osent pas?" Peut-être' (p. 49, my emphasis).

13. '"Quand même, répète Anaïk, ce n'est pas bien. On aurait pu accepter le thé de Mme Zineb"' (p. 60).

14. As Sylvie Durmelat suggested at the IRS conference on 'Women and Ethnicities in France' (November 1998), organized by Jane Freedman and Carrie Tarr, the interviewee's story opens up a space where the interviewer can reminisce about her own childhood. This in itself is a model of discursive hospitality.

15. 'Et la fête de l'Aïd étant venue, ma mère, dans un élan de générosité dont elle avait le secret, m'avait demandé d'apporter aux voisins, comme le veut la coutume, le plat de gâteaux que l'on offre à la mémoire d'un parent décédé. "Tu vas aller chez la voisine, et tu lui diras bien que les gâteaux, c'est de la part de mon oncle Moussah. – Oui, maman", avais-je répondu, en jeune fille obéissante, du haut de mes 13 ans. Je me revois pétrifiée, sonnant à la porte, l'assiette de gâteaux bien droite pour ne rien renverser, et j'entends encore la voix aigre et peu engageante: "C'est qui, qui sonne? – C'est moi, Yamina, la fille de votre voisine, ma mère m'a dit de vous apporter des gâteaux de la part de mon oncle Moussah! – Tu diras à ta mère que je le connais pas, ton oncle!" avait sèchement riposté la voix de la voisine. Bien sûr puisqu'il est mort, me disais-je en moi-même, en haussant les épaules. L'année suivante, j'avais renouvelé la tentative en frappant à la porte de la voisine d'en face. Elle avait une maison et un beau jardin rempli de roses, mais je n'avais pas eu davantage de succès. Aussi, l'année d'après, avec ma soeur qui s'était vu infliger, elle aussi, une assiette identique, nous avons décidé d'un commun accord, d'enterrer dans un terrain vague, assez éloigné, les gâteaux de l'Aïd. Ce souvenir me fait involontairement sourire . . .' (pp. 182–3).

16. For a good analysis of what happens when superior knowledge and powerlessness coexist, see the beginning of Eve Kosofsky Sedgwick's *Tendencies* (1993).

17. Western cultures stereotypically think of the recipient of a gift as the obligated party, but Mauss's analysis of the Maori legal system reveals more complex forms of debt that resemble what occurs between the

little girl and the neighbour. Mauss notices that the ritualizing of gift-giving practices has consequences over who has or loses power. If the gift is correctly given, 'Coming from one person, made or appropriated by him, it gives him power over the other who accepts it. In the case where the prestation provided is not rendered in the prescribed juridical, economical, or ritual form, the giver obtains power over the person who has participated in the feast and has taken in its substances, the one who has married the girl or has bound himself by blood relations, the beneficiary who uses an object enchanted with the whole authority of the giver' (Mauss, 1997, p. 30).

−10−

Where Women Tread: Daughters and Mothers in *Souviens-toi de moi* and *Sous les pieds des femmes*[1]
Carrie Tarr

If French cinema in the 1980s and 1990s has gradually been forced to acknowledge on screen the presence of its post-colonial ethnic others (Tarr 1997a), women of Maghrebi origin − be it first generation women immigrants or their more integrated daughters − have continued to be confined to the cinematic margins. In the last few years of the decade, however, two women of Algerian origin have made their first feature films and offered new representations of what it means to be a woman of Algerian origin living in France to-day. This article sets out to analyse how *Souviens-toi de moi* (*Remember Me*) by Zaïda Ghorab-Volta (1996) and *Sous les pieds des femmes* (*Where Women Tread*) by Rachida Krim (1997) address the gaps and inadequacies in dominant representations of women of Maghrebi origin and, in particular, how they represent the ways in which both daughters and mothers negotiate their problematic bicultural identities.

It is notable that, despite the creative activities of 'second generation' women since the early 1980s,[2] and despite the fact that young men of Maghrebi origin (the 'Beurs') first started to make films in the mid-1980s (Bosséno, 1992; Tarr, 1993), women filmmakers of Maghrebi origin were not able to make their voices heard in the cinema until the mid to late 1990s. *Souviens-toi de moi* and *Sous les pieds des femmes* are historically significant as, respectively, the first medium-length and full-length feature films to be written and directed by French women of Algerian origin.[3] Neither Ghorab-Volta nor Krim came to filmmaking through the traditional routes, that is, through professional training at the FEMIS (the French National Film School) or by working their way up through the industry. Zaïda Ghorab-Volta, born in 1966, grew up in the Parisian *banlieue*, the fifteenth child of an immigrant Algerian family (Robinson, 1999, p. 203), and started off in social work before becoming an actress,

Figure 4. Rachida Krim shooting *Sous les pieds des femmes* (photograph by Sébastien Raymond, courtesy of MPA).

writer and director. She took nine years to complete *Souviens-toi de moi*, which was made on a shoestring budget with an amateur cast. She also co-wrote the script for Romain Goupil's 1996 television film, *Le Voile du silence* (about a schoolgirl whose decision to wear the veil confounds her family and friends), and since *Souviens-toi de moi* has directed a television film, *Laisse un peu d'amour* (1998), about mother-daughter relationships within a white single parent working-class French family. Rachida Krim, born in 1955, was brought up in Alès (in the south of France), where her father worked as a miner, her parents having emigrated from Algeria in the 1950s. She went to art school and worked and exhibited as an artist before making a short documentary, *El Fatha* (1992), about the rituals involved in an Algerian wedding. Thanks to the success of this film, described as being 'full of magical beauty, palpable emotion and unusual sensuality' (Chauville, 1998, p. 134), she was able to get funding to research *Sous les pieds des femmes*, which developed into a full length feature film with an international cast.

Both films appear to draw their inspiration from auto/biographical sources. Ghorab-Volta not only wrote and directed *Souviens-toi de moi*, she also plays the main role, lending a patina of authenticity to her fictional character, Mimouna, a contemporary young woman of Algerian origin living in the Parisian *banlieue*. Furthermore, the film is dedicated to the director's cousins in Algeria, who play an important role within the film's diegesis. *Sous les pieds des femmes's* autobiographical sources are not inscribed within the text in the same way, but Krim has acknowledged in interviews that her script (co-written with Catherine Labruyère Colas) is based on interviews with her immigrant mother and with women who chose to return to Algeria at the end of the War of Independence (1962). The film, which centres on Aya, a first generation immigrant woman, can thus be read as a fictionalized tribute to the memories and experiences of Krim's mother and other Algerian women living in France and active within the FLN (Front de Libération Nationale/National Liberation Front) at the time of the struggle for independence, a time which is coterminous with Krim's own early childhood.[4]

Both films thus focus on women of Algerian origin, albeit women of different generations. Such a choice of protagonist is in itself a challenge to dominant cinematic expectations, the only previous film to foreground such a character being Anne Fontaine's *Les Histoires d'amour finissent mal en général* (*Love Stories Usually End Badly*) (1993) (in which Ghorab-Volta makes a cameo appearance).[5] Both films situate their main protagonist in relation to the Algerian immigrant family and Algerian cultural traditions.[6] And both avoid the stereotypical representations typical of the dominant culture which either associate the young Arab woman with exotic sexuality and the older Arab woman with superstition and tradition or, alternatively, construct women as the victims of the Arabo-Berber-Islamic sex-gender system. Instead, both films dramatize the complex, fragmented subjectivity of the woman of Algerian origin, divided between her (problematic) allegiance to her culture of origin and her need to construct a meaningful life in France.

Though they share a common focus on women's experiences, there is a striking difference between the two films in terms of genre. By locating its starting-point in the Parisian *banlieue*, *Souviens-toi de moi* offers a woman-centred re-writing of the male-authored *banlieue* films of the mid-1990s, the most successful of which was *La Haine* (Mathieu Kassovitz, 1995) (Tarr, 1997c; Vincendeau, 2000). To date, the *banlieue* film has typically focused on the lifestyles of young, streetwise male protagonists, normally including their (often reluctant) involvement in drugs, crime and violence, and has tended to marginalize or stereotype both young women and immigrant mothers of Maghrebi origin (Tarr, 1999).[7] Ghorab-Volta's concerns lie primarily in the sphere of interpersonal relationships and her film evacuates the 'masculine' themes characteristic of the *banlieue* film. As for *Sous les pieds des femmes*, whose setting somewhere in the south of France avoids all references to the *banlieue*, the film's

reconstruction of a hitherto hidden history invites comparison with two
period films of the late 1990s which reconstruct immigrant life in the
bidonvilles (or shantytowns) of the 1950s and 1960s, namely *Le Gone
du Chaâba* (Christophe Ruggia, 1998), based on Azouz Begag's best-
selling autobiographical novel, and *Vivre au paradis* (Bourlem Gherdjou,
1999), loosely based on the novel of the same name by Brahim Benaïcha.[8]
What distinguishes *Sous les pieds des femmes* is not only its representation
of a suppressed episode in Franco-Algerian relations through the eyes,
voice and actions of an immigrant woman, but also its complex negotiation
of the connections between past and present which make it a potentially
hard-hitting political drama rather than a nostalgic period piece.[9]

In the rest of this article, I will analyse the ways in which each film
represents the woman of Maghrebi origin, and then compare and contrast
the two films, particularly in terms of their representation of daughters
and mothers and the relationships between different generations of
women. I will argue that differences in emphasis between the two films
point to significant shifts in the way women directors of Maghrebi origin
are able to come to terms with their bicultural heritage.

Figure 5. Generational conflict between mother and daughters in *Souviens-toi de moi*,
with Zaïda Ghorab-Volta as Mimouna in the foreground (courtesy of Pierre Grise).

Souviens-toi de moi

Souviens-toi de moi expresses the existential anguish of a young woman trying to negotiate between the strains and stresses of immigrant family life and the equally stressful life she leads in the outside world. Mimouna's fragmented self is manifest in an episodic narrative structure which cuts between the enclosed family/domestic space in the *banlieue* and the more open, public spaces of the city. Punctuating shots of Mimouna dashing through the streets of Paris or crossing the road back to the *banlieue* housing estate mark her inbetweenness. Abrupt transitions in the editing and the poignant strains of the original string-based musical score reproduce her inner anguish. Her lack of a coherent, centred sense of self is reinforced by the off-centre framing, and by the naturalistic, semi-improvised acting style which allows her to vent her feelings of frustration and rage.

Mimouna's experiences are embedded within the context of the immigrant Algerian family. The space of the family home is dark and enclosed, and marked by conflict. The diegesis opens with a shot of the mother kneading the couscous, visually trapped by the window frame, but also shot in close-up to invite the audience's sympathy. Her appearance in traditional dress, her preoccupation with domestic activities, and her deference to her husband are also seen through the eyes of her Westernized daughters, and account for their revolt against conventional women's roles in Algerian culture. Her husband is a silent, severe patriarchal figure who expects to be waited on and attempts to exert his authority by chiding his son, Hamid, for not being a proper man (Hamid is unemployed and does not supervise his sisters' honour as he is expected to). One daughter has already left home, the youngest is dreaming of escaping too, and Hamid refuses the conventional patriarchal role his father wants him to assume. The daughters have no real communication with their father, despite declaring that they are 'not afraid of him' any more. Their communication with their mother consists of screaming and shouting at her in French, while the mother screams back at them in Arabic. The parents only speak Arabic (which is subtitled for the audience), whereas the children understand Arabic but will not speak it. The film thus offers a disturbing image of the immigrant family, where there is little intimacy or communication, and individuals are shot separately within the frame, or caught alone and lost in doorways or at windows. The *mise en scène* invites sympathy for the parents as well as their children, however, showing how they, too, have lost their bearings, and are ineffectual except in causing their children misery by attempting to impose the values of their culture of origin. The only relief within the home is to be found in the scene of

Figure 6. Mimouna and friends: multi-ethnic female solidarity in *Souviens-toi de moi* (courtesy of Pierre Grise).

intimacy between Mimouna and her younger sister, their two faces shot upside down in close-up as they lie on the bed, laughing together and dreaming of escaping to 'la mer de Chine' ('the sea of China', also a play on the word for 'mother').

Mimouna's life outside the home is compartmentalized into various relationships with 'indigenous' white French people, which she is obliged to hide from her family. She is emotionally dependent on her lover, Jacques, but her transgressive love affair looks as though it is about to end and she reacts violently and hysterically when Jacques tells her to lead her own life, and refuses to be a father, a hero, or a saint for her. She has a dead-end job working in a school canteen (not in a hospital as she tells her parents), which she decides to leave. But she is able to find comfort in the company of her girlfriends, who insist that they all share the same problems, be it Claude, her co-worker (who holds hands with her on the bus); or Cordelia and Marie (with whom she goes to the café and the disco). The film suggests that what these young women have in common, moaning about their relationships with men and the lack of direction in their lives, is more significant than any cultural or ethnic differences.[10]

The tension Mimouna experiences between home and the outside world is temporarily halted by the introduction of a third term in the third part of film, that is, the family holiday which Mimouna spends in Algeria with her parents. There is a change in film style, the pace of the editing slows down and the camera pans calmly to and fro over the domestic interior settings, where Mimouna laughs and chats with her cousins and wears Algerian dress. So what does Algeria represent here? Not a historically realistic space in that the episode contains no references to the contemporary political situation (no doubt because the screenplay dates back to the late 1980s). Not either the exotic space of the harem, held up for a Western gaze, as argued by Danielle Robinson (1999).[11] Rather the Utopian space of the extended Algerian family, where the separation of the sexes allows groups of people to come together and talk as they are unable to do in France, so affirming the value of the parents' cultural background. The mother is able to share with the other women her longing to return to Algeria, but her fear of losing her children if she does so; the father speaks of the sacrifices he has made in emigrating to France and articulates an awareness of the difficulties facing his son. As a result, the spectator (and implicitly Mimouna) gains more respect for the parents through a sense of their personal histories, and more of an understanding of their inability to integrate into French society. As for Mimouna herself, her conversations with her female cousins allow her to enjoy the warmth of the gynocentric aspect of her Algerian heritage. At the same time, her cultural difference from them prevents her from sharing all her cultural (and specifically sexual) knowledge with them, and their good-humoured but resigned criticisms of Algerian men and the way women are treated in Algeria confirm for her that her place is back in France. At the end, though, Mimouna manages to articulate a few words of Arabic, while the cousins tell her that they will always be with her.

The final sequence of the film concerns Mimouna's return to France, visualized through a subjective tracking shot alongside the Seine in the centre of Paris (as opposed to the tracking shot into the *banlieue* with which the film opens), followed by a brief scene of Mimouna and her girlfriends walking by the river, discussing their holidays and their relationships, then going off to have a drink. There are no more migrations between different spaces. Mimouna is a different person, less aggressive, more at peace with the world, able to laugh at her problems, and put her relationship with Jacques behind her. The last scene offers an image of interracial friendship and female solidarity, and though there is no attempt to show any change within the immigrant family, the film's fluid ending allows the hope that Mimouna's reclamation of her roots, her more

Figure 7. Rachida Krim on the set of *Sous les pieds des femmes* with Nadia Fares (Fusilla) and Claudia Cardinale (Aya) (photograph by Sébastien Raymond, courtesy of MPA).

positive awareness of her Algerian cultural heritage, will enable her to be more at ease with her hybrid status in France.

Sous les pieds des femmes

Sous les pieds des femmes centres on the mental turmoil of a woman, Aya (Claudia Cardinale), who has chosen to settle with her family in France, but who is forced by a visit from her former lover, Amin, in France for the first time since the Algerian War ended some thirty-five years ago, to confront her memories of what took place during the struggle for independence and her problematic relationship with post-war Algeria. The autobiographical dimension of *Sous les pieds des femmes* is not inscribed within the film by a dedication or an authorial presence (as in *Souviens-toi de moi*), but Krim's position as the daughter who knows the truth of her mother's history, having thought she had been abandoned as a child when her mother was in prison, is replicated in the film through the role of Aya's daughter, Fusilla (Nadia Fares). Unfortunately, *Sous les pieds des femmes* at times betrays the fact that it is a first film, particularly in its awkward pace and editing, its poor lighting, its at times overly didactic tone, and the continuity problems caused by its ambitious intercutting of past and present. Nevertheless, its more formally stylized, studied representation of an Algerian immigrant woman and her family provides a striking alternative to *Souviens-toi de moi*'s more aggressive, 'naturalistic' approach.

Aya differs from the mother of *Souviens-toi de moi* in her apparently successful assimilation into French society, expressed not just through the casting of Claudia Cardinale (to be discussed below), but also through the *mise en scène* of her elegant, spacious family home and the pattern of relationships between the members of her family. In *Sous les pieds des femmes*, the parents speak French and wear elegant Western clothes. Moncef, a retired miner and former FLN activist, is not a stereotypical, authoritarian father figure, but a thoughtful, caring man who respects his wife's desires. (It becomes apparent that he would have preferred to return to Algeria after the war and that he still nurses illusions about Algeria's post-war achievements). The parents have an affectionate relationship with their Westernized daughter, Fusilla, who is (apparently) happily married to a white Frenchman, has a daughter of her own, drives her own car, and is able to criticize both events in Algeria and France's response to those events. In cinematic terms, this is an unconventional (because so Westernized), but nevertheless completely unthreatening representation of an apparently integrated immigrant Algerian couple and their household, where Aya's only concessions to her Algerian origins consist in wearing the same ear-rings that she wore as a young woman and serving a *tagine* to her French son-in-law. However, the eradication of all but the most superficial traces of the family's Algerian heritage soon proves to be a sign not just of their assimilation (their immigration dates back to the 1950s rather than to the 1960s, as is presumably the case in *Souviens-toi de moi*), but of a more pathological attempt to achieve a distance from the past.

The eruption of the past triggered by the visit of Amin calls into question Aya's identity as an assimilated woman, drawing attention to the inner conflicts that she has hitherto suppressed but not resolved. In the opening sequence, Aya pores over her reflection in the bathroom mirror, as she attempts to field the questions about the past put to her by her young grand-daughter. What we see is the split and doubled image of Cardinale's heavily made-up face, the mask of the integrated, Westernized woman that requires constant work to keep it in place. Repeated shots of Aya examining her image in the mirror, adjusting her lipstick and eye make-up, and fingering her shoulder-length hair (so different from the long braids she wore as a young woman), punctuate the film right up to the penultimate sequence, by which time the grand-daughter (and the spectator) has found out about her past as an FLN activist and her subsequent trial and imprisonment. What Aya (and the spectator) sees, however, is not just the Westernized woman of the present but also the self she once was, and the contemplation of her image leads to the memory flashbacks which explain her 'split' identity.

The film cuts between the present of Amin's overnight visit and the past of events beginning back in 1958 before Amin and Aya went their separate ways. The flashback structure splits the film into two separate but interwoven strands, on the one hand the intimate personal drama of Aya's confrontation with Amin and all he represents, taking place in the present (and shot mostly within fixed frames which emphasize how Aya has become trapped), and on the other the historical drama taking place in the past, in which Aya becomes involved in the activities of the FLN and is sentenced to life imprisonment after impersonating a French woman and assassinating a police officer (and which includes dynamic action sequences, like the horrifying police raid and, more awkwardly, the assassination). The disjunction between past and present and between the woman's film and the historical action film, is compounded by the choice of casting, since Fejria Deliba, who plays Aya as a young woman, bears little resemblance to Cardinale, who plays her some thirty-five years later. (The casting of different actors in the roles of Moncef and Amin is far more convincing in terms of continuity.) Leaving aside the question of the political correctness or otherwise of casting Cardinale as an Algerian woman (or the choice of a star like Cardinale as a commercial ploy to bring in audiences), the unavoidable difference between the two incarna-tions of Aya produces a Brechtian distanciation effect, which may work to alienate the spectator but at the same time draws attention to the radical (and impossible) change of identity that Aya has undergone.

That change is described by Fusilla as the difference between the traditional Algerian mother she remembered as a child, and the French woman who returned from prison. Aya's initial transformation from illiterate immigrant wife and mother to sophisticated FLN activist who can pass for French is motivated by her transgressive (and reciprocated) desire for Amin, the handsome young FLN cell leader who first teaches her to write her name (the content of the first flashback). Out of (repressed) love for Amin and obedience to the cause with which she identifies, Aya starts to become involved in FLN activities, aided and abetted at various times by other (French) women, for example, the FLN supporter who gives her friendly advice (a cameo appearance by Bernadette Lafont), the hairdresser who allows her to take refuge in the shop with her children during the police raid, the elderly neighbour who shelters her from the police, whose sons had been taken away by the Gestapo in World War Two. She stops behaving like a traditional Algerian wife and mother and instead takes to the street to collect FLN dues, witnesses her husband's arrest, organizes Amin's escape, and eventually agrees to abandon her children and take on the identity of Rose Benoît, a Frenchwoman, in order to carry out more important missions (and be closer to Amin).

Dressed first of all in a sleeveless, blue-spotted summer dress (the same dress Fusilla wears thirty-five years later at the beginning of the film), Aya manages to pass for French (like the Arab women who carry bombs in Gillo Pontecorvo's *Battle of Algiers,* 1966), even though she has to learn how to walk in high heels and avoid contact with the men in the streets of Marseille. As Rose Benoît, she obediently transports arms and successfully (if reluctantly) carries out the assassination of a high-ranking police officer. Her problem comes with her supposition that the freedom of movement and action that she has assumed in her disguise as a Frenchwoman will not interfere with her 'original' identity as Aya. When, after the assassination, she at last gets Amin to express his love for her, she tries to please him by changing from her dark, tailored French suit into a beautiful embroidered Algerian dress, wanting to demonstrate to him that there are aspects of Algerian culture that French colonial rule has been unable to destroy. However, Amin is appalled and angry and orders her not to wear the dress again, presumably since her transgressive sexual and political behaviour is not reconcilable with the traditional image of Algerian womanhood that her dress invokes. In a key scene, for the first (and last) time Aya disobeys his orders and refuses to be confined to her French identity as Rose Benoît. She asserts that she is 'Aya, the daughter of Mohammed and Fatima Bouziane', and challenges Amin either to kill her or to accept that she will never lower her eyes to a man again. The moment confirms the ineradicable distance separating the repressed, islamic FLN male activist who earlier in the film, in line with FLN policy, had authorized the execution of a couple of adulterous lovers (a decision that continues to haunt Aya); and the woman who, thanks to her involvement in the revolutionary process, has become conscious of her own desires, but is forced to recognize that they are not compatible with the goals of the Algerian revolution.

After her confrontation with Amin, Aya is subjected to the processes of French justice: torture, imprisonment and trial. The camera pans over a number of other women prisoners, but Aya's voice-over recounts how numb and isolated she felt because, unlike them, she no longer has any illusions about the future. At the trial, shot schematically against blank backgrounds, red for the prosecution, blue for the defence and white for

Aya, Aya, dressed once again as Rose Benoît, goes through the motions and, as a prisoner of war, refuses to accept the jurisdiction of the court. The scene is used to make familiar points about the problematic identity of Algerians in France since, as the (Algerian) defence lawyer points out (a cameo performance by Hammou Graïa), as an Algerian living in France at the time of French colonial rule in Algeria, Aya is neither fully French (she does not have full rights of citizenship) nor fully Algerian (since she is a colonized subject). But attention is also drawn to her problematic gender identity. The prosecution vilifies her in the name of both French and Algerian values because she has abrogated her role as wife and mother. The defence, in contrast, offers an interpretation of her behaviour that, although unconvincing as a statement from the period, speaks perhaps for what the director would like spectators to believe, namely, that Aya is a model of female emancipation, a woman who has broken free from traditional constraints. Undoubtedly, the representation of Aya's active participation in the struggle for independence and defiance of Islamic law do challenge conventional representations of the subordinate, immigrant woman. But the idea that Aya is fully emancipated is undermined by her voice over, which draws attention back to the present day in which, having made the decision to stay in France on her release from prison rather than return to Algeria, she has exchanged her revolutionary ideals for the more conventional roles of wife and mother within the immigrant family, albeit in an apparently exemplary, Westernized fashion.

The surfacing of Aya's memories, which at first leads her to avoid contact with Amin, finally allows her to confront him, and to express her bitterness and disappointment in him. She tries to make him (and the spectator) see that the seeds of the fanaticism to come in an independent Algeria were already present in the way he allowed the application of Islamic law to police their personal relationship. She criticizes what is happening in Algeria to-day, in particular the imposition of the Family Code, and people's failure to speak out against it, and she chides Amin for standing by and allowing his own son to impose the wearing of the veil on his wife. (The fact that Amin's son is an Islamic fundamentalist likely to denounce his own father underlines the failure of the revolutionary project for Amin, too.) The film ends with Aya, who at the beginning of the film had refused to leave her domestic interior, accompanying Amin to the bus stop with her daughter and grand-daughter. The rural setting and musical accompaniment of this sequence recall the moment in the past when Amin and Aya had first embraced and Amin had expressed his vision of the future. This time it is Aya who comforts Amin, and expresses her own vision of an Algeria where men would themselves achieve liberation by recognizing that the country's wealth and strength lies in the liberation of its women. As the camera pulls away, the image of Amin travelling back towards a troubled Algeria is intercut with images of what he is leaving behind, namely, Aya, her daughter and her grand-daughter, three women of three different generations whose place is now in France. At the same time, Amin's voice-over from the future suggests that he has been able to learn something from Aya. When they first embraced, he quoted the Islamic saying, 'Where mothers tread lies paradise.' Now he can respond to Aya's question about women (as opposed to mothers) with the answer, which explains the film's title, 'Where women tread lies truth.' The film's ending thus brings together the two narrative strands, past and present, woman's film and action drama, through the common thread of a feminist consciousness, the truth of which Aya is at last able to transmit to Amin. The film closes with a close-up of Aya's face, this time looking out on the world rather than within and, at last, with the hint of a smile on her lips.

Conclusion

Both these films construct active but troubled female subjects through fragmented narratives which cut from place to place in *Souviens-toi de moi*, and between present and past in *Sous les pieds des femmes*. In each case, however, the film's ending allows the central protagonist to piece together the fragments and move towards some form of acceptance of herself and her conflicting loyalties (in *Souviens-toi de moi*) or suppressed dreams (in *Sous les pieds des femmes*), in a resolution which firmly recognizes that her place and future lies in France. In the process, both offer significant challenges to contemporary male-authored films treating the same material. *Souviens-toi de moi* turns away from questions relating to violence and criminality in the *banlieue* and constructs a series of feminized spaces where male figures can be marginalized or mocked (though it remains sympathetic to the disempowered immigrant Algerian father and his son). *Sous les pieds des femmes* similarly refuses to locate historical agency in a story of male heroism, even though Aya's menfolk are both FLN activists. Instead, the film is constructed through the reflections of an intelligent, heroic woman, and relegates the two men to the role of either domesticated partner (Moncef) or (unsatisfactory) object of desire (Amin). Moreover, Krim's re-working of the past functions not just as a contribution towards the construction of a collective memory for second-generation Algerian immigrants, nor as a feminist counter-history to dominant histories of the Algerian War (though these elements

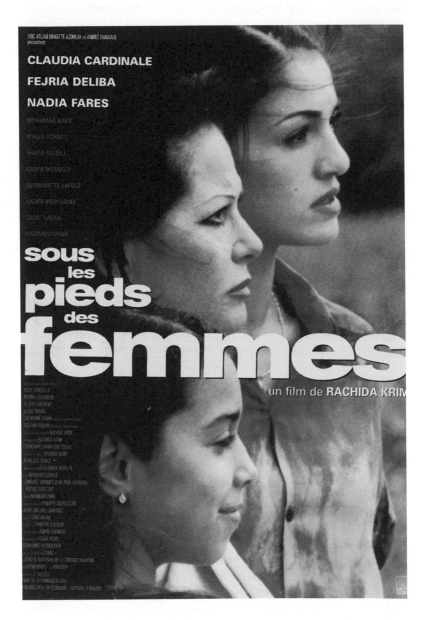

Figure 8. Three generations of women, taken from the poster of *Sous les pieds des femmes* (photograph by Sébastien Raymond, courtesy of MPA).

are important), but also as a way of demonstrating how the past informs the present, and so offering a critical purchase on current conflicts in Algeria and the injustices of traditional Algerian/Islamic patriarchal values.

Taken together, these films also represent an important shift in focus, the first foregrounding the 'second generation' daughter, the second foregrounding the 'first generation' immigrant mother. It is interesting, therefore, to compare their representations of the different generations and daughter-mother relationships. *Souviens-toi de moi* draws at first on the idea of a second generation 'torn between two cultures', even as it shows how Mimouna is eventually able to draw strength from her hybrid identity, thanks to her relationships with her Algerian cousins and her French girlfriends. Mimouna's (nameless) unassimilated immigrant mother, who is herself torn between her longing for her homeland and her duty to her children, represents one of the cultures against which the daughter needs to rebel, and the resulting tensions between daughter and mother are not resolved within the film's diegesis (even if Mimouna's change in attitude opens up the possibility of future accommodation). In *Sous les pieds des femmes*, in contrast, the second generation daughter, Fusilla, shows none of the anxiety and distress that characterizes Mimouna and appears to assume, quite unproblematically, a stable, hybrid identity (though her role is not explored in any depth). Instead the film foregrounds her love and admiration for the mother whose assimilation is revealed to have been a knowing masquerade. Aya's critique of the way Algerian women are treated in Islamic law, and her demonstration through her own life of what Algerian women can achieve (and at what cost), establish her as an important role model for the younger generations, not just through Fusilla (who identifies with her defiant spirit by wearing her blue-spotted dress), but also through Fusilla's daughter (and thereby, hopefully, the spectator) who hangs on to her every word.

The two films, then, seem to be representing different stages in the process of integration, the difference between them being due in part, perhaps, to the fact that Ghorab-Volta's film project first took shape in the 1980s. However, in each case, by telling their mothers' stories as well as their own, the two daughter-filmmakers are contributing to the process by which the younger generations of French citizens of Algerian origin can construct a collective memory, assume their Algerian heritage and come to terms with their hybrid identity. In both films, it is the ability to recover and integrate aspects of the suppressed Algerian dimension of their identity (whilst maintaining a critique of the Islamic sex-gender system) which offers the women based in France most hope for the future.

The appearance of these films, with their particular emphasis on how women contribute to Algerian history and culture, suggests, paradoxically, that women of Algerian origin are now sufficiently confident of their place in France to be at last able to claim their roots.

Notes

1. An earlier, shorter version of this chapter was given as a paper at the conference on *Refocusing: Women Filmmakers*, Vancouver, March 1999. Some of the material on *Souviens-toi de moi* has also appeared in an earlier article (Tarr, 1997b).
2. In fact, since the early 1980s, Maghrebi women have been making documentary videos and short films, predating the 'Beur' cinema phenomenon of the mid-1980s. Among these are two fictionalized, autobiographical shorts by Farida Belghoul: *C'est Madame la France que tu préfères?* (1981), in which the 'Beurette' character (played by Belghoul herself) has to convince her brother that it is acceptable for her to live independently in Paris, having told her family that she is at University in Grenoble; and *Le Départ du père* (1983), in which Belghoul accompanies her father to Algeria and is unable to decide whether to persuade him to return to France or to stay there with him. Two more recent shorts, *Le Petit chat est mort* (1992) by actress Fejria Deliba and *Le Silence* (1996) by Saafa Fathy, show a continuing preoccupation with women's problematic identity in relation to the patriarchal values of the Algerian immigrant family. In *Le Petit chat est mort*, a teenage daughter confronts her mother over their different attitudes towards appropriate gender roles; and in *Le Silence*, a young girl suffers in silence from the lack of communication between herself and her father.
3. Despite the work of Caribbean filmmakers like Euzhan Palcy (Martinique) and Elsie Haas (Haiti), not to mention numerous West African women filmmakers, there have as yet been no French feature films by metropolitan-based women of Caribbean or African origin. However, in 1998, a short, experimental film exploring issues relating to white/black bodies, *Le Génie d'Abou* (1997), directed by Isabelle Boni-Claverie, of Ivoirian origin, was shown at the Créteil International Women's Film Festival (Thackway, 1999).

4. See Amrane-Minne (1994, pp. 164–77) for testimonies by Algerian women active within the FLN's French Federation. See also Stora (1992, pp. 340–2, 310–13) for the historical background to the FLN's activities in the Alès and Avignon region, and a few facts and figures about Algerian women's active participation in demonstrations and hunger strikes in France during the Algerian War.
5. See Tarr (1997b).
6. Most films by male filmmakers of Maghrebi origin also situate their characters in relation to the immigrant Algerian family and Algerian culture, whereas white-authored *banlieue* films tend to isolate characters of Maghrebi origin from their family background (Tarr, 1999).
7. The films of Malik Chibane, *Hexagone* (1994) and *Douce France* (1995), exceptionally, provide sympathetic, realistically constructed, young female secondary characters (Tarr, 1995; 1999) and are open to the possibility of shifts in gender roles within the Maghrebi community for both women and men. Karim Dridi's *Bye Bye* (1995) includes a complex portrait of the contemporary immigrant mother.
8. The documentary film, *Mémoires d'immigrés* by Yasmina Benguigui (1997), similarly contributes to the work of constructing a collective memory for its French citizens of Algerian origin (see Durmelat, next chapter).
9. *Vivre au paradis* also constructs strong (though secondary) female characters active within the FLN. However, the film's period setting makes it less open to reflection on gender roles in the present.
10. The film also suggests that integration may be easier for women than for men in that, in the typical *banlieue* film, access to a disco/nightclub regularly figures as a trope of exclusion for its young male protagonists.
11. This analysis treats one particular sequence of the film in terms of its similarity to nineteenth-century orientalist paintings, whilst, paradoxically, indicating how the film inscribes the spectator quite differently from these paintings and foregrounds its subjective standpoint.

–11–

Transmission and Mourning in *Mémoires d'immigrés: l'héritage maghrébin*: Yamina Benguigui as 'Memory Entrepreneuse'

Sylvie Durmelat

Mémoires d'immigrés: l'héritage maghrébin (1997), a 160-minute documentary film directed by Yamina Benguigui, has already established itself as 'the great film' on the topic of immigration (Leclère, 1997, p. 78). Benguigui's aim was to tell the stories of Maghrebi immigrants in France, first and foremost to their children who know only fragments of these stories, but also to the indigenous French ('les Français de souche') who share this history (p. 80). This objective is clearly set out from the beginning of the film. One of the fathers interviewed declares: 'Our children are here today. They must know why we are here, why we came, how we came, what conditions we worked in, and how our life has been spent.'[1] Benguigui's basic task, then, is to construct, with the help of oral accounts, a place for the collective memory of Maghrebi immigration in France, a memory that has hitherto been marked by national amnesia (Noiriel, 1995), the silence of the parents, and the ignorance, or rather, the indifference of French society.

The frequently cited figures – 350 interviews, two years of preparation, nine months of editing, 600 hours of rushes and a budget of fifty million francs – present the documentary as the result of a long gestation (nine months on the editing table) and endow it with an accrued legitimacy. They also attest to its aim to represent a wide range of opinion, ensured by interviews with all the 'great' and 'small' actors, firstly politicians, then the fathers, mothers and children, who have together woven the history of Maghrebi immigration in France.

The documentary was jointly produced by and for the private television channel, Canal Plus, and Bandits Productions. It was funded not just by the typical institutional sponsors of projects related to immigration, such as the FAS (Fonds d'Action Sociale pour les travailleurs immigrés et leurs familles/Social Action Fund for immigrant workers and their families) and the Ministère de l'Aménagement du territoire, de la ville et de l'intégration (Ministry of Integration and National, Regional and Urban Development),[2] but also by a few, somewhat less typical sponsors, those normally devoted to the mainstream culture industry, such as the Centre National du Cinéma (National Cinema Centre) and the Ministère de la Culture (Ministry of Culture). Benguigui, director of an earlier, successful television documentary for France 2, *Femmes d'Islam* (1994), had already proven herself a competent filmmaker, and gained the trust of the principal film and television production networks.

Mémoires d'immigrés was first broadcast on Canal Plus in May 1997, then again in June 1997. It was hailed unanimously by the critics as a necessary testimony: 'THE document on immigration' (Leclère, 1997, p. 157), and in January 1998 it was released in the cinema, the ultimate recognition for a documentary. Before and after its release on the big screen, Benguigui accompanied public screenings of her film in schools and local communities, participating in the ensuing debates.[3] In this manner, she was able to coax other fathers and mothers into speaking, encouraging them to go out of their way to come and 'see themselves', and thus allowing their words a hitherto unheard-of circulation.

Since its broadcast on Canal Plus, *Mémoires d'immigrés* has received the 'Sept d'or' (the French television award) for best documentary, the Special Prize at the Festival International de Production Audiovisuelle (International Festival of Audiovisual Production), and the Golden Gate Award in San Francisco (Mauraisin, 1998, p. 37). Finally, Benguigui's book, *Mémoires d'immigrés: l'héritage maghrébin*, which brings together various testimonies (apart from those of the officials), including some which do not appear in the documentary, was released shortly afterwards in July 1997 by Editions Canal Plus, then by Albin Michel. A CD reprising the music of the film is also in the pipeline. *Mémoires d'immigrés* thus constitutes a successful, even profitable televisual, cultural and economic operation, indicating that 'immigration' as a cultural object is finally *showable* and, more importantly, acceptable. At the start of the 1998 television season, Benguigui became the co-host of a bi-monthly programme entitled *Place de la République*, which addressed issues relating to integration and the communities emerging from immigration. This new role suggests the need to rethink the place that the documentary and its director seek to hold in this same Republic.

It seems to me that the notion of 'memory entrepreneur', as defined by Gérard Noiriel (using texts on memory by Max Weber and Maurice

Yamina Benguigui as 'Memory Entrepreneuse'

Halbwachs) allows for a good understanding of Benguigui's project. According to Noiriel (1995, p. 380), for a collective memory to emerge, individual recollections must necessarily be objectivized by a process of naming, fixed in writing, but also continuously recalled by monuments and other forms of commemoration. Individual actors can thus link their personal experiences to a shared, collective representation of the past. In order to do this, the role of 'memory entrepreneurs' is crucial, for it is they who choose which individual experiences best represent their cause and then transform these into collective memory.

Throughout her research and the nine months of editing, Yamina Benguigui fully assumed the function and mission of a 'memory entrepreneuse'.[4] Indeed, her function as a transmitter of memories was reinforced by the fact that, on an individual level, her documentary allowed her to give meaning to her own experiences:

> Through filmmaking I thought I could distance myself from my own story. But it was cinema which brought me back to it. It's not as though I had forgotten where I came from or who I was. It is just that I rarely thought about *why* . . . Cinema lent me an identity – as a director – so that I could reconstruct the one I was neglecting – as a daughter of immigrants.' [5] (Groupement national des cinémas de recherche, 1998, p. 3)

Benguigui has not spoken to her father since the age of eighteen, when she left home after breaking his rules concerning marriage and reproduction (though according to her mother, her father closely follows her career) (Chane-Tune, 1997, p. 134; Leclère, 1997, p. 78). Through her film, Benguigui has found a subterfuge to make herself her father's heir, practically despite him. Since, as she claims: 'I still don't know my father's story. I've never known exactly how he came to France'[6] (Leclère, 1997, p. 80), she has been forced to find a detour via a cultural artefact, the documentary, to create a heritage that her father, due both to the disruption created by immigration and to his daughter's rupture with the rules of his culture of origin, was either unable or unwilling to pass on.

As a 'memory entrepreneuse', Benguigui has begun to accumulate symbolic, cultural and economic capital, which accredits her as a legitimate representative and agent of the transmission of memories about the history of Maghrebi immigration, and so enables her to become, finally, her father's daughter. If, as she states: 'behind this film is the idea of a reconciliation'[7] (p. 80), it is played out on several levels: between the Maghrebi community and the so-called host society, between immigrant parents and their children, and, symbolically, between Benguigui

Figure 9. Yamina Benguigui (courtesy of Bandits Productions).

and her father. The film thus constitutes a kind of image-based homage to the absent, silent father. The choice of Super 16, requiring a large technical team and heavy equipment, rather than video, a lighter, more flexible and intimate technology, contributes towards the aim of constructing a commemorative monument and reinforces the film's ultimate message about the need for/lack of burial places for immigrant parents in French soil.[8] A poetic and occasionally elegiac work, *Mémoires d'immigrés* serves as a kind of *tombeau* in the dual sense of the term, both a burial place and a poetic work dedicated to the dead or to those who are soon to die.

The legitimacy enjoyed by this documentary, its undisputed level of authority, its wide circulation, and Benguigui's explicitly stated objective, namely, to make a work of reconciliation, beg the question as to how the conditions of production and broadcasting by and for television (and subsequently the cinema) have conditioned her discourse, all the while making it possible. Because the director seeks to provoke her audience's emotion and empathy towards immigrants and their families, while presenting an eminently respectable, dignified and often nostalgic image of the Maghrebi community, the film tends to euphemize or omit less consensual elements. Through an analysis of the film's structure and images, as well as through a few comparisons with the book released shortly afterwards, I would like to examine those aspects of Benguigui's project that give it its strength and originality, as well as its paradoxes and compromises, necessary for the transmission and acceptance of its message.

Mémoires d'immigrés is composed of three sections of equal length that both separate and link the 'fathers', 'mothers' and 'children'. This structure has been variously qualified as a triptych, a trilogy, and a saga. The pictorial quality of the Super 16 image, the unique character of each of the three sections, and the way they are articulated, chronologically and thematically, emerge from the triptych. As in a trilogy or saga offering an epic family history, Benguigui steers away from an event-based, historical chronology, such as that espoused by politicians, historians and sociologists. Instead, she uses time markers extracted from the real-life experience of both families and individuals, 'I didn't want any more political or historical discourses on immigration, either. It is important to get back to ordinary people and their experiences.'[9] (p. 79). By showing the history of immigration as a family history in terms of filiation and genealogy (although she also integrates, as a kind of guiding chronological thread, interviews with the politicians and economic decision-makers of the time), Benguigui makes her narrative much more accessible. Through the model of the family saga, a popular French television genre, Benguigui introduces a recognizable, easily reproducible periodization with which each of the participants can identify, as well as the audience.

This family temporality is crucial for the film's goal of commemoration. As Alfred Grosser emphasizes, so-called 'collective memory' is less an actual memory than 'transmission via the family, school and the media' (Nicolaïdis, 1994, p. 208). In the case of Maghrebi immigration, this memory has only been transmitted by its absence. In her book (and in the leaflet that accompanied the film at the time of its cinema release), Benguigui asks: 'What have you done to my father? What have you done to my mother? What have you done to my parents to make them so mute? What did you say to them to make them so unwilling to root us in this land where we were born?' [10] (Benguigui, 1997, p. 9). The construction of an audio-televisual memory seeks to combat the illegitimacy that plagues the children's generation, both in the eyes of their parents and in the perspective of the host society: 'Our parents never gave us roots. Neither did the state and French society, obviously. No-one ever said, you are citizens. We have to create our own roots. Through the vote and many other ways.' [11] (Leclère, 1997, p. 81). The expression 'creating roots' highlights the fact that this documentary, a kind of prosthetic root, is an attempt at constructing a collective memory (rather than a more obviously historical project), the clearly stated objective of which is to promote, shamelessly, a discourse in favour of integration. Her documentary, like the electoral vote she mentions, is a civic and republican act. The rehabilitation of the immigrant father and mother paradoxically allows for access to the national symbolic.

The tripartite structure establishes a temporality for Maghrebi immigration that insists on the children's rightful presence in France and so seeks to produce a social space in its own right for the new generations (rather than a problematic space inbetween two cultures). Thus Benguigui's documentary, like other recent cultural productions emphasizing the memory of immigration,[12] clearly breaks with *le mythe du retour* ('the myth of the return home'), as well as with other types of differentialist discourses (like the celebration of marginality and inbetweenness, or the exoticism of hybridity). This break is effected by a vigorous reclamation of Frenchness (Labro, 1997, p. 64). But at what price? The choice of the three groups, fathers, mothers and children, excludes other possibilities. The Maghrebi populations settled in France since the first half of the twentieth century go unmentioned, as do non-economic migrants like the *harkis* (Algerian soldiers who fought for the French during the Algerian war of independence) and their families, the inclusion of which would render the notion of a Maghrebi heritage less self-evident.

On the other hand, the choice of three sections emerges from the strategic use of a certain ethnic logic. Benguigui claims: 'The fathers would not have been able to speak in front of their wives and children about the brutality of their recruitment. I had to respect cultural codes and question them separately'[13] (Humblot, 1997, p. 3). She thus emphasizes that cultural codes, the sense of honour and the duty of modesty, are as rigorous for the fathers as for the mothers; she thereby avoids reproducing the stereotype of the silenced, oppressed Arab woman, and shows how men are also silenced. Consequently, each section possesses its own colouring and tone. Benguigui films the fathers alone, most often outside, in their place of work. The mothers are filmed in pairs, inside or on their doorstep, a space with connotations of femininity. The section devoted to the children includes testimonies from both sexes, emphasizing throughout the rapidity of the phenomenon of acculturation. They are filmed either in groups of well-behaved youths in their early teens, or individually, and in their workplace, at home, or in the urban spaces that have marked their childhood – what remains of an *hôtel dortoir* (a long-stay dormitory hotel) for Mounsi, the site of the former shantytown in Nanterre for Ahmed Djamaï.

For the fathers, Benguigui favours workplace locations – defunct Renault warehouses on the Ile Séguin for Khémais Dabous, dilapidated mines in the north of France for Abdellah Samate and Mohamed Toukal. Using panning shots to present the industrial landscape, she marks out the limits of the men's horizons, bounded as they have been by daily labour. In one mine, a tower filmed from a low angle with a backward zoom, appears both crushing (compared with Abdellah's silhouette) and derisory, the mine being abandoned and decrepit. The image implicitly compares the fathers to their work tools, rusted and defunct. However, the sound track avoids exploiting the fathers and dispossessing them of their labour yet again, for their voice-over statements become a guiding commentary that organizes the image. When, filmed on his balcony, Khémais Dabous appears quite small in contrast with the background formed by the factory premises, his voice-over commentary recalls the indifference of Renault towards its immigrant workers.[14] Despite his smallness on screen, his voice overlaps with the images that illustrate his words, and his status as the interpreter and analyst of his own experience is thereby consolidated. The interjection of black-and-white archive film, punctuated with songs of exile by Slimane Azem and Dahmane El Harachi, give this section a comparatively less warm and colourful tone than that of the mothers. The fathers barely speak about their family lives, though they always mention their children as the ultimate rationale for their lives as workers in France.

A series of dissolves presents the faces of the mothers, filmed in extreme close-up, in slow motion, in colour, and bathed with a warm light, all to the sound of a slow, nostalgic song by Dalida (female singers here replacing the male ones). This mini video-clip sequence coaxes forth the emotion and support of the audience, and compensates for the relative absence of archive material about the women, otherwise made up for by

Figure 10. Two of the mothers in *Mémoires d'immigrés* (courtesy of Bandits Productions).

the recourse to private archives and family photos, enlarged and detailed by the camera. The industrial landscapes give way to interiors. The mothers' horizons are bounded by the walls of their houses, covered with trinkets and photographs of their children. This universe is more corporeal, less ghostly than that of the fathers. It is also distinguished by the emphasis on the women's suffering – imposed marriages and children, being shut up in insalubrious hovels, illiteracy, finding difficulty in getting their bearings as well as merely getting around, and all without the security blanket of the extended family – retold here through the medium of conversation and often punctuated by laughter with the other woman present. Once again, Benguigui sets out to make characters out of her speakers. Following the interview with Khira Allam, the camera lingers on the decor of her room, on her photographs, but also on the impressive number of alarm clocks and other clocks placed here and there, six or seven in total. These shots do not serve the needs of the argument, but rather create what Barthes (1982) calls a 'reality effect'. This woman is more than a Maghrebi immigrant, she is a person with her own tastes and her own funny little manias.

The final section presents groups of young teenagers as well as the individual testimonies of relatively well-established young adults in their thirties. Exterior shots of blocks of flats (HLM) repeatedly fill the screen. We see clusters of young teenagers gesturing, running, or walking around the housing estates, without hearing them. We also see interviewees at home, with books, pianos and a more contemporary decor in the background. The change in *mise en scène* discreetly emphasizes how some of the 'children' have achieved social advancement. A panning shot that highlights this transition begins with a view of the HLM façades, only to dissolve mid-way to a view of the more opulent-looking façades of apartment buildings in the city centre. Is this transition, then, simply a question of façades?

Thanks to the way the three sections are balanced and separated, Benguigui ensures the free speech of each of the interviewees and shows how differences in sex and generation affect the experiences of all three groups. However, this structure also tends to give the impression that events and experiences are on an equal footing, and that the balance that governs them in the film translates their balance in reality. By avoiding confrontation and reproducing the division between masculine and feminine spheres, does Benguigui not in fact limit the representation of the power relations that inform both family and community? At the heart of the section on the mothers, the speakers make reference to various tensions and conflicts. 'Freedom, I took it and I gave it to my children', says Yamina Baba Aïssa, 'I would never have done to my daughters what was done to me.'[15] 'My parents never wanted me to attend school. I got my revenge with my children,' recalls Aldjia Bouachera.[16] Four of the five interviews with the mothers describe how they have progressively assumed non-traditional roles. By positioning this questioning within the section on the mothers, whilst reinforcing the family structure as a presentation strategy, Benguigui chooses not to foreground questions of sexual difference, preferring to concentrate on the need to construct a collective memory, her ultimate goal. Far from silencing these questions, however, she puts them at the heart of her documentary.

Several technical and aesthetic effects combine to create a strong sense of unity between the three sections. One of the most remarkable is the way in which the director's presence is effectively erased from the proceedings. Benguigui prepared and led the interviews, 'telling her own story to gain people's trust' (Humblot, 1997, p. 3). In the editing process, however, she chose to erase signs of her presence, both on the screen and on the sound track, in order to privilege what her interviewees have to say. This, in conjunction with the absence of a guiding voice-over commentary and the relative paucity of insert titles, reinforces the impact of the speakers' voices. The witnesses on the screen seem to address the audience directly, a method of presentation which allows the parents to be constructed as historical agents rather than victims. The film thus avoids the pitfall of *misérabilisme* while producing an effect of objectivity.

The absence of voice-overs, an effect usually employed to guide the audience, is compensated for by precise and meticulous editing. For example, the testimony of Abdellah Samate, a Moroccan immigrant, echoes earlier statements made by workforce selector Joël Dahoui. Abdellah speaks about the selector's handshake, intended to check for calluses and thus to verify that the candidate is well suited for manual labour. Benguigui chooses not to include the harshest comments made by Joël Dahoui (Leclère, 1997, p. 80), nor does she explicitly highlight the often shocking comments made by certain officials. She prefers to comment on them indirectly, using other testimonies or archive images as a counterpoint. This presentation technique corresponds with her desire to avoid 'the pitfalls of the denunciatory film' and 'attacking the television viewer' (pp. 79–80).

Despite her visible absence, the framing of the image allows Benguigui to channel the viewer's sympathies. In general, she first presents the fathers, mothers and children in their environment, using a long shot or medium shot. Then, as soon as the interview begins, we move with the camera into the house, office or factory. The camera then favours the close-up, framed just below the shoulders or at chest-level. At the most affecting moments, when the speakers describe their suffering or humiliation, an extreme close-up focuses on their faces, corresponding both to the plunge into the past and to its recollection. At the end of the interviews, a reprised long shot re-establishes a distance from each individual, like a goodbye to a person we have grown close to. This play on distance cues the emotion and support of the audience. In contrast, the officials of the period are most often filmed in their offices – with their books or the insignia of the Republic in the background – and positioned behind a table, a supplementary obstacle between them and the camera. This creates a greater distance between them and the viewer (while the use of a few extreme close-ups assumes an ironic function). Rather than eliciting the viewer's support and conviction through indignation and indictment, Benguigui prefers to facilitate emotional identification with her characters, all the while retaining the legitimizing seal of objectivity.

The film is punctuated by recurring images of the boat and the liner, the use of emotionally charged songs in Arabic and Berber and the recurrence of certain archive images which establish a certain progression between the three sections. The images of the liner and the boat function like a *mise en abîme*, both of the voyages undertaken by the immigrants themselves, and of the documentary and its establishment of lines of communication. A brief shot of the shimmering sea echoes Khémais' dreams about life in France as he recounts his first Mediterranean crossing. A few seconds later, the liner in the Mediterranean gives way to a barge passing the Île Séguin in the Seine and the Renault warehouses, thus designating the culmination of Khémais's odyssey in the grey landscape of the car industry. The imagery of boats arriving in the first section is mirrored by the image of a young girl staring at a boat leaving the port of Marseille in the second section, symbolic of the implantation of the newly arrived mothers on the other shore of the Mediterranean. The interview with two Algerian mothers from the Panier district of Marseille concludes with a shot of Mekia Gomri and her grandson on the 'Ferry Boat', a miniature liner, giving a birds-eye view of the crossing of Marseille's Old Port. This reprise of the theme of crossing, at a more low-key, local, everyday level, signals that the voyage is continuing within metropolitan France, albeit with new issues at stake.

The songs of Kabyle singers Slimane Azem and Dahmane El Arachi give way to Idir, Dalida, and Enrico Macias, the latter a *pied noir* artist chosen by Kira Allam to speak of her nostalgia for Algeria, then to the *raï* of Cheb Mami and Cheb Hasni and, finally, to Rachid Taha, formerly of the group Carte de Séjour, to accompany the children's section. These songs, embedded throughout the film, signal moments of emotion, endow the film with greater unity, and win the audience's collective participation and sympathy, while at the same time serving as a kind of cement for the various fragments of the cut-and-pasted interviews. Aside from their function as entertainment, for the immigrant audience this familiar music confers a seal of authenticity upon the documentary, reinforcing the adherence of individual memories to the collective representation being offered them. Songs and music also accompany the opening and closing black-and-white archive images. These images represent silhouettes of slow-moving men, whose silence accentuates their ghostly quality. The songs and music render them even more poignant and seek to fill the emptiness left by the fathers' silence, the silence which Rachid Kaci claims in the third section to be so loud in his head.

At the beginning of the film, inserted within a series of black-and-white, slow motion archive images in which the camera focuses on a man's face, is the image in colour of Abdellah Samate, followed by that of Mohammed Toukal, both of whom ask the questions that open the film. The slow motion proceeds in part from a desire to pause on the anonymous faces that viewers have never really taken the trouble to look at before, with the hope of turning them into characters. The editing establishes a continuity between them and the contemporary witnesses before us in the film, as well as a decisive rupture in the way they are treated in the televisual and media image. In the present time of the film, they address the viewer directly, without an intermediary, and their silence gives way to their testimony. The move to colour functions as an exorcism of the ghostly images of furtive-looking men which haunt the memory of their children. It allows them to be reincarnated in flesh and blood and also rooted in French soil, a rooting whose final stage, the documentary suggests, would be burial in French ground.

At the end, after a few images of Muslim sections in French cemeteries and inscriptions in Arabic on the tombs, a statement reads, 'In France there are currently 50 designated Muslim burial sections, 1 Muslim cemetery'.[17] This image then slowly dissolves to show figures of men in slow motion, using the same archive material presented at the very beginning of the film. The editing here creates an effect of circularity and return, accentuated by the fact that these images of men literally emerge from the cemetery, like poorly buried ghosts coming back to reclaim their due. The last image of the film is also a quotation, duplicated from a black-and-white archive image already present at the beginning of the film. A man, an immigrant, passes furtively in front of a piece of graffiti, 'France for the French' ('La France aux Français'), on which the image focuses. Benguigui's camera sends this graffiti to the viewer as an echo, reminding us how these words have continued to circulate. However, on its second appearance within the film, the graffiti assumes quite a different meaning. This time it is accompanied by a contemporary song by Rachid Taha: 'Look, look, it's starting again, everywhere, everywhere throughout sweet France',[18] which alludes to the eternal return of anti-Maghrebi racism. The placing of this last image at a final point is more than a quiet warning against rampant racism. The choice of a song in French from an offspring of immigration is a way of saying that France is for the French of Maghrebi origin too.

The slow motion endows the filmic image with a photographic quality, frozen in time. It also has the effect of creating a kind of patina and increasing the nostalgia that the documentary distills, often ambiguously, as in the reuse of old songs currently back in fashion.[19] Through the reuse of songs of exile and the repetition of archive images in slow motion, Benguigui succeeds in creating a temporal 'thickness' and an authoritative periodization (the fathers, the mothers, the children), which recreate the past as a lost, distant time that can only be transmitted as absence, or phantom.

For Derrida: 'To be haunted by a ghost is to have a memory of something one has not lived through in the present, to have the memory of something which, basically, has never had the form of presence. Cinema is a "fantomachie" (a struggle with ghosts)'[20] (Derrida, 1996, p. 129). In this respect, Benguigui's documentary participates in a form of ambiguous nostalgia, a call to memory not intended to confront history directly but rather to shrug it off, and thus render it less sorrowful. The aestheticization of the archive image, filled with emotion, endows the documentary with what Arjun Appadurai (1996, pp. 75–85) calls a 'patina'. This patina accords a legitimacy and a kind of seniority to France's Maghrebi community that some have hitherto refused to acknowledge. It also sparks in the children of migration, as well as in the non-Maghrebi audience, a certain nostalgia for the memory they have not lived firsthand. Nostalgia aroused in such a manner renders the collective experience more digestible, and participates in the construction of a temporality and a periodicity that allow for the imagining of a new social space.

However, this project of reconciliation, with its strong integrationist message, strategic and necessary though it may be, is conceived on the basis of certain important gaps and silences. The most important of these concerns the absence of youths from the *banlieue* and, especially, of the young adolescents whom we notice in groups around the tower blocks, but who are not given a voice. Benguigui preferred to use professionally and socially well-established young adults in their thirties, claiming:

> I interviewed young people aged between 18 and 25, but I put these images aside. They are not mature. They shout out their hatred for society. It's always 'France's fault'. They live in a state of resentment. For this reason I preferred to let people speak who had gone beyond this stage, people whose discourse is better worked out.[21] (Leclère, 1997, p. 81)

But what exactly is a discourse which has been 'worked out'? The 'beurgeoisie' that she presents has, in effect, learned how to code its demands in a language palatable to the host society, just as Benguigui has done with her documentary. One of Benguigui's objectives was to show the suffering of both parents and children and, at the same time, win the support of her audience. Clearly it is much more difficult to coax an audience into identifying with young men whose suffering often has no other outlet than verbal and sometimes physical, albeit highly ritualized, violence. By not giving a voice to these teenagers, one might ask whether Benguigui is not actually reproducing the social, professional and symbolic exclusion through which this section of the adolescent population is victimized. She convincingly breaks down the mechanisms that have led to the exclusion of the fathers, but she does not shed any light on the ways in which these same mechanisms are reproduced, at least in part, to victimize their children. By lingering on the past in slow motion, Benguigui does not show the urgency of the present or the more negative aspects of the Maghrebi heritage.

In a sense, Benguigui is striving to defuse the stereotypical imagery typical of the French media, by avoiding controversial subjects in vogue and refusing worn-out debates, the terms of which are beyond her control. Since assertions of difference and movements of resistance tend to reinforce the system they oppose (Certeau, 1994; Chambers, 1991), conciliation may serve to defuse the perverse effects of such a reappropriation. However, it may be that a class distance is emerging between the first-generation élite, endowed with the legitimacy granted them by the host society in search of token representatives, and the children of immigrants suffering the full consequences of the economic crisis, as well as the accumulation of various social, geographic and cultural exclusions and handicaps.

Other important absences result from this project of reconciliation. The Algerian War is presented very rapidly as a backdrop with the help of archive images of the period. This may be due to the fact that the war did not have a lasting impact on the continual flux of migration into France, as both Benguigui, in her book, and Jean-François Ceyrac, the ex-manager of the CNPF (the French employers' association) in the documentary, emphasize. Indeed, the number of immigrants actually increased both during and after the war. However, there is no mention of the fact that this same immigrant population, both men and women, played a decisive role in the war for Algerian independence by collecting funds for the armed struggle in Algeria, guaranteeing supply bases to the FLN (Front de Libération Nationale/National Liberation Front) and constituting a meeting place between students, migrants and future political leaders. A stronger emphasis on the Algerian War might have reawakened old internal antagonisms and conflicts within the immigrant community, most notably between the rival nationalist groups, the MNA (Mouvement National Algérien/Algerian National Movement) and the FLN. Furthermore, the racial attacks of October 1961 are only briefly recalled by a few journal clippings, perhaps not explicitly enough for those members of the audience who have never heard of them, though these events are decisive in the history of Algerian immigrants in France.

Moreover, no mention is made of controversial issues such as the so-called 'headscarves' affairs, the construction of mosques on French soil, or the fathers' and mothers' religious practices. Benguigui includes testimonies about Ramadan, the burial of Maghrebis in France, outside Islamic lands, and the repatriation of bodies, but the emphasis here is on their function as identity markers in the perspective of a symbolic integration on and (literally) into French soil, rather than on their religious and ritual nature. On the other hand, she does include the two Algerian mothers from Marseille who declare with broad smiles, with the jubilation of someone telling a good joke, that they are going to the church of Notre Dame de la Garde to visit *la bonne mère*, the city's patron saint, at the Christmas midnight mass. The book which followed the film includes a dialogue with a young girl who had chosen to take the Islamic veil. This particular account was not kept in the film, perhaps because of the negative reactions it might have sparked among majority French audiences. In the book, the chapter is entitled, 'Naïma ou l'inconsciente tentation du couvent' ('Naïma, or the unconscious temptation of the convent'). The title betrays an explanatory, pedagogic project, intended both to make this choice understandable and to translate it into terms which would be familiar to a Christian readership, but also to render it less threatening, to soften it, while carefully handling the fears of the mainstream public by stressing that it proceeds from a new interpretation of the Muslim faith.[22]

The paradoxes of Benguigui's documentary stem from the fact that she wishes to create a common ground at the heart of the community as well as between the community and the society in which it has established itself. She is thus forced to euphemize references to both Islam and the colonial past, and she places the emphasis on other registers of collective self-representation that the Maghrebi community has at its disposal: their ethno-social belonging and the condition of immigrants, as highlighted by the title.[23] With this documentary, Benguigui acts as a symbolic operator of integration, to use Vincent Geisser's expression. As such, she is subjected to a double constraint: 'Demonstrating a relative intellectual and ideological conformity with the advocates of the system in place, that is, adhering to a discourse on integration' while at the same time 'remaining "ethnically visible"', so maintaining 'the illusion of a dialogue amongst the various cultural components of the national community'[24] (Geisser, 1996, p. 129). This is, perhaps, the creative constraint of Benguigui's work: to proclaim herself in favour of integration within the Republic, all the while consolidating the symbolic, historical and cultural capital of a potential Maghrebi community. She manages to weave a problematic continuity between these two projects which both elevates

Democratic
paradox

the parents' dead body to the realm of the sacred and avoids the anti-establishment violence, which is sporadically stirred up by the body of the younger generations.

Translated by John Ryan Poynter and Carrie Tarr

Notes

1. 'Nos enfants, ils sont là aujourd'hui. Il faudrait bien qu'ils sachent pourquoi on est ici, pourquoi on est venus, comment on est venus, et dans quelles conditions on a travaillé, et comment notre vie a passé.'
2. The FAS is a state agency that collects part of the social security and pension fund contributions paid by immigrant workers in order to fund and control a variety of cultural and social projects aimed at and/or organized by migrant communities and their children. The Ministry of Integration and National, Regional and Urban Development was created in the late 1980s, following riots between youth and the police in a Lyon suburb. Its main objective is to address the integration of disenfranchized youth from the *banlieues* (the peripheral working-class housing estates largely inhabited by immigrant populations and severely hit by unemployment).
3. On this subject, see the *Télérama* article (no. 2534-5, August 1998) entitled 'Le tour de France de Yamina Benguigui' ('Yamina Benguigui's Tour de France'), in which Véronique Brocard recounts the series of public debates in which Benguigui participated after the release of her film, including the strong exchanges and emotions she shared with the public. The title of the article and its overt allusion to the Tour de France seem to me more than an amusing wink at the reader. By comparing Benguigui to a racing cyclist who 'goes around the country, from city to city, reels under her arm' and 'makes herself available to the point of exhaustion' (Brocard, 1998, p. 40), Brocard identifies Benguigui's deep desire to inscribe herself within the heart of the national territory, a desire which informs her documentary. In his article on 'Le tour de France', published in *Lieux de mémoire*, Georges Vigarello reminds us that the tour is an 'inventory-cum-race' of the nation intended to illustrate and glorify the territory. In Benguigui's case, her impromptu tour of France, sparked off by the success of the

film, describes the extent to which the territory of the 'Hexagon' has been informed by the presence and history of Maghrebi immigration, each site and each visit becoming an occasion for the evocation of this history and its contribution towards the fashioning of the national territory. In this sense, her tour of France becomes indeed 'a take-over [of the territory] by force and skill' (Vigarello, 1990, p. 892). Thus, by integrating a previously unknown section of the population, a new human geography emerges from the old paradigm of the tour.

4. In her interview with Thierry Leclère (1997, p. 80), Benguigui states, 'I felt I was on a mission, with a huge responsibility on my shoulders. I was doubtful the whole time.'

5. 'Par le cinéma j'ai cru pouvoir m'éloigner de mon histoire. C'est précisément lui qui m'y ramène. Ce n'est pas que j'oubliais d'où je venais ou qui j'étais. C'est tout simplement que je songeais rarement au *pourquoi* ... Le cinéma m'a prêté une identité – celle de réalisatrice – pour reconstruire celle que je négligeais – fille d'immigrés.'

6. '[J]e ne connais toujours pas l'histoire de mon père. Je n'ai jamais su exactement comment il était venu en France.'

7. '[D]errière ce film, il y a l'idée d'une réconciliation.'

8. Benguigui explains, 'I didn't want a video. I wanted a real film'.

9. 'Je ne voulais pas non plus de discours politique ou historique sur l'immigration. Il faut en revenir aux hommes, et à ce qu'ils ont vécu.'

10. 'Qu'avez-vous fait de mes parents? Qu'avez-vous fait de ma mère? Qu'avez-vous fait de mes parents pour qu'ils soient aussi muets? Que leur avez-vous dit, pour qu'ils n'aient pas voulu nous enraciner sur cette terre, où nous sommes nés?'

11. 'Nos parents ne nous ont jamais enracinés. L'État et la société française non plus, c'est évident. Il nous faut fabriquer des racines. Cela passe par le vote aux élections et par bien des choses'

12. See for example the films *Sous les pieds des femmes* (Rachida Krim, 1998), *L'Autre côté de la mer* (Dominique Cabrera, 1997), *Le Gône du Chaâba* (Christophe Ruggia, 1998), adapted from the novel by Azouz Begag, and *Vivre au paradis* (Bourlem Guerdjou, 1999), adapted from the novel by Brahim Benaïcha.

13. '[L]es pères n'auraient pu dire, devant leur femme, leurs enfants, la brutalité de leur recrutement. Je devais garder les codes culturels, les interroger séparément.'

14. Immigrants were mostly employed as Ouvriers Spécialisés (OS), meaning assembly-line workers specializing in a particular task, unchanged and constantly repeated.

15. Yamina Baba Aïssa: 'La liberté, je l'ai prise et je l'ai donnée à mes enfants . . . Jamais je n'aurais fait à mes filles ce qu'on m'a fait.'
16. Aldjia Bouachera: 'Mes parents n'ont jamais voulu que je fasse d'études. Je me suis vengée sur mes enfants.'
17. 'Actuellement en France 50 carrés musulmans 1 cimitière musulman.'
18. 'Voilà, voilà que ça recommence, partout partout dans la douce France . . .'
19. The same work of memory is notable in Rachid Taha's 1998 album, *Diwan*, which brings together several classic titles, passionately reinterpreted and adapted to current musical tastes.
20. 'Etre hanté par un fantôme, c'est avoir la mémoire de ce qu'on n'a jamais vécu au présent, avoir la mémoire de ce qui au fond n'a jamais eu la forme de la présence. Le cinéma est une "fantomachie".'
21. 'J'ai interviewé ces jeunes, entre 18 et 25 ans, mais j'ai mis ces images de côté. Ils ne sont pas mûrs. Ils crient leur haine de la société. C'est toujours de "la faute de la France". Ils ne vivent que dans le ressentiment [. . .] C'est pour cette raison que j'ai préféré faire parler des gens qui ont dépassé ce stade et qui ont un discours construit.'
22. In the Muslim tradition, a religious and pious woman demonstrates her faith by marrying and having several children. In this respect, Naïma's choice seems more Christian than Muslim.
23. I refer here to the four registers of collective representation defined by Jocelyne Césari (1996): ethno-social belonging, the condition of immigrants, the postcolonial past, religious practice and/or identity.
24. '[F]aire preuve d'un relatif conformisme intellectuel et idéologique avec les tenants du système en place, c'est-à-dire adhérer au discours sur l'intégration', 'rester "ethniquement visible"', 'l'illusion d'un dialogue entre les diverses composantes de la communauté nationale'.

Bibliography

Abdelkrim-Chikh, R. (1988), 'Les femmes exogames: Entre la loi de Dieu et les droits de l'homme', *Annuaire de l'Afrique du Nord*, 27: 235–54.

Abou Saada, G. and Millet, H. (1986), *Générations issues de l'immigration*, Paris: Editions Arcantère.

Appadurai, A. (1996), *Modernity at Large: Cultural Dimemsions of Globalization*, Minneapolis: University of Minnesota Press.

Bachollet, R., Debost, J.-B., Lelieur, A.-C. and Peyrière, M.-C. (1994), *Négripub: L'image des Noirs dans la publicité*, Paris: Somogy.

Balibar, E. (1998), *Droit de cité*, La Tour d'Aigues: Editions de l'Aube.

Barison, N. and Catarino, C. (1997), 'Les femmes immigrées en France et en Europe', *Migrations Société*, 9, 52: 17–19.

Barlet, O. (1996), *Les Cinémas d'Afrique noire: le regard en question*, Paris: L'Harmattan.

Baron, B. (1989), 'Unveiling in early twentieth century Egypt: Practical and symbolic considerations', *Middle Eastern Studies*, 25, 3: 45–78.

Barthes, R. (1982), 'L'effet de réel', in G. Genette and T. Todorov (eds), *Littérature et réalité*, Paris: Seuil.

Basfao, K. (1990), 'Arrêt sur images: Les rapports franco-maghrébins au miroir de la bande dessinée', *Annuaire de l'Afrique du Nord*, 29: 225–35.

Benani, S. (1995a), 'Les Nanas Beurs', in *Immigrant women and integration,* Council of Europe Publications.

Benani, S. (1995b), 'Le voile et la citoyenneté', in M. Riot-Sarcey (ed.), *Démocratie et représentation,* Paris: Kimé.

Benguigui, Y. (1997), *Mémoires d'immigrés: l'héritage maghrébin*, Paris: Albin Michel.

Bentaieb, M. (1991), 'Les femmes étrangères en France', *Hommes et migrations,* 1141: 4–12.

Bentichou, N. (ed.) (1997), *Les femmes de l'immigration au quotidien,* Paris: L'Harmattan.

Beski, C. (1997), 'Les difficultés spécifiques aux jeunes filles issues de l'immigration Maghrébine', in N. Bentichou (ed.), *Les femmes de l'immigration au quotidien,* Paris: L'Harmattan.

Bibliography

Bhabha, H. K. (1994), *The Location of Culture*, London and New York: Routledge.

Bloul, R. (1994), 'Veiled objects of (post-)colonial desire: forbidden women disrupt the republican fraternal sphere', *The Australian Journal of Anthropology*, 5, 1–2: 113–23.

Bloul, R. (1996), 'Victims or Offenders? "Other" Women in French Sexual Politics', *European Journal of Women's Studies*, 3, 3: 251–68.

Bosséno, C. (1992), 'Immigrant cinema: national cinema – the case of Beur film', in R. Dyer and G. Vincendeau (eds), *Popular European Cinema*, London and New York: Routledge.

Bouamama, S. and Sad Saoud, H. (1996), *Familles maghrébines de France*, Paris: Desclée de Brouwer.

Boucebi, M. (1982), *Psychiatrie, société et développement*, Algiers: SNED.

Boulahbel-Villac, Y. (1992), 'Les femmes algériennes en France', *Revue française des affaires sociales*, 46, 2: 105–23.

Bousquet, G. (1991), *Behind the Bamboo Hedge: The Impact of Homeland Politics in the Parisian Vietnamese Community*, Ann Harbor: University of Michigan Press.

Brah, A. (1993), 'Difference, Diversity, Differentiation: Processes of Racialisation and Gender', in J. Wrench and J. Solomos (eds), *Racism and Migration in Western Europe*, Oxford: Berg.

Brocard, V. (1998), 'Le tour de France de Yamina Benguigui', *Télérama*, 5 August.

Castel, R. (1995), *Les métamorphoses de la question sociale*, Paris: Fayard.

Certeau, M. de (1994), *La Prise de parole et autres écrits politiques*, Paris: Seuil.

Césari, J. (1996), *Etre musulman en France aujourd'hui*, Paris: L'Harmattan.

Chambers, R. (1991), *Room for Maneuver: Reading (the) Oppositional (in) Narrative*, Chicago and London: University of Chicago Press.

Chafiq, C. and Khosrokhavar, F. (1995), *Femmes sous le voile: face à la loi islamique*, Paris: Félin.

Chamoiseau, P. and Confiant, R. (1991), *Lettres créoles: Tracées antillaises et continentales de la littérature: Haïti, Guadeloupe, Martinique, Guyane, 1635–1975*, Paris: Hatier.

Chane-Tune, M.-C. (1997), 'Yamina Benguigui. Pour qu'immigration ne rime plus avec humiliation', *Télé 7 Jours*, June 26.

Chauville, C. (ed.) (1998), *Dictionnaire du jeune cinéma français: Les Réalisateurs*, Paris: Scope.

Bibliography

Cissé, M. (1996), 'Sans-papiers: les premiers enseignements', *Politique la revue*, 2: 9–14.

Cissé, M. (1999), *Parole de sans-papiers!* Paris: La Dispute.

Costa-Lascoux, J. (1995), 'Immigrant women: out of the shadows and on to the stage', in *Immigrant Women and Integration*, Council of Europe Publications.

Costa-Lascoux, J. and Live Yu-Sion (1995), *Paris-XIIIe, lumières d'Asie*, Paris: Autrement.

Dayan-Herzbrun, S. (1995), 'Cheveux coupés, cheveux voilés', *Communications*, 60: 158–84.

Delesalle, N. (1999), 'En France l'égalité se fait attendre', *Télérama*, 2597, 20 octobre.

Derrida, J. and Steigler, B. (1996), *Echographies de la télévision. Entretiens filmés*, Paris: Galilée-INA.

Dewitte, P. (ed.) (1999), *Immigration et intégration: l'état des savoirs*, Paris: La Découverte.

Djebar, A. (1995), *Vaste est la prison*, Paris: Albin Michel.

Djeghloul, A. (1989), 'L'Irruption des Beurs dans la littérature française', *Arabies*, 30: 80–7.

Douglas, A. and Malti-Douglas, F. (1994), *Arab Comic Strips: Politics of an Emerging Mass Culture*, Bloomington: Indiana University Press.

Durmelat, S. (1998), 'Petite histoire du mot beur', *French Cultural Studies*, 9: 191–207.

Eagleton, T. (1983), *Literary Theory: An Introduction*, Oxford: Basil Blackwell.

Fanon, F. (1952), *Peau noire, masques blancs*, Paris: Seuil.

Fassin, D., Morice, A., and Quiminal, C. (eds) (1997), *Les lois de l'inhospitalité: les politiques de l'immigration à l'épreuve des sans-papiers*, Paris: La Découverte.

Ferré, N. (1997), 'La production de l'irregularité', in D. Fassin, A. Morice and C. Quiminal (eds), *Les lois de l'inhospitalité: les politiques de l'immigration à l'épreuve des sans-papiers*, Paris: La Découverte.

Ferreol, G. (ed.) (1994), *Intégration et exclusion dans la société française contemporaine*, Lille: Presses Universitaires de Lille.

Franchini, P. (1993), *Métis*, Paris: Jacques Bertoin.

Gaspard, F. and Khosrokhavar, F. (1994), 'Sur la problématique de l'exclusion: de la relation des garçons et des filles de culture musulmane dans les quartiers défavorisés', *Revue française des affaires sociales*, 2: 6–15.

Gaspard, F. and Khosrokhavar, F. (1995), *Le foulard et la République*, Paris: La Découverte.

Bibliography

Geesey. P. (1995), 'North African Women Immigrants in France: Integration and Change', *Sub/Stance*, 76/77: 137–53.

Geisser, V. (1996), Les élites politiques françaises d'origine maghrébine: à la conquête d'une légitimité', *Hérodote*, 80: 104–29.

Goldberg-Salinas, A. and Zaidman, C. (1998), 'Les rapports sociaux de sexe et la scolarité des enfants de parents migrants', *Recherches féministes*, 11, 1: 12–28.

Göle, N. (1993), *Musulmanes et modernes*, Paris: La Découverte.

Golub, A., Morokvasic, M. and Quiminal, C. (1997), 'Evolution de la production des connaissances sur les femmes immigrées en France et en Europe', *Migrations Société*, 9, 52: 17–36.

Groupement national des cinémas de recherche and Cara M. (eds) (1998), *Mémoires d'immigrés: l'héritage maghrébin*.

Halen, P. (1993), 'Le Congo revisité: Une décennie de bandes dessinées "belges" (1982–92)', *Textyles*, 9: 365–82.

Hargreaves, A. (1995), *Immigration, 'race' and ethnicity in contemporary France*, London and New York: Routledge.

Hargreaves, A. (1997a), 'Ni immigrés, ni jeunes issus de l'immigration', *Bulletin of Francophone Africa*, 11: 8–12.

Hargreaves, A. (1997b), *Immigration and Identity in Beur Fiction: Voices from the North African Community in France*, second expanded edition, Oxford and New York: Berg (first edition, 1991).

Hargreaves, A. and McKinney, M. (eds), (1997), *Post-Colonial Cultures in France*, London and New York: Routledge.

Harris, W. (1960), *Palace of the Peacock*, London: Faber & Faber.

Hearn, J. and Collinson, D.L. (1994), 'Theorising Unities and Differences between Men and between Masculinities', in H. Brod and M. Kaufman (eds), *Theorizing Masculinities*, London: Sage.

Hitchcott, N. (1997), 'Calixthe Beyala and the Post-Colonial Woman' in A. Hargreaves and M. McKinney (eds), *Post-Colonial Cultures in France*, London and New York: Routledge.

Humblot, C. (1997), '"Mais qui va nous écouter ma fille?" Entretien avec Yamina Benguigui', *Le Monde, Section Télévision, Radio, Multimédia*, May 26.

Ireland. S. (1996), 'L'exil et le conflit culturel dans les romans des écrivaines beures', *Multi-Culture, Multi-écriture; La voix migrante au féminin en France et au Canada*, Paris and Montreal: L'Harmattan.

Jamieson, N. L. (1993), *Understanding Vietnam*, California: University of California Press.

Jazouli, A. (1985), 'Autonomie, contestation et intégration conflictuelle', *La 'Beur' génération, Sans frontière*, 92, 3: 49–53.

Jelen, C. (1993), *La famille: secret de l'intégration*, Paris: Robert Laffont.

Kincaid, J. (1988), *A Small Place,* New York: Penguin Books.

Kristeva, J. (1984, [1974]), *Revolution in Poetic Language*, trans. by M. Waller, New York:

Kristeva, J. (1986), 'Women's Time', *The Kristeva Reader*, Oxford: Basil Blackwell.

Kristeva, J. (1988), *Étrangers à nous-mêmes*, Paris: Fayard.

Labro, M. (1997), 'Immigration: Notre devoir de mémoire', *L'Express*, May 29.

Lacoste-Dujardin, C. (1988), 'Renier les parents pour s'intégrer? Le dilemme des enfants des parents maghrébins immigrés en France', *Hérodote*, 50, 4: 138–52.

Lacoste-Dujardin, C. (1992), *Yasmina et les autres de Nanterre et d'ailleurs: filles de parents maghrébins en France,* Paris: La Découverte.

Lacoste-Dujardin, C. (1994), 'Relations des jeunes filles à leur mère dans l'immigration maghrébine en France', in N. Bensalah (ed.), *Familles turques et maghrébines aujourd'hui. Evolution dans les espaces d'origine et d'immigration*, Paris: Maisonneuve et Larose.

Lacoste-Dujardin, C. (1996), *Des mères contre les femmes. Maternité et patriarcat au Maghreb*, Paris: La Découverte.

Laronde. M. (1993), *Autour du roman beur*, Paris: L'Harmattan.

Le Huu Khoa (1985), *Les Vietnamiens en France: insertion et identité. Le processus d'immigration depuis la colonisation jusqu'à l'implantation des réfugiés*, Paris: L'Harmattan.

Le Huu Khoa (1993), *L'Interculturel et l'Eurasien*, Paris: L'Harmattan.

Le Huu Khoa (1996), *L'Immigration confucéenne en France*, Paris: L'Harmattan.

Lê, L. (1995), 'Les Pieds nus', in Le Huu Khoa (ed.), *La Part d'Exil*, Aix-en-Provence: Publications de l'Université de Provence.

Lê, L. (1997), *Les Trois Parques*, Mesnil-sur-l'Estrée: Christian Bourjois.

Leclère, T. (1997), 'Nous ne repartirons nulle part', *Télérama*, May 21.

Lefèvre, K. (1989), *Métisse blanche*, Paris: Éditions Bernard Barrault.

Lefèvre, K. (1995), *Retour à la saison des pluies*, Marseille: Edition de l'Aube.

Lelièvre, F. (1997), 'Quelques repères à propos des femmes migrantes', in N. Bentichou (ed.), *Les femmes de l'immigration au quotidien*, Paris: L'Harmattan.

Lesselier, C. (1999), 'La législation sur l'entrée et le séjour des personnes étrangères en France: pour une analyse féministe', *Brochure de RAJFIRE*. Paris: RAJFIRE.

Lloyd, C. (1998), 'Rendez-vous manqués: feminism and anti-racisms in France', *Modern and Contemporary France*, 6, 1: 61–73.

Lochak, D. (1997), 'Les politiques de l'immigration au prisme de la législation sur les étrangers', in D. Fassin et al (eds), *Les lois de l'inhospitalité: les politiques de l'immigration à l'épreuve des sans-papiers*, Paris: La Découverte.

Madoc, N. and Murard, N. (1995), *Citoyenneté et politiques sociales*, Paris: Flammarion.

Maspéro, F. (1990), *Les passagers du Roissy-Express*, Photographs A. Frantz, Paris: Seuil.

Maspéro, F. (1994), *Roissy Express*, trans. P. Jones, London: Verso.

Mauraisin, O. (1998), 'Vidéo: l'immigration maghrébine en France. *Mémoires d'immigrés*', *Le Monde*, Section Télévision, Radio, Multimédia, December 13–14.

Mauss, M. (1997), 'Gift, gift' (trans. K. Decoster), *The Logic of the Gift*, New York and London: Routledge, 28–32. [Originally published in *Mélanges offerts à M. Charles Andler par ses amis et ses élèves*, Strasbourg: Istra, 1924.]

McKinney, M. (1997a), 'Haunting figures in contemporary discourse and popular culture in France', *Sites*, 1, 1: 51–76.

McKinney, M. (1997b), '*Métissage* in post-colonial comics', in A. Hargreaves and M. McKinney (eds), *Post-Colonial Cultures in France*, London: Routledge.

McKinney, M. (1998), '*Beur* comics', in A. Hughes and K. Reader (eds), *Encyclopedia of Contemporary French Culture*, London: Routledge.

McKinney, M. (forthcoming), '*L'art de la fugue*: runaways in post-colonial French-language comics', in T. Inge and G. Spielmann (eds), *Comics: An International Idiom*.

Mohamed, A. R. J. (1983), *Manichean Aesthetics: The Politics of Literature in Colonial Africa*, Amherst: University of Massachussetts Press.

Mokaddem, Y. (1995), 'Filiation et identité. Transmission, rupture et/ou écarts chez deux romanciers de l'immigration: Ahmed Kalouaz et Tassadit Imache', in C. Bonn (ed.), *Littératures des immigrations 1: Un espace littéraire émergent*, Paris: L'Harmattan.

Morgan, D.H. (1992), *Discovering Men*, London: Routledge.

Morrison, T. (1987), *Beloved*, London: Chatto & Windus.

Nader, L. (1989), 'Orientalism, occidentalism and the control of women', *Cultural Dynamics*, 2, 3: 323–55.

Nederveen Pieterse, J. (1992), *White on Black: Images of Africa and Blacks in Western Popular Culture*, New Haven: Yale University Press.

Bibliography

Nicolaïdis, D. (ed.) (1994), *Oublier nos crimes: l'amnésie nationale: une spécialité française*, Paris: Autrement.

Nicollet, A. (1993), *Femmes d'Afrique noire en France*, Paris: L'Harmattan.

✗ Noiriel, G. (1995), 'Immigration: Amnesia and Memory', *French Historical Studies*, 19, 2: 367–80.

Pigeon, G. (1996), 'Black icons of colonialism: African characters in French children's comic strip literature', *Social Identities*, 2, 1: 135–59.

Pilloy, A. (1994), *Les Compagnes des héros de B.D.: Des femmes et des bulles*, Paris: L'Harmattan.

Porterfield, T. B. (1998), *The Allure of Empire: Art in the Service of French Imperialism, 1798–1836*, Princeton: Princeton University Press.

Powrie, P. (ed.), *French Cinema in the 1990s: Continuity and Difference*, Oxford: Oxford University Press.

Pratt, A. (1981), *Archetypal Patterns in Women's Fiction*, Bloomington: University of Indiana Press.

Pratt, M. L. (1992), *Imperial Eyes: Travel Writing and Transculturation*, London and New York: Routledge.

Prencipe, L. (1994), 'Famille-Migrations-Europe: Quelles relations possibles?', *Migrations Société*, 6, 35: 27–42.

Quiminal, C. (1991), *Gens d'ici, gens d'ailleurs*, Paris: Christian Bourgois.

Quiminal, C. (1997), 'Familles immigrées entre deux espaces', in D. Fassin, A. Morice and C. Quiminal (eds), *Les lois de l'inhospitalité: les politiques de l'immigration à l'épreuve des sans-papiers*, Paris: La Découverte.

Rio, F. (1998), 'Immigrés franco-algériens et conflits identitaires', *Tumultes*, 11, 177–97.

Robinson, D. (1999), 'Beur culture: a new voice or Orientalism revisited?' in K. Salhi (ed.), *Francophone Voices*, Exeter: Elm Bank Publications.

Rosello, M. (1993), '*Georgette!* de Farida Belghoul: Télévision et départenance', *L'Esprit Créateur*, XXXIII, 2: 35–46.

Roze, A. (1995), *La France arc-en-ciel: les Français venus d'ailleurs*, Paris: Juillard.

Rude-Antoine, E. (1995), *Jeunes de l'immigration*, Paris: Karthala.

Rude-Antoine, E. (1997), *Des vies et des familles: les immigrés, la loi et la coutume*, Paris: Odile Jacob.

Savarese, E. (1995), 'La femme noire en image: Objet érotique ou sujet domestique', in P. Blanchard, S. Blanchoin, N. Bancel, G. Boëtsch and H. Gerbeau (eds), *L'Autre et nous: 'Scènes et types'*, Paris: ACHAC/Syros.

Bibliography

Sayad, A. (1977), 'Les trois âges de l'émigration algérienne en France', *Actes de la recherche en sciences sociales*, 15: 59–81.

Sebbar, L. (1984), *Le Chinois vert d'Afrique*, Paris: Stock.

Sedgwick, E. K. (1993), *Tendencies*, Durham: Duke University Press.

Sherzer, D. (1999), 'Comedy and Interracial Relationships: *Romuald et Juliette* (Serreau, 1987) and *Métisse* (Kassovitz, 1993)', in P. Powrie (ed.), *French Cinema in the 1990s: Continuity and Difference*, Oxford: Oxford University Press.

Sherzer, D. (forthcoming), 'French colonial and postcolonial hybridity: "condition métisse"', *Journal of European Studies*.

Silberman, R, (1991), 'Regroupement familial: ce que disent les statistiques', *Hommes et Migrations,* 114: 13–17.

Stora, B. (1992), *Ils venaient d'Algérie: L'immigration algérienne en France 1912–1992*, Paris: Fayard.

Stora, B. (1994), 'Cicatriser l'Algérie', in D. Nicolaïdis (ed.), *Oublier nos crimes*, Paris: Autrement.

Taarji, H. (1990), *Les voilées de l'Islam*, Paris: Balland.

Tahon, M. (1998), *Algérie, la guerre contre les civils*, Quebec: Nota Bene.

Tai, Hue-Tam Ho (1992), *Radicalism and the Origins of the Vietnamese Revolution*, Cambridge, Massachusetts and London: Harvard University Press.

Tarr, C. (1993), 'Questions of identity in Beur cinema', *Screen*, 34, 4: 321–42.

Tarr, C. (1994), 'Violence, Gender and Identity in *Le Thé au harem d'Archi Ahmed* by Mehdi Charef and *Shérazade* by Leïla Sebbar' in R. Günter and J. Windebank (eds), *Violence and Conflict in Modern French Culture*, Sheffield: Sheffield Academic Press.

Tarr, C. (1995), 'Beurz in the hood: the articulation of Beur and French identities in *Le Thé au harem d'Archimède* and *Hexagone*', *Modern and Contemporary France*, 4: 415–25.

Tarr, C. (1997a), 'French cinema and post-colonial minorities', in A. Hargreaves and M. McKinney (eds), *Post-Colonial Cultures in France*, London and New York: Routledge.

Tarr, C. (1997b), 'Ethnicity and identity in contemporary French cinema: the case of the young Maghrebi-French woman', *Iris,* 24: 125–35.

Tarr, C. (1997c), 'Ethnicity and identity in *Métisse* and *La Haine*', in T. Chafer (ed.), *Multicultural France: French Working Papers Series 1*, Portsmouth: University of Portsmouth.

Tarr, C. (1999), 'Ethnicity and identity in the *cinéma de banlieue*', in P. Powrie (ed.), *Contemporary French Cinema: Continuity and Difference*, Oxford: Oxford University Press.

Bibliography

Thackway, M. (1999), *Reverse Angles: Representation, Cultural Identity, and Voice, in Francophone West African Film*, Unpublished thesis.

Tiffin, H. (1987), 'Post-Colonial Literatures and Counter-Discourse', *Kunapipi*, 9, 3: 17–34.

Tournier, M. (1970), *Le Roi des Aulnes*, Paris: Gallimard.

Tournier, M. (1986), *La goutte d'or*, Paris: Gallimard.

Tribalat, M. (1995), *Faire France. Une enquête sur les immigrés et leurs enfants*, Paris: La Découverte.

Van Renterghem, M. (1997), 'Le sabbat de Lady Lê', *Le Monde des livres*, October 31.

Vigarello, G. (1990), 'Le tour de France', in P. Nora (ed.), *Les Lieux de mémoire*, Paris: Gallimard.

Vincendeau, G. (2000), 'Designs on the banlieue: Mathieu Kassovitz's *La Haine*', in S. Hayward, and G. Vincendeau (eds), *French Film, Texts and Contexts*, Revised and expanded edition. London and New York: Routledge.

Wihtol de Wenden, C. (1988), 'De l'émigration à l'Islam: L'immigration maghrébine dans l'imaginaire politique français', in B. Etienne (ed.), *L'Islam en France: Islam, état et société*, Paris: CNRS.

Wihtol de Wenden, C. (1990), 'L'immigration maghrébine, entre une représentation figée du passé et une perception fantasmatique du présent', *Annuaire de l'Afrique du Nord*, 29: 391–400.

Woodhull, W. (1993a), 'Exile', in *Post/Colonial Conditions: Exiles, Migrations and Nomadisms*, Yale French Studies, 82, New Haven: Yale University Press.

Woodhull, W. (1993b), *Transfigurations of the Maghreb: feminism, decolonization, and literatures*, Minneapolis: University of Minnesota Press.

Yeager, J. A. (1987), *The Vietnamese Novel in French: A Literary Response to Colonialism*, Hanover and London: University Press of New England.

Yeager, J. A. (1993), 'Kim Lefèvre's *Retour à la saison des pluies*: Rediscovering the landscapes of Childhood', *L'Esprit Créateur,* 33: 47–57.

Yeager, J. A. (1997), 'Culture, citizenship, nation: the narrative texts of Linda Lê', in A. Hargreaves and M. McKinney (eds), *Post-Colonial Cultures in France*, London and New York: Routledge.

Yuval-Davis, N. and Anthias, F. (1989), *Woman-Nation-State*, London: Macmillan.

Zehraoui, A. (1996), 'Processus différentiels d'intégration au sein des familles algériennes en France', *Revue française de sociologie,* 37, 2: 237–61.